THE COMPLETE GUIDE TO THE BRITTANY

Candace Darnforth

LP Media Inc. Publishing
Text copyright © 2021 by LP Media Inc.
All rights reserved.

www.lpmedia.org

Publication Data

Candace Darnforth
The Complete Guide to the Brittany – First edition.
Summary: "Successfully raising a Brittany Dog from puppy to old age" – Provided by publisher.
ISBN: 978-1-954288-30-0
[1. Brittany – Non-Fiction] I. Title.

Design by Sorin Rădulescu
First paperback edition, 2021

TABLE OF CONTENTS

CHAPTER 11

Grooming Your Brittany

CHAPTER 12

Preventative Medical Care

CHAPTER 13

Breed-Specific Diseases

CHAPTER 14

INTRODUCTION

Did you just bring home your new Brittany?

Welcome! You have joined the legion of those whose lives will be forever enriched by the unconditional love and selfish devotion shared with their Brittany.

From the first minute you lay eyes on your Brittany – his bold, striking coat, soft eyes, and floppy ears will steal your heart. But the Brittany is not just another pretty face, as he is packed with personality.

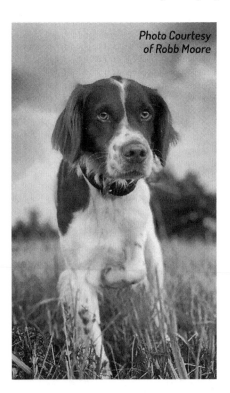

Photo Courtesy of Robb Moore

Often, this breed is referred to as an English Lady or Gentleman, due to their gentle demeanor and respectful personality. Brittanys have a reputation for being the perfect family dog and for good reason. The Brittany is friendly, loyal, patient, and their intelligence makes them highly capable working dogs. It is hard to find another breed that tries harder to please its owner.

Brittanys are often described as one of the most loyal and devoted dog breeds. They are considered "Velcro dogs" who love to be with their family.

Brittanys make excellent therapy dogs and life-long companions.

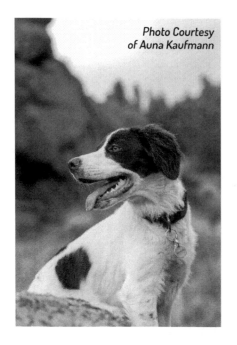

Photo Courtesy of Auna Kaufmann

They quickly adapt to new situations and can be trained to do just about anything. The only thing your Brittany cannot learn is something you did not teach him.

The Complete Guide to Brittanys not only covers basic obedience training, but fundamental field-training lessons. The Brittany is considered to be one of the most versatile of bird dogs. The dogs' medium-length coat is long enough to protect them from thorns without getting stuck in the bushes and hedgerows. Besides having an excellent sniffing nose, they can flush out and retrieve on land and water and have more than enough energy to go all day.

Whether you are a veteran Brittany owner or are new to the breed, this book will provide you with everything you need to help you care, train, and bond with your new lovable friend. You will learn what your Brittany needs to be a healthy and happy dog, long into his senior years.

So, without further ado, continue reading to embark on your exciting journey with your new best friend!

CHAPTER 1
Meet the Brittany

The Brittany is an athletic, agile, and medium-sized dog who loves spending time with you in the Great Outdoors. He thrives on an active lifestyle of long walks, fetch games, or hiking in the woods. Brittanys have a great enthusiasm for life, and their joie de vivre is contagious!

The Brittany is known for having a soft temperament and sensitive personality. Smart almost to a fault, Brittanys are very easy to train. This is due to their innate and eager desire to please plus their intelligence.

Even though they are praised for their hunting skills, they make wonderful family companions. They especially adore children. When properly socialized, they can get along with other dogs and even cats. You will love bonding and training your new best friend. First, however, you should learn a few things about the breed to understand how to train your Brittany in the ideal fashion.

Photo Courtesy of Adam Paine

What is a Brittany?

> "
>
> *The Brittany is first and foremost a bird dog. But they do make great companion, family dogs as well because of their intelligence and desire to please.*
>
> **ROBERT FLEURY**
> *Birch Hill Brittanys*
>
> "

The Brittany is one of the world's most beloved hunting breeds. They also excel in agility, obedience, flyball, rally, and as therapy and service dogs. The breed adapts to all types of climates and absolutely adores water.

Brittanys have a long history of field work alongside their human companions. There has always been a strong bond between man and dog when it comes to the Brittany. In fact, the solid relationship is so formidable that it has become one of the defining characteristics of this breed.

Often, these pups are called Brittany Spaniels, Brittanys, or Britts. They are one of several dog breeds that fall under a sporting group. Sporting and field breeds are renowned for being alert and energetic. Your Britt is no exception to the rules, as he is full of energy and does not tolerate a couch potato lifestyle. Your pooch requires mental stimulation, exercise, and plenty of attention.

The keenness and versatility that make Brittanys unrivaled hunters can be channeled into sports. Agility, dock diving, obedience, flyball – you name it; this easy-to-train breed is up for it. The Brittany is the perfect fit for those searching for a hunting partner, dog-sport partner, or a companion for a family with an active, outdoorsy lifestyle.

Due to a Brittany's extraordinary energy levels, it is important to provide your pup

FUN FACT
Black Coloration?

The breeding of Brittanys stopped in France during WWII. By the time breeding began again, the gene pool was severely depleted. As a result, France decided to allow black-spotted Brittanys in the standard to expand the gene pool. American breeders have never allowed black-spotted Brittanys in the breed standard, and America and Canada are the only countries where black spots are forbidden on Brittanys.

Photo Courtesy of Barbara Brandreth

with plenty of exercise. A walk around the block a few times a day does not suffice. If your Brittany's basic exercise needs are not met daily, he may become stressed and hyperactive, expending his energy in ways that you most likely will not approve of, such as chewing up your furniture. As a rule of thumb: Brittanys require at least an hour of exuberant exercise each day, making them unsuitable pets for most apartment dwellers.

As mentioned before, Britts have a very gentle personality. Generally, a stern look or a sharp word is enough to get the point across to your dog when he is acting up. Be gentle yet firm when training, avoiding all types of harsh punishments. The Brittany breed does not cope well in a tense, stressful home environment with loud voices or noises.

Whether you have a puppy or an adult dog, your new best friend will enrich your life for at least a decade or more. Your Britt will not only provide you with hours of amusement, but he will protect your family, home, and your possessions.

Grooming a Britt is relatively easy as they have a short coat with longer feathering on the legs and belly. A weekly brushing session will keep his coat looking healthy and prevent loose hair from piling up on your floor or furniture.

As with any dog, you must begin to establish a good, solid relationship the minute you bring your new pup home. Brittanys, in general, are very easy to train, but if you do not start training right away, you may end up with a disobedient, uncontrollable dog who is no fun to be around.

Brittanys crave companionship, so they are susceptible to separation anxiety when left alone for long periods of time, expressing their anxiety by chewing and barking. As with all breeds, Brittanys need to be properly trained and socialized.

History of the Brittany

Some claim that the Brittany first appeared around the 2nd century, however, there is no evidence to validate this belief. Historians have discovered tapestries and paintings from the 17th century depicting Brittany-type dogs with a bobtail. In 1850, Reverend Davies wrote about a medium sized hunting dog who could retrieve, point, and flush out gamebirds.

The exact history of the Brittany is surrounded in mystery. However, around 1850, it was common for the English upper-class to travel to Brittany, France, to hunt game birds. These noble Englishmen brought along with them their well-trained Pointers, Irish, English, Gordon and Llewellyn Setters. At the end of each hunting season, the dogs were often left behind with the locals until the following shooting season.

It is believed that the Brittany residents mated their brown and white "traditional" spaniel breeds with the English dogs, which would explain the variety of colors observed today in the Brittany.

According to historical records, in 1896, a Brittany was shown at a Paris exhibition and won one of the top prizes. The breed began to gain popularity in 1904 when a Brittany named "Max de Callac" was the first French champion. Soon after, in 1907, the breed received official recognition when a French club was formed. The club still exists and carries the original name of "Club de L'Epagneul Breton – France." In 1907, the breed standard was drawn up in Nates, France, and officially adopted by the club on June 7, 1908.

The Club de L'Epagneul Breton's motto is "A maximum quality in a minimum volume." The quote sums up Brittanys perfectly as they are extremely versatile dogs yet perfectly proportioned.

In 1928, the first Brittany was imported to the United States, with the first litter registered the same year. In 1934, the American Kennel Club adopted the Brittany's breed standards.

LONG HISTORY
Old Breed

The Brittany has been around for hundreds of years. There are depictions of Brittanys in tapestries and paintings dating as far back as the 17th century.

In 1982, the American Kennel Club shortened the name to Brittany to reflect the breed's hunting style, as it resembled the style of a setter more than a spaniel.

In France, the breed is referred to as the Brittany Spaniel. However, many countries have dropped the word "spaniel" in recognition that the Brittany points, rather than flushing out its game. Also, the Brittany will not compete against other spaniels in dogs shows or field trails.

It is suspected that the use of "spaniel" was caused by a translation error from the original name "L 'Epangneul." This word is derived from the French verb "s 'espaigne" which means to lie flat. In the past, before the existence of forearms, pointing dogs would lie flat on the ground indicating the direction of the game. The hunters would capture the game by throwing a large net over them.

In France and other European countries, the breed is referred to as L 'Epangneul Breton. However, in Canada, Ireland and the United Kingdom, the breed is referred to as Brittany Spaniel. New Zealand and the United States simply refer to the breed as Brittany.

Photo Courtesy of Sarah Hull

American Brittany or French Brittany

Despite the fact that the American Brittany and the French Brittany share the same ancestry and are genetically the same breed, there are a few notable differences.

How do these so-called differences affect a bird hunter or a new pet owner?

Appearance – The French Brittany has the black color gene. It is common to see French Brittanys with black roan. Even if a French Brittany has an orange or light brown coat, it will almost always have black pigmentation on its nose. Early American breeders only imported foundation stock with orange and white, or liver and white, and eliminated any dogs with black markings or dogs carrying the black coloring genes.

Another difference is the French Brittany is slightly smaller in size when compared to its American counterpart. Often, the French Brittany is described as having a "cobby" body shape, which means the dog's height is equal to its length. The American Brittany tends to be longer and lankier.

Hunting style – Both breeds excel at a variety of hunting styles. However, according to popular opinion, the French Brittany tends to hunt closer and quarter tighter. On the other hand, the American Brittany adapts to a wider range of hunting techniques and can cover a wider range due to longer legs and faster running speed. Both dogs are capable retrievers and water dogs and are hard-working.

Temperament – Both the American and French Brittany are considered to be sweet-natured, high-energy, and loyal companions. They are both known for their love of life and their ability to trick you into letting them cuddle on the couch next to you after a long day of hunting or hiking. French and American Brittanys both have strong pointing instincts and are excellent sniffers.

Some breeders state that the only difference is that American Brittanys are born in America, and French Brittanys are born in France. However, many other breeders believe the split between the French and American Brittanys is irrevocable, as the two have been moving in different directions for more than eighty years. In recent years, breeders in the United States and France compared DNA tests and discovered that the breed markers for both American type and French type Brittany are identical.

The United Kennel Club recognizes the American and French Brittany as two separate breeds. However, the American Kennel Club and the North American Versatile Hunting Dog Association register both types under the breed's name "Brittany."

Difference Between Working and Show Lines

Working Brittanys are less nervous, incredibly energetic, and are always on a mission. Their appearance may vary, but they tend to have a leaner, athletic build, whereas show line Brittanys may be slightly taller, longer, and broader. Typically, working Britts are smaller in size with their ears perched higher on their head, with shorter coats and less feathered fur on their legs and bodice than their counterparts.

Working Brittanys are not recommended for the average pet owner unless they intend to put the dog to work by hunting or performing sports. A Brittany from working bloodlines will never win in the show ring because he was bred for working, not showing.

The average cost for a working Brittany can be anywhere from $900 and upwards. On the other hand, a Brittany with top breed lines and a superior pedigree for shows may cost anywhere from $1,500 to $6,500.

Physical Appearance

The Brittany has long legs and is a medium-sized dog with muscular shoulders. A graceful long neck complements a square-proportioned bodice. The breed's energetic and graceful gait is due to its broad, muscular thighs. The rugged hunter's shoulders are slightly wider and higher than the rear end. The leggy build gives the Brittany the ability to run fast and cover large amounts of ground quickly.

A full-grown Brittany stands at between 17 to 19 inches and weighs approximately thirty to forty pounds.

The Britt's amber or hazel eyes give a unique softness to the dog's face that will melt your heart instantly. There are a few different eye color possibilities, such as dark brown, hazel, brown, and amber.

Generally speaking, the Brittany has a tri-color coat. Colors may be clear or blotchy patches, with streaks of color showing through the white markings. Some coat possibilities may be brown, liver, red, cream, Isabella, fawn, blue, pied or brindle. If you prefer your puppy to have a certain color of fur, consult a breeder.

A Brittany's coat is not prone to tangles, but to maintain coat health, it is recommended you brush your pup daily. Extra care will be required if you are planning to exhibit your dog at shows. A Brittany's coat is quite fine and easily snags leaves, grass, or small twigs while on walks through the woods, so you need to brush his coat out afterward.

The dog's medium-length muzzle has a brown or beige button nose. Your Brittany has a keen sense of smell that may get him into trouble at times, so only let him off the leash when you know you can trust him to come and stay by your side. Often, the Brittany is referred to as an inquisitive sniffing machine who will follow his nose right out of your sight.

Brittany's are famous for their short tail, and many are actually born without a tail. It is considered to be acceptable to have this breed's tail docked, and it is rare to see a Brittany with a tail longer than four inches. Traditionally, Brittany's tails were docked to prevent injury to the full tail while working. Today, the tail is docked to maintain the tradition of the standardized look of the Brittany.

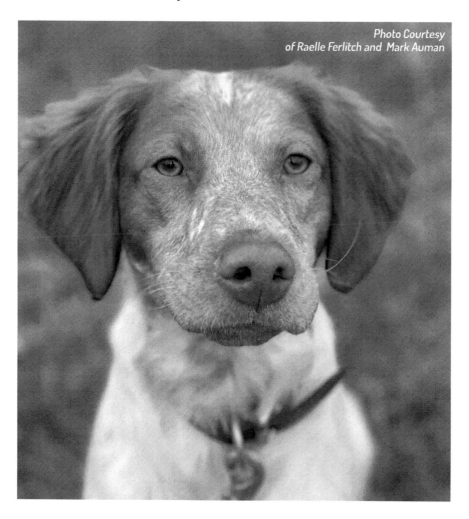

Photo Courtesy of Raelle Ferlitch and Mark Auman

Behavioral Characteristics

The floppy, triangular-shaped ears are encased in short yet wavy, dense hair. The Brittany has an acute sense of hearing and is sensitive to loud noises. Your dog will alert you of any unusual happenings. This breed is protective of his family but generally is not aggressive unless taught to be.

The Brittany is a hardy dog that requires little maintenance, but he is a very social dog who needs constant human interaction. This energetic dog requires regular mental stimulation, exercise, and attention otherwise he will quickly become bored and may display destructive behaviors. Like most breeds, the Brittany needs to be properly trained and well-socialized in order to grow up into a gentle, peaceful dog who gets along with everyone and other animals.

Even though Brittany's are renowned for hunting, they are recognized as one of the top breeds for families with children due to their happy, friendly demeanor. This rugged, high-energy breed has a sensitive personality and responds to positive reinforcement. Brittanys do not respond well to stressful environments with yelling or tense situations.

Younger Britts often are excessively submissive and may accidentally urinate or dribble urine when they become overly excited or feel frightened. This is not a housebreaking issue and will go away as your dog matures. If your Brittany is left alone for long periods of time, he may start to whine, bark, or chew on your furniture.

Your Brittany will make it his mission in life to befriend any other furry friends who live in the same household. However, your pooch will also not hesitate to chase off any cats he may believe are trespassing on his property.

Don't be fooled by your dog's small stature. He is a fast learner and is eager to please, which makes him quite easy to train.

One of the downsides to the Brittany's intelligence is that he will learn bad habits just as fast as good habits. This means that your dog will need to receive consistent obedience training as early as possible in life. Brittanys respond favorably to all types of positive-reinforcement training methods, especially when there is a delicious treat involved. Later on in this book, we will discuss how to successfully use these methods in training your Brittany.

Your Brittany will test his boundaries and limits throughout his life. This is why training needs to be consistent and fair.

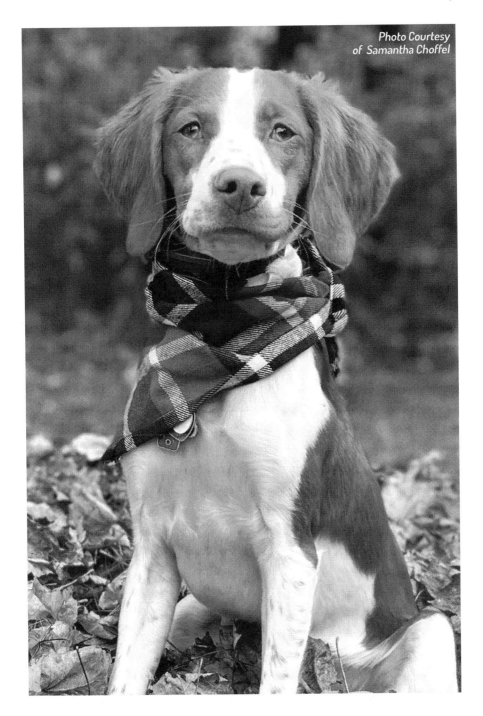

Photo Courtesy
of Samantha Choffel

Exercise Requirements

> "
>
> *The Brittany requires an active family that enjoys outside activities. They need a home with a fenced in yard so they can safely play and exercise. Brittanys can be apartment dwellers but their owner must understand and be able to fulfill their exercise requirements. It is very rare for me to place a puppy to a family in an apartment unless they have previous Brittany experience or are very physically active.*
>
> JESSIE SCHULZ
> *Credit Brittanys*
>
> "

Brittanys are highly energetic and require at least one hour of vigorous exercise each day. This active breed excels at all types of canine sports and has won the most Dual Champions of all American Kennel Club sporting breeds.

A couple of laps around the park or local pond will not only give you a workout but will help your dog burn off excess energy. Switch things up by going for a hike or snowshoeing. Your pooch will be happy to accompany you wherever you go. You will find your Britt's love of life contagious, and without even realizing it, you will be more active than ever with your new best friend by your side.

Age Expectancy

The Brittany has an average lifespan of twelve to fourteen years. This active breed is prone to health concerns like canine hip dysplasia, hypothyroidism, and epilepsy. These conditions can be treated if caught in time, so your veterinarian may recommend annual thyroid and hip exams for your dog.

Brittanys are generally healthy and hardy dogs, and the leading cause of death is cancer in their golden years. Quality of life and diet will directly impact your Brittany's life span. Obesity can cause serious health problems in this breed, such as joint problems, heart disease, back pain, and digestive disorders. Even though it may be tempting to share your food with your furry friend when he looks at you with those big soulful eyes, too many treats may cause extra weight gain and future health issues.

Is a Brittany the Right Fit for You?

> *A family with an active lifestyle is a great one for a Brittany! They love to run and play and this makes them great dogs to live with. Their size (1 71/2 to 20 1/2 " tall - 35 to 45 lbs.) makes them perfect for most families! They love children, so encourage them to take part in all areas of training!*
>
> DIANA L KUBITZ
> *Renegade Brittanys*

Brittanys are excellent pets for veteran and first-time pet-owners, as they are one of the easiest dogs to train. But, as with all dogs, certain breeds are best suited for families with certain characteristics.

Here are some general questions to ask yourself to see if you will make a good match for a Brittany:

- Can I give my Brittany at least one hour or more of vigorous exercise a day, in addition to playing, training, and socializing?
- Do I have enough energy to keep up with my Brittany?
- Will there be someone in the house most of the day so as to avoid my Brittany being left alone for extended periods?
- Can I reciprocate the unfailing love that my Brittany will show to me day after day?
- Am I disciplined enough to train my Brittany to be obedient?
- Is there tension in my home? Are there frequent arguments or fights that may stress out my Brittany?
- Do I have the time and energy to properly socialize my Brittany?

If you decide that a Brittany is the ideal choice for you and your family, you are not getting just a pet – you are gaining a new member of the family, who will be dedicated to showing his new family how much he adores them and depends on them.

CHAPTER 2
Choosing a Brittany

Congratulations on making the exciting decision to bring a Brittany puppy or adult dog into your home. Selecting the right dog can be fun, but it also requires some careful thought – even more so if you are looking for a hunting companion that is true to its breed.

Before you even see your future Brittany, you need to see beneath the surface, beyond those soft, warm brown eyes looking up at you. Often this is referred to as the "Iceberg Principle," which involves learning about the dog's bloodline, its siblings and parents, and possibly, a breeder's reputation and ratings.

In this chapter, we will discuss everything you need to know about how to see "beneath the surface" so you can find the best Brittany for your lifestyle.

Photo Courtesy of Seth and Kelly Urtel

Purchasing or Adopting

> 66
>
> *Whether getting a Britt from a breeder or rescue, one thing remains the same, you want it to be a healthy animal. Breed rescues always try to make sure dogs are up to date on shots, worming and heartworm prevention, and are usually spayed or neutered. If you buy from a breeder, make sure that the parents have had testing for any genetic defects, the pups have had adequate shots and worming, and are healthy.*
>
> DIANA L KUBITZ
> *Renegade Brittanys*
>
> 99

Should I adopt a Brittany or buy a puppy?

Before you can start looking for your new Brittany, you will need to choose between adopting vs. buying a dog or a puppy. Neither option is better than the other as there are pros and cons to both options.

You should never feel pressured to buy or adopt your new furry friend. However, being well-informed about your options will help you make the best choice for you and your family.

ADOPTING A SHELTER DOG

Adopting an older dog does not have the same cute factor that a puppy has, but a Brittany who has received a second chance has a boundless capacity to love. Also, an older shelter dog will prove to be more manageable as he will have already bypassed the early training stages that can make puppies so challenging.

Unfortunately, there is a lot of negative stigma surrounding shelter dogs. The facts show, though, that the majority of shelter dogs have been surrendered to a shelter not because of the dog's behavior but because of the pet owner's change of circumstances.

PROS TO ADOPTING A BRITTANY:

- Adult Brittanys are more likely to already be trained in the basics like potty training. Although, it should be noted that this is not a foregone conclusion and should be confirmed with the shelter.

16

- The majority of shelter dogs are already neutered/ spayed and microchipped.
- In adult dogs, their personality and temperament are already more evident, so you can get a better idea of how they will fit with your family and lifestyle.
- You are saving the life of the Brittany by giving him a new forever home and making space in the shelter for another dog in need.

HELPFUL TIP
"American" vs. "French" Brittanys

When looking for a Brittany puppy, it's important to note that there are two different lines. American Brittanys are faster and taller than their French cousins. French Brittanys tend to work more closely with hunters than American Brittanys.

- Adult Brittanys are likely to have less energy than a puppy. That's not saying your Brittany will be low energy, as they are high-energy dogs, just that the hyper-activity of a puppy may have subsided.
- The love and appreciation from a shelter dog are incomparable!

The costs for adopting a dog can be considerably lower than buying a puppy from a reputable breeder. According to the Animal Humane Society, adoption fees for dogs can run between $120 to $650, depending on the shelter. On the other hand, purchasing a Brittany from a reputable breeder can cost $900 and upwards.

CHALLENGES TO ADOPTING AN ADULT BRITTANY:

- Some dogs may have had a traumatic past, which could lead to challenging behavioral issues.
- Bad habits can be ingrained in adult dogs and may be difficult to break.
- Finding a younger Brittany in a shelter can be more difficult than adopting an older Brittany. Age often is accompanied by health problems, especially if previous owners did not look after the dog properly.
- Many shelters have strict requirements for adopting one of their dogs to ensure the animal does not end up in a shelter again in the future.
- After life in the shelter, the dog may have developed phobias to new situations and things such as children, cats, or even the vacuum cleaner.
- Depending on the dog's experiences and previous training, some Brittanys may be trained to hunt, but not all older dogs can successfully be trained to hunt later in life.

Choosing a Shelter or Rescue

Animal shelters throughout the United States are overburdened with millions of pets each year. By making the decision to adopt your Brittany, you are making room in the shelter for another dog desperately in need of help. Plus, you are giving your Brittany a second chance at finding a loving home. An added bonus is that any costs associated with adopting your pooch will go directly towards the shelter. So, they can continue providing quality care to other dogs in need.

Many Brittanys are patiently waiting for someone to adopt them and take them to their new forever home. The majority of these dogs are loyal, devoted, well-trained dogs who just got the short end of the bone for one reason or another and have no place to go.

Before you rush out to adopt your canine companion, though, there are a few things you should consider. Make sure you are adopting a Brittany that matches your real lifestyle and not your aspirational one. As mentioned before, Brittanys, even if older, are high-energy dogs and need an active lifestyle.

Although you may want to adopt your Brittany from a rescue or shelter, it can seem overwhelming to know where to begin. Start by phoning local veterinarian clinics to ask for recommendations. They often know of dogs who might need re-homing or of reputable shelters in the area that might have a Brittany up for adoption. Another option is to do a Google search online for shelters or rescues in your county or state who specialize in Brittanys.

Even though the majority of shelters are honest and great to work with, there are some rescues and shelters that are just out to make a quick buck. They flat out lie to adopters, leaving them with aggressive, sick, pregnant, or even terminally ill dogs. Adopting your Brittany from an unethical shelter can quickly turn into a nightmare.

Here are some warning signs to watch out for when adopting:

The shelter refuses to let you meet your Brittany before the adoption day. Any reputable and trustworthy shelter will let you meet with your future best friend as often as you like, even if you are still thinking it over. Just remember, though – someone can still adopt your Brittany while you are in the "thinking it over" stage.

They refuse to take the dog back. Any reputable shelter or rescue will have a clause in the contract that will permit you to return the dog within a specified time frame if necessary.

They adopt out puppies younger than eight weeks. Federal law states that a shelter or rescue has to vaccinate, neuter, or spay animals before they are put up for adoption. It is considered to be unethical and illegal to spay or neuter a puppy younger than eight weeks in many states.

The shelter provides little or no proof of vaccinations. Avoid any shelter or rescue that is unwilling to provide proof of vaccinations. A reputable shelter will go over the dog's known medical history with you, including what vaccines the shelter administered and when. You will need to pass those records on to your vet so that future vaccines are administered on schedule.

The shelter employees remind you of pushy used-car salesmen. A good shelter is more concerned about the dog's long-term care than making a sale. They will give you the time you need with the dog to make your decision without feeling pressured.

When you find a shelter that you are interested in, ask them to send you a free pamphlet or information regarding their adoption process, requirements, and information on how to care for your Brittany. Each shelter or rescue organization has different requirements before starting the adoption process.

The following is a general guideline. The requirements will vary from shelter to shelter:

- Most shelters will require you to show a government-issued photo ID proving you are twenty-one years or older.
- You will need to fill out a straightforward application form or an in-depth questionnaire.
- In some cases, you will need to provide references, such as permission from your landlord, verifying you are allowed to have pets.
- Some shelters or rescues will send a representative to your home to make sure it is safe and suitable for a dog.
- The shelter will observe how you and your family interact with the dog during a meet and greet before taking him home.
- Adoption fees will vary depending on the institution. Generally, the fee covers basic veterinary care, food, housing, and care the dog received while in the shelter or foster care.

Just a word of caution – once you start meeting different Brittanys up for adoption, your emotions will be running in full gear. For this very reason, you need to do your research beforehand. Take your time to read the adoption contract before signing, and don't be shy to ask any of the following questions:

IS THE SHELTER RESPONSIBLE FOR ANY IMMEDIATE HEALTH PROBLEMS?

Some reputable shelters offer two-week health coverage in case a health-related problem occurs. Other shelters expect adopters to assume full responsibility for the canine the minute they sign the contract.

IS YOUR BRITT ALREADY NEUTERED OR SPAYED?

Most shelters or rescues will include the price of neutering or spaying in the adoption price, but others may charge you extra for the surgery. Always ask to avoid an unwanted surprise later on.

CAN THE SHELTER PROVIDE YOU WITH COPIES OF YOUR DOG'S MEDICAL RECORDS OR BACKGROUND INFORMATION?

Find out what kind of life your Brittany had before ending up in the shelter. Be aware, the shelter might not know if the dog was abandoned or found. Ask if the dog has any health conditions or dental issues and if it is up to date with its vaccines. Be sure to ask the estimated age of the dog.

WHAT IS THE SHELTER'S RETURN POLICY?

Many shelters have rules in case the adoption does not work out. The contract often will state the adopters have to return the dog to them, even if it is years later.

WHAT ARE THE DOG'S PERSONALITY AND TEMPERAMENT LIKE?

You can inquire about how the dog reacts around other dogs and children or if he is easily startled by sharp, loud noises. Is there anything in particular that makes them anxious, scared or aggressive? The shelter should be able to inform you about the Brittany's training and whether he is potty trained and obeys basic commands.

CAN YOU SPEND TIME WITH THE DOG BEFORE ADOPTING HIM?

Some shelters or rescues let a potential adopter bond with the dog before signing the contract. If so, ask to take him out for a few walks on and off the leash. Take the dog for a car ride to see how he reacts in the car.

By asking questions, you will have a better understanding of your Brittany and his background so that you can care for his needs and provide a safe environment for him. Plus, you will be better prepared to meet the shelter's requirements and will increase the probability of having many happy years with your Brittany.

If you are still on the fence about whether you should adopt your Brittany, here are a few common myths about adopting a dog:

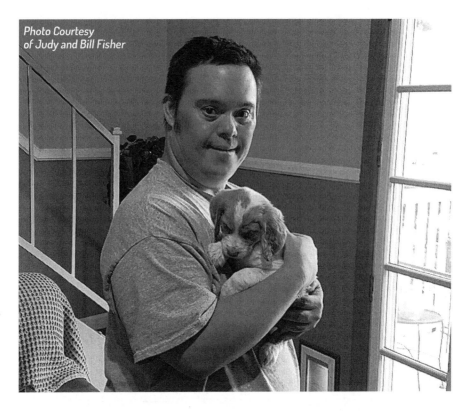

Photo Courtesy of Judy and Bill Fisher

Shelter dogs were abandoned because they have behavior issues – Quite often, dogs are given up because of an unexpected change of circumstances such as divorce, allergies, moving into housing that does not allow pets, financial issues, or lack of time.

Shelter dogs have emotional baggage – Rescued dogs have a past, but their history often is a blessing in disguise as they are already potty trained and have received basic obedience training, saving you time.

I cannot find a shelter or rescue that has Brittanys – The majority of shelters maintain a waiting list for specific breeds, so ask to be added to their list. An excellent option is the *National Brittany Rescue & Adoption Network (NBRAN)*, a non-profit organization, dedicated to finding Brittanys in need a loving forever home.

I do not know what I am getting – The shelter should be able to tell you in great detail about your Brittany's personality and temperament. On most occasions, the shelter will be able to tell you the reason why the original owner had to surrender the dog to a shelter. The only time the shelter will be unable to provide extra information is when the dog was found as a stray on the street.

Beware of Puppy Farms

A puppy farm is often referred to as a puppy mill. Puppy mills are inhumane, mass-breeding facilities, where puppies are bred in poor conditions, increasing their risk of ill health and resulting in high vet bills for the owner.

Puppy mills are only concerned with churning out puppies for profit and completely ignore the needs of the pups and their mothers. When choosing to buy your Brittany, avoid pet stores or online websites, as the majority of puppies come from puppy mills. Often, puppy mills sell through social media, online classified advertisements, and flea markets.

Mother dogs will spend their entire life in a cramped cage with little personal attention, and when they are unfit to breed, they will simply be dumped on the side of the road or killed. Many dogs never leave the confinement of the so-called breeding facilities alive, whether it's a concrete pen in a shed or in a cage in someone's garage. They live and die in a few square feet of pure misery.

Due to a lack of sanitation and medical care, the majority of puppy mill dogs suffer from health issues and are prone to hereditary conditions, like respiratory disorders and heart diseases. There are more than 10,000 puppy mills in the United States alone, and they sell more than two million puppies each year.

Puppies from puppy mills also have a difficult time adapting to a normal home environment, and often grow up into anxious, aggressive, and fearful dogs. Lack of early socialization skills can cost thousands of dollars to treat.

Most puppy buyers usually have no clue of the dreadful conditions their puppies start life in or the conditions the parent dogs are left behind to endure. If the buyers do, they believe they are saving the puppy, but the puppy mill market gains another sale, and the demand continues in the lucrative puppy mill trade.

Here are some warning signs to look out for before purchasing a puppy

- The seller does not ask any questions, and you can pay for the puppy up-front without any previous screening.
- Look for the seller's profile online. If they are advertising many litters from different breeds, then it is a red flag.
- Beware of offers to meet somewhere convenient, e.g., a car parking lot or a gas station that is separate from the puppy mill.
- The breeder is located in another state but is willing to ship you the puppy, no questions asked.

- Puppies should never be sold if they are under eight weeks or younger.
- The seller makes no future commitment to you or the puppy. Reputable breeders always require you to sign a contract promising you will return the dog to them if you are unable to care for him in the future.
- Copy and paste the phone number into a search engine. If the number is being used on lots of different sites, then this is likely a deceitful seller.

As with everything in life, it is important to remain vigilant and to do plenty of research before signing the contract with the seller.

Photo Courtesy
of Dwayne Parkinson

Researching Reputable Breeders

> "
>
> *If you are looking for a Brittany breeder, search for those involved in the American Brittany Club, and that do all health clearances. These breeders are involved in bettering the breed through competition and using only the best dogs to breed (selective breeding). You can search for breeders using the American Kennel Club or American Brittany Club websites. Look at how often they breed and how many dogs they have. Also, look at the health guarantees and conditions the puppies are raised in. For a rescue Brittany, I would consider using the American Brittany Rescue or National Brittany Rescue, both are endorsed by the American Brittany club.*
>
> **DARLENE VANHOEVE**
> *Shamrock Brittanys*
>
> "

Responsible breeders do not sell their puppies to the first person who shows up. A reputable breeder will NEVER sell their puppies through a pet store or any other way that does not allow them to meet with you and thoroughly evaluate you to make sure you are a good match for one of their dogs.

Breeders do not only connect you with your adorable Brittany, but you can rely on them throughout your dog's life. Breeders are often likened to being your own private guide as they provide invaluable information from choosing the best puppy for you and how to care for him year after year.

Your Brittany will likely live from twelve to sixteen years, so it is worth investing time now to be sure you are working with a responsible breeder who breeds healthy, happy Brittanys and keeps them in clean, humane conditions.

You can find a reputable breeder by asking for referrals from your veterinarian or close friends, by contacting local Brittany clubs, or even by visiting a professional dog show. If you have your mind set on purchasing a French Brittany, then start your search with the Club L 'Epagneul Breton of the United States.

A RESPONSIBLE BREEDER ...

Keeps numbers small – A responsible breeder only breeds one type of dog and is knowledgeable about the breed's requirements and needs. Often, they will only have one or two litters a year, meaning you will be placed on a waiting list for at least six months or more before you can welcome your little pup home.

Wants to know you – Any trustworthy breeder cares about their puppies and want to know where they are going. They may ask you to fill out an application form to allow them to see if you are a good fit for one of their pups. If you have other pets, breeders may ask for a veterinary reference.

Will require you to sign a contract – Reputable breeders will ask you to sign a contract stating that you will have your Britt neutered or spayed by a certain date. The contract will also state that you will return the dog to the breeder if you are suddenly unable to care for the dog at any point in your life.

Encourage you to visit – Responsible breeders want you to come and see where the puppy was born and raised. The best way to get a glimpse into how your puppy will be as an adult is to observe his parents. During the meet-and-greet session, observe the breeder and the dogs. Does the breeder seem genuinely concerned about the well-being of the dogs? Are they kept in clean, roomy, comfortable areas? How do the dogs interact with the breeder and strangers?

Will show you a full medical record – Responsible breeders will proudly show you a complete record of the dogs' parents' and grandparents' medical records. At the same time, the breeder will inform you of your Britt's personality traits, behavior, size, and appearance.

Are active in breed specific clubs – Responsible breeders are often active in local, state, and national clubs that specialize in their specific breed. The majority of them compete with their dogs in field, tracking, obedience, and agility trials or other performance events.

Take the time to find a reputable breeder, and you will be thanking yourself for the rest of your dog's life.

Gun Dog Brittany Breeders

If you are primarily looking for a hunting companion, you will need to look for a breeder who maintains a "dual quality" line. This means the breeder can prove the dogs' past field and show performance. Be sure to ask the breeder if it is possible to see both the dam and the sire. If the sire is off-site, you may be able to do a video conference with the owners to see their dog in action.

Take the time to personally talk with people who previously purchased puppies from the line you are considering. If they live in your area, meet those dogs in person so you can get an idea of what their temperament is like. Most Brittany owners love to show off their dogs and share details about their dogs' personalities and training.

If you are looking for a good hunting companion, make sure the breeder is an avid hunter. Dogs bred to hunt ought to come from a history of hunters. If the breeder seems apathetic in regard to this notion, it is a red flag.

A pedigree may just be a piece of paper, but it is very important, as it gives you a glimpse into the line's bloodline, siblings and parents.

Ask about the family history. For example: Is there a history of genetic birth defects such as hip dysplasia and epilepsy? The breeder should provide health certification and put the return policy in writing.

Now that you have identified the litter you want to see, choose a pup that makes direct eye contact, as this is a clear sign of intelligence and a willing hunting spirit that can be trusted. Brittanys are one of the most intelligent dogs, and the breeder should start engaging the pup in learning activities from six weeks of age.

Even though puppies are still awkward, you can observe their "prey drive" from six weeks of age. Look for a strong hunting instinct that can be observed by watching the pup try to retrieve something – does he dash after it or simply ignore it and continue playing with his littermates?

Look at the coat quality of the dam as it will give you an idea of her health and, thus, of the pup's. It should have a consistent texture with no bald patches and brilliance to her fur. A Brittany's coat should be fine yet dense, with the hair lying flat with a slight wave.

Ask the breeder if there are dogs in the puppy's background (roughly two to four generations back) from both field and show stock. Most Brittanys come from dual backgrounds. Look for a pedigree with DCh. (Dual Champion), FCh. (Field Champion), and Ch. (Show Champion), or combined with the dog's points towards these titles. Look for hunting test titles such as JH, SH, and MH (Junior, Senior, and Master Hunter), which are hunter companion titles.

If you are interested in one of the many activities the Brittany is able to compete in, be sure to discuss the details with the breeder. Here are a few of the activities Brittanys often compete in:

- **Field Trials** – For a polished field dog or a promising junior.
- **Dog Shows** – A show for Brittanys who meet the AKC's standard of perfection.
- **Hunting tests** – For hunting companions of all levels.
- **Obedience Trials** – For Britts trained specifically in obedience training.

- **Tracking** – For certified tracking dogs who can follow and track a scent on the ground.
- **Agility Trials** – For Britts trained to go through an obstacle course.
- **Junior Showmanship** – For children ages 10 to 18 with any dog breed – handling is judged, not the dog.

Important Questions to Ask the Breeder

Buying a Brittany is a big commitment and investment. Ideally during your first visit or over the phone, there are some questions you should ask any breeder you may be considering. Their answers matter, as does their willingness to provide them. Any sign of hesitation is a definite warning sign.

Here are a few questions to consider asking the breeder:

WHAT ABOUT THE SIRE AND DAM CAUSED YOU TO CONSIDER THEM FOR BREEDING?

This question can tell you so much about the breeder's philosophies. If he simply paired two Brittanys together to make some extra cash, he will not have a good answer. A trustworthy breeder will provide a long list of reasons, such as genetic tendency of the pedigree, hunting skills, trainability, intelligence, and personality.

IS THE PEDIGREE AND HEALTH INFORMATION AVAILABLE?

Make sure the breeder has tested and evaluated both parents and has the proper documentation to prove that neither parent has genetic diseases. A good breeder should have certification of the dam and sire and at least three generations' documentation to show pedigree records and certify the bloodline's health (hips/eyes/elbows).

CAN I MEET THE PARENTS?

It might not always be possible to meet the dog's father, but it is essential to see how the pup interacts with his mother and his littermates. Is the mother aggressive, shy, or well-adjusted? Are the puppies hyperactive or docile? Observe the size of the parents and their temperament. This will give you a general idea what your puppy will be like.

WHAT HEALTH GUARANTEES DO YOU OFFER?

Health guarantees vary from breeder to breeder, but any reputable breeder will offer a health guarantee. Given the unpredictability of genetics, there is no real guarantee you will get a champion hunting dog, but a health guarantee is a nice backup. Let's say you are sold a Brittany puppy that quickly proves to have serious health issues; you will have peace of mind knowing a refund is in order.

CAN YOU PROVIDE REFERENCES?

Any good breeder will have an extensive list of happy clients who have purchased a Brittany from them in the past. Give these folks a phone call and ask them the following: What are their likes and dislikes regarding the breeder? What are the pros and cons of the breeder's line of dogs? Also, be sure to ask for a veterinary reference, as any reputable breeder will be in good long-term standing with one.

HOW OLD IS THE MOTHER, AND HOW MANY LITTERS HAS SHE HAD?

Make sure that the mother was not mated before two years of age and is not older than eight years old. During her lifetime, she should not have been bred more than four times, including this litter. If a C-section was required, she should not have had more than two in her lifetime.

HOW DO YOU SOCIALIZE THE PUPPIES?

Puppies learn proper social skills from their mother and littermates. Ideally, the breeder is raising the puppies in a family environment, where the pups are exposed to adults, children, and a variety of noises. If the puppy is going to be trained as a hunting companion, be sure to ask what training techniques will be taught before the puppy is twelve weeks old.

Breeder Contracts and Guarantees

Reputable breeders always require anyone who purchases one of their dogs to sign a contract. For first-time pet owners, the requirement to sign a contract may come as a surprise. We often associate signing a contract with purchases of big items such as a car or house, but not a puppy.

For many breeders, contracts are the ideal opportunity to share their philosophies, advice, and expectations with the new pet owner. Breeders are taking a leap of faith as they are entrusting you with one of their puppies. Signing the contract reminds you of the enormous responsibility you are about to undertake.

Contracts vary from breeder to breeder, but they contain some basics such as the puppy's AKC registration number, the name and the registration numbers of the dam and sire, and the purchase price.

If you have never seen a breeder's contract, here are common elements:

- In the case the buyer is unable to care for the Brittany, then the buyer will return the dog to the breeder immediately.
- If the dog will be used for breeding or as a professional show dog, then the contract will specify the terms.
- The buyer must follow the specified schedule of vaccinations.
- If the dog is not planned to be used for breeding, then the contract will specify when the dog is required to be spayed or neutered.
- Some contracts guarantee against certain genetic health defects such as hip dysplasia.

If there is anything unclear or that makes you feel uncomfortable, ask before you sign the contract. Ask the breeder to send you a copy of the contract in advance, so you can take your time reading it over without feeling pressured.

SHOW VERSUS PET CONTRACT

You will notice in your contract that the breeder will make a distinction between a puppy that is "pet quality" or "show quality." It should say "show potential," as it is impossible for a breeder to predict whether a puppy will be show quality when fully grown.

The main differences between a show and pet contract are the responsibilities attached to each. The breeder will determine which pups in a litter are pet quality or show quality. Pet quality pups are those the breeder deems unsuitable for being a future candidate for showing or breeding. Often, pet quality dogs will have a limited registration, meaning they can participate in certain AKC events, and their offspring can be registered.

Show dog contracts can vary depending on the breeder. Some breeders stipulate in the contract that they want to reevaluate the dog at a certain age to ensure the dog is developing as expected. Other breeders require the dog owner to hire a professional handler to show their dog. These clauses may seem strict, but your show dog will be representing their bloodline, so the breeders want to guarantee positive publicity.

If you are planning on breeding your Brittany, then the contract will list all of the health screenings that you will need to perform beforehand. Also, the contract will establish when the breeding will happen and a long list of other details, including financial arrangements.

Inquire About the Parents and Health Tests

Puppies are not toys. If they were, they would be interchangeable, and a defective one would just be a slight inconvenience to change without accompanying heartache. Reputable breeders do everything in their power to ensure their puppies are as healthy as possible, but sometimes things do not work out as planned.

The majority of breeders' contracts guarantee against genetic defects up to a certain age, whereas others only guarantee against specific illnesses such as heart problems. For example, some breeders will guarantee against hip dysplasia only if the owner takes certain precautions, such as not letting the puppy run up and down the stairs until a year old, perhaps even longer for larger breeds.

HELPFUL TIP
Brittany Rescues

Unfortunately, many people aren't prepared to meet a Brittany's exercise requirements, and the dogs therefore end up in rescues or shelters. Consider adopting an older Brittany from a rescue rather than buying a puppy from a breeder. For a list of Brittany rescues nationwide visit the National Brittany Rescue and Adoption Network (NBRAN) at - www.nbran.org

The American Kennel Club requires all certified Brittany breeders to complete a hip and ophthalmologist evaluation. Look for a breeder with the Bred with H.E.A.R.T program, which educates breeders on the best breeding practices and intensive health testing. Look for a breeder who provides an OFA or PennHIP certification on at least the parents.

Feel free to ask the breeder to show you any health screening certificates for both parents. Ask the breeder about the medical history of the dog's parents, grandparents, and great-grandparents. Consider carefully whether to purchase the puppy if one of these diseases is in the family line:

- Otitis externa
- Sterile nodular panniculitis
- Cancer – thyroid neoplasia
- Spinal muscular atrophy
- Eye disease: primary lens luxation (PLL)
- Renal amyloidosis.

Male vs. Female

People often have personal preferences as to the sex of their pets. Characteristics such as loyalty, affection, and intelligence are not gender-specific. Characteristics vary from dog to dog and not between the sexes. Instead of focusing on the sex of the dog, make sure the dog's personality and energy level is a match for yours.

It is worth mentioning that many of the biological differences between female and male dogs are related to their reproductive hormones, and a dog's behavior is affected by hormones. Once the dog is neutered or spayed, the hormonal behavior will disappear over time.

There are a few hormonal and behavior differences that you should be aware of:

BEHAVIORAL DIFFERENCES – Your Brittany's behavior and personality will be molded by his training, upbringing, and surroundings. However, studies show that dogs tend to get along better with the opposite sex. If you are bringing a second dog into your home, create a balance with one female and one male.

HORMONAL DIFFERENCES – Unneutered males have a tendency to roam about the neighborhood in search of a mate. Female dogs that have not been spayed will experience a heat cycle twice a year, producing a secretion to attract male dogs. If you do not get your female Brittany spayed, then you will have to deal with her heat cycle generally every six months. Heat cycles can impact your Britt's ability to hunt and train with other male dogs, as she will cause the male dogs to become distracted. Also, there can be a messy discharge or bleeding during the heat cycle that is unpleasant.

PHYSICAL DIFFERENCES – Male dogs tend to be slightly larger in size when compared to their female littermates. Female dogs tend to mature faster than male dogs, making them easier to train. Some hunters prefer a bigger dog to handle while hunting bigger game or battling tough terrain. Others prefer the smaller, compact size of a female Brittany as they take up less space and use a smaller crate, etc. However, the size differences between a Brittany male and female generally are only two inches and a pound or two.

MARKING – Male dogs, especially unneutered dogs, have a tendency to mark their territory. Some hunters find this trait to be distracting or even annoying, as it may startle or warn potential prey to your whereabouts. If your Britt is more concentrated on marking his territory, he might not be completely focused on the job at hand. Most hunters are not put off by this and accept it as one of their dog's tendencies.

Spaying and neutering can be advantageous if you want to avoid the risk of unwanted puppies or have a more affectionate and less aggressive dog. However, if you plan on entering your Brittany into shows or professional field trials, then you need to remember that neutered or spayed dogs are ineligible.

In the end, it comes down to personal preference and what you consider annoying or not. If you're specifically looking for a hunting companion, most hunters agree that the sex does not affect the dog's hunting skills. That said, early obedience training is vital to make sure the dog knows its place and its job, regardless of sex or breed.

Picking the Correct Puppy

> *Let the breeder know what your goals are for your Brittany pup. If you are looking for just a companion or one that only hunts occasionally, you won't need a highly competitive pup that has a higher drive to hunt and run. If you want to compete in trials, or are hard core hunters you will not want a laid back non-competitive pup who, while he likes to hunt isn't concerned about getting to the bird first. So talk to your breeder about having them pick the pup that has the best potential to suit your purposes.*
>
> **ARLETTE HENNESSEY**
> *K Nine Birddog Brittanys*

Often the breeder will recommend a certain puppy for you, taking into consideration your lifestyles, circumstances, and whether your dog will be a working or show dog. If you have the opportunity to choose your Brittany, here are some suggestions to take into consideration.

Observe how your Brittany interacts with his mother and littermates. Is he the bully of the litter or shy and fearful? How does he react when he is apart from them? Assessing the Britt's reaction will give you a general idea how he will react when he is left alone for a short period of time.

Puppies raised in a family environment are often more socially adjusted to the typical commotion of an everyday household. Your Brittany should feel comfortable around strangers and not shy away from you. If the puppy

Photo Courtesy of Sherri Hooker

seems anxious around the breeder or you, he most likely will grow up to be a nervous dog.

Never get a dog on impulse. A Brittany puppy can be adorable, but he will quickly grow out of the cute stage, and it is entirely up to you whether he grows into a devoted and obedient companion or an unruly, disobedient dog. The more time you put into your Britt's training and socialization, the more you will get back.

Avoid puppies that tuck their tails under their legs or pull away from you when you try to pat them. Shy dogs often grow up into adult dogs who are easily frightened and may snap at younger children.

Give the puppy a quick health check by making sure he is in tip-top shape. Your Brittany's ears should be clean and odorless. The pup should be alert and aware of his surroundings. Even though it is typical for all dogs to have smelly breath, the pup's breath should not be offensive, and his curly coat should look soft, clean, and shiny. There should be no signs of fleas or ringworm.

If the puppies do not look healthy, then walk away. Even though the thought of leaving those adorable puppies behind will be difficult, it will save you from heartbreak in the future.

> Decide on the activities you want your new puppy to be involved in and the characteristics that will aide in their involvement in those activities. For example, if you want to compete in agility you will need to look for different traits than someone looking to do therapy work with their Brittany. If you can, try to visit the litter more than once. You will get a better evaluation of each puppy's personalities. For example, you might think one of the puppies has a calmer, more laid back personality but when you visit the litter a second time that puppy might be extremely outgoing. It's possible that puppy had been playing really hard before you visited the first time so he/she acted more laid back. Always remember, trust your breeder. They spend eight weeks with the puppies and they can give suggestions on which puppy you should take based on the personality traits you are looking for in your new puppy. Also be sure you feel comfortable and get along well with your puppy's breeder. Breeders can be a great source of knowledge throughout your dog's life and it's really important you have a good relationship with them. They are always there to answer questions, celebrate your accomplishments, and share in the love of this wonderful breed.

JESSIE SCHULZ
Credit Brittanys

CHAPTER 3

What to Expect the First Few Months

As the owner of a new puppy, you can expect your life to turn upside down within seconds. You can count on finding your leather shoes chewed apart and having to wake up at 5:15 in the morning to a barking dog only to find a variety of liquid and solid deposits on your living room carpet.

Considering some of the drawbacks of getting a new Brittany, you may ask yourself about the upside. The benefits to bringing home a new dog are limitless! Even though the first few months may be a challenge, thoughtful preparation and planning can give your bundle of energy a head start into settling into his new family. Any initial bumps in the road will transform into happy memories.

Photo Courtesy
of Kelly Pascoe

35

Puppy Proofing Your Home – Inside and Out

> *First and foremost you want to 'puppy-proof' your house much as you would for a toddler. Remove things you don't want your puppy to chew on. Don't give them an old shoe or piece of clothing as a chew toy - they can't tell the difference between their shoe and your $200 shoes!*
>
> **DIANA L KUBITZ**
> *Renegade Brittanys*

Before bringing your new dog home, you will need to puppy proof your entire home – inside and out.

Dogs, especially puppies, are like toddlers and can get themselves into trouble very fast. All dogs are curious and will investigate every nook and cranny of your house. You will want to take precautions to protect your Brittany and your house from a potential disaster. It is extremely important that you take certain precautions and create a safe environment.

Before you bring home your Brittany, get down on your knees and crawl from room to room, looking out for any possible hazards at a puppy's eye level. The Brittany's personality is often compared to Velcro. This means that where you are, your pooch will be right by your side. For this reason, be sure to pay extra attention to rooms where you will be spending the majority of your time.

IN THE KITCHEN

Food is, of course, the most attractive element of your kitchen for your Brittany. Most Britts love to eat, so never under estimate your pup being alone in the kitchen with food on the table. You may want to install a puppy gate to keep your pooch out of the kitchen while you are cooking.

Your cabinets and drawers are ideal cubby holes to crawl into and explore. You can buy child-proof latches at the local hardware store, which will help to prevent your curious pup from getting into trouble and, at the same time, keep him away from harmful cleaning supplies and foods. In chapter ten, you will find an extensive list of human foods that are considered toxic for all dogs.

Your Brittany's nose can sniff out the tiniest morsel of food on the floor, and your garbage bin will be almost impossible to resist. Be sure your

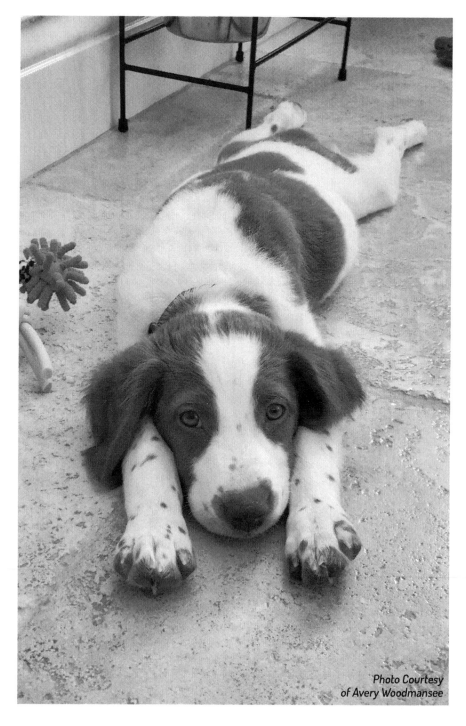

Photo Courtesy
of Avery Woodmansee

garbage bin has a tight lid that tightly closes, or better yet, keep it tucked away under the sink with a childproof lock on the door.

IN THE LIVING AREAS

Be vigilant in keeping living areas organized and tidy. Make sure that there are no small objects lying around, such as shoes, cell phones, or glasses – all of these items will tempt your curious and teething Brittany. Make sure that all blind cords and power cords are tucked away, out of sight, or placed inside of chew-proof PVC tube.

If you have a fireplace, your Britt may be harmed by ashes and flames. A quick and easy solution is using a protective fire screen. Another overlooked danger is fire-starter sticks; some dogs cannot resist the temptation of munching on them.

Another hazard is house plants. Many house plants are toxic if consumed by dogs such as lilies, orchids, Christmas cactus, jade plants, ivy, and aloe vera. Place any house plants on a table, counter, or inside an off-limits room with the door shut.

Be sure there is nothing up high that can fall on your Brittany if he accidentally bumps into a piece of furniture. If your puppy accidentally displaces a heavy vase, your dog may get seriously injured and/or damage your possessions.

IN THE OFFICE

Your office is full of everyday items that will make your Brittany feel like he is inside of a candy shop with so many temptations: papers, magazines, paperclips, staples, power cords, rubber bands, just to name a few. These items might be fun for your Britt to play with, but if swallowed, they can cause serious issues, even fatal in some cases. If you are into arts and crafts, be sure that any sharp objects, including needles, are out of reach. Plastic bags and plastic wrap can also cause suffocation.

Wires and cords can be a problem, as chewing on a plugged-in cord could electrocute your dog. Be sure to tuck away any cords to keep them out of your puppy's way.

IN THE BATHROOM

Some hazards in the bathroom are quite obvious, such as dental floss, medications, razors, cotton swabs, or soap. These can all be dangerous if eaten or swallowed by your Brittany. Expensive emergency visits to the veterinarian's office are quite common for puppies. Be sure to place all shampoos, conditioners, tissue paper, etc., inside of the bathroom cabinet or on a shelf out of the dog's reach.

Drinking from the toilet never is a good idea for dogs, especially if you use harsh chemical cleansers. Furthermore, sinks and tubs filled with water may present a drowning hazard for your puppy. So always close the toilet lid and keep the bathroom door closed. Tuck away any dangling power cords, and place childproof latches on the cabinets.

IN THE BEDROOM

Brittanys are scent-orientated and will gravitate towards anything that smells like you. Aside from the threat of your Brittany chewing on your leather shoes, bedrooms are generally benign when it comes to puppy hazards. But to be on the safe side, make sure any jewelry, hair clips, hair pins and bands are out of your curious dog's reach.

Mothballs are another potential hazard. They are extremely toxic, so if you use them, make sure they are stored in a place your Brittany cannot reach. Dirty, smelly clothes are especially tempting for your Brittany, so be sure to place them inside a laundry hamper. Brittanys love to crawl and squeeze their way into small spaces. If you do not want your puppy crawling under your bed, then make a temporary blockade with boxes until he learns house rules.

IN THE GARAGE OR THE BASEMENT

Garages and basements tend to be storage areas for just about everything, including pesticides, rat and rodent poison, fertilizers, antifreeze, solvents, coolants, gasoline, and so on. The simple solution is to place these items inside of a closed cabinet or on a high shelf. The same is true for smaller items such as bolts, nails, and screws. If you live in a colder climate, be aware that many de-icing compounds are made from harmful chemicals, so look for a product that is pet-safe.

IN THE LAUNDRY

Brittanys are tempted to chew on and even swallow dish towels or stray socks, which can lead to serious gastrointestinal issues and a costly veterinarian bill. Washers and dryers can seem like a tempting place for a short nap, and you may not notice the sleeping dog if you put in a load of clothes. Quick fix: keep any appliance doors closed at all times. Make sure laundry detergents, cleansers, bleach, and fabric softeners are up on a shelf and not on the floor.

IN THE YARD

Brittanys love the great outdoors and the plants in your flower garden. There are a number of indoor and outdoor plants that can cause gastrointestinal issues such as diarrhea and vomiting. Some of the most common outdoor plants that are toxic for your dog are daffodils, foxglove, tulips, bird of paradise, and lupines. Be sure to block off access to your plants while your puppy is roaming the yard. You can find a more extensive list of toxic plants for dogs on the Animal Poison Control website.

Compost, mulches, pesticides, insecticides, fertilizers, and other garden chemicals can cause health issues for your pooch. Your best line of defense is to use products on your lawn and garden that are pet-friendly.

Walk through the grass in your bare feet, looking for any objects that could potentially harm your puppy, removing any rocks, nuts, or pinecones. Just as fireplaces can be a danger indoors, ashes and flames from fire pits and barbecues can be hazardous. When you are barbecuing, keep an eye on your Brittany and keep the lighter fluid out of reach.

If your yard is fenced, check to make sure that there are no holes that your pet can squeeze under and escape. If you have holes in your fence, block them off with boards or chicken wire. Your Brittany can squeeze through a space much smaller than you would imagine. Be sure your fence is high enough so your Brittany cannot jump over it.

If you have a swimming pool or pond, be sure to block off access to them. Even though your Brittany can swim, he could still drown if he falls in and is unable to get out. Also, many of the chemicals used in maintaining swimming pools and ponds are toxic. If your Brittany drinks the water, it could cause an upset tummy or diarrhea.

BETTER SAFE THAN SORRY

As a general precaution, put away anything of value or that could be a chewing or choking hazard (puzzle pieces, Air-pods, small toys, or so on) out of reach and sight when you are not around.

Open doors and windows are great at letting in fresh air, but they can also tempt your Brittany outside into the world of cars and other risks. Make sure, if your dog can get outside on his own accord, that he will be heading into a safe, enclosed place, such as a fenced-off backyard.

By taking time to puppy-proof your home, you are setting him up for success. As your Britt gets older, he will learn basic obedience training and what is expected of him, so you will not need to be so vigilant with him.

Shopping List

> " Brittanys can be climbers and jumpers. A baby gate may work for containment, or you may need a taller gate. Some people have resorted to putting two gates on top of each other! They can also get bored easily and then may become destructive to furniture or other easily reached items. Give them plenty of stimulation and safe chewing options.
>
> **DARLENE VANHOEVE**
> *Shamrock Brittanys* "

Once you bring your new dog home, whether he's an adult or a puppy, you will not want to leave your furry bundle of joy alone while you go shopping, so make sure you get the following items beforehand.

The most indispensable item on the list? Your unconditional love – it may sound cheesy, but it is true.

APPROPRIATE FOOD – Puppies need proper nutrition to grow into healthy adult dogs. When you pick up your Brittany, the breeder or shelter will often give you a few days' worth of the food they were feeding your dog. To avoid tummy upset during what is already a stressful time, gradually transition your dog to a new food by mixing the two foods together.

CLICKER – An essential training tool for training your Brittany from day one, a clicker is a handheld device that makes a clicking noise, used in positive-reinforcement training.

CRATE – Crate training provides your Brittany with a safe place to call his own while minimizing accidents on the carpets and destructive behavior such as chewing on the furniture.

There is no need to buy a puppy-sized crate and then another crate when the dog is adult-sized. Instead, save some money and time by getting a crate that is designed for your Brittany when he is full-grown. The crate should provide enough room for your Brittany to stand up, turn around and stretch. In chapter five of this book, we will discuss everything you need to know and more about crate training.

I personally prefer metal crates for the following reasons:

- Wire crates can easily be collapsed and can take up less space in storage. Plastic crates only come in two pieces, and they take up more room.

- Some puppies can feel claustrophobic in a plastic pen, as there is less visibility. Wire crates provide a clearer view, allowing your pup to see everything around him. When the dog needs quiet time, you can easily place a blanket on top.

- The majority of wire crates come with a divider that allows you to adjust the size of the crate as your puppy grows.

Photo Courtesy of Dan Thomas

- The plastic tray on the bottom of the crate makes for easy clean-up as it simply slides up. Plastic crates need to be taken apart to thoroughly disinfect them.

DOGGY TREATS – Doggy treats play a vital role in training your four-pawed companion. Look for treats that are soft, chewable, and low in calories and sugar. Remember that while treats help in bonding and reinforcing good behavior, they should never make up more than 10% of your pup's overall diet.

FOOD AND WATER DISHES – Your Brittany should have his own food and water dishes. Even though you may decide to only put out your Britt's food dish at meal times, fresh water should be available at all times. If you find your dog devours his food too fast, maybe consider investing in a slow-feeding bowl to teach your dog to eat at a more appropriate pace.

SHAMPOO AND GROOMING TOOLS – Even if you plan to get your Britt professionally groomed, you should have all the basics at home. Dog-friendly shampoo, a comb, a brush, and nail clippers are essential grooming tools. If you live in an area with skunks, it is always handy to have a neutralizing skunk shampoo on hand. You can find more information on how to groom your Brittany in chapter 11 of this book.

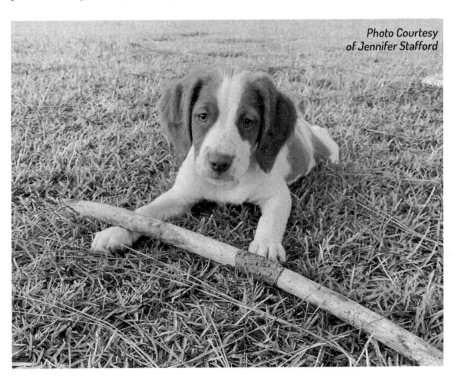

Photo Courtesy of Jennifer Stafford

COLLAR, LEASH, HARNESS, AND I.D. TAGS – Walking your new Brittany is one of the best ways to bond, stay active, and socialize your dog. You will need a secure and sturdy leash and collar from day one. Collars can be adorned with an identification tag that includes your contact information in case he gets lost. A no-pull harness will teach your energetic Brittany not to pull while on his walk. Trust me – your Brittany will love his harness just as much as you!

PEE PADS – Pee pads are essential for potty training, even if you are planning on training your Brittany to go outside. In the beginning, your puppy will have a hard time not urinating, so you can place the pee pad in an area close to his crate and slowly move towards the designated bathroom area.

POOP BAGGIES – Being a responsible dog owner means picking up after your puppy. Look for poop baggies that are made from durable material and are easy to dispose of. It's even better if they are made from biodegradable materials.

PUPPY BED OR BLANKET – The crate will provide a sense of security for your pooch, but a soft, warm blanket will make it feel like home. Look for an orthopedic mattress designed for the crate size. Also, your puppy will greatly appreciate having a soft, fluffy bed to relax on while watching television with his new family.

PUPPY GATE AND PLAY PEN – This can give the puppy an area to play that is safe. This comes in handy when you are busy, have company, or have to leave the puppy alone.

PUPPY TOYS – All dogs need mental stimulation, including your Brittany, no matter how old he is. Toys are a fantastic way to bond and interact with your pooch. If your Brittany is a puppy, look for toys designed for puppies during their teething stage. Consider interactive treat toys and puzzle toys to keep your dog engaged when you cannot be with him.

STAIN AND ODOR REMOVER – Puppies do not come potty trained, and even if you adopted an older shelter Brittany, he might need to be reminded about proper indoor potty etiquette. You need to anticipate accidents. Look for a stain and an odor remover that is designed to destroy pet urine enzymes. These enzymes are like a red flag calling out for your dog to return to the exact same spot to urinate again.

TOOTHPASTE– You will need to get your Brittany used to having his teeth brushed from the very first week of bringing him home. Never use human toothpaste on your puppy. It contains an artificial sweetener called Xylitol, which is extremely toxic for dogs. Instead, look for toothpaste specifically designed for large-sized dogs. You can find more information on how to brush your pup's teeth in chapter 11 of this book.

By being prepared for your new Brittany's arrival, you will be able to concentrate on bonding with him as soon as you bring him home. Besides everything that you need to do to make your Brittany feel like a member of the family, do not forget to capture your memories together through your camera or phone.

Establish Puppy House Rules and Daily Routines

> 66
>
> *Brittanys should never run, jog, jump, bike, or walk on hard surfaces until they are two years old. This is true for all breeds of dogs. Their joints and skeletal system develop until two years old and constant impact from activities on hard surfaces can damage or hinder their development. While they are young, let your puppy play on grass or exercise in safe bodies of water. Teach them how to retrieve a ball or just let them run and play in a fenced in yard. Once your Brittany turns two, they can join you in all activities.*
>
> JESSIE SCHULZ
> *Credit Brittanys*
>
> 99

As you recall, you have just taken your puppy away from the only world he has ever known, leaving his mother and littermates behind. Your dog just had a frightening car ride and has now arrived in a strange, new world with new smells, sounds, and people. Your Brittany needs to learn how to live in this strange new environment. Helping your Britt grow into a well-behaved and well-mannered family member is the responsibility of everyone in your house.

HAVE A FAMILY MEETING

Before bringing a Brittany into your life and home, it is extremely important to sit down with all of the members of your household and agree upon a set of rules for your new dog that everyone has to respect. By this, I am not referring to a set of rules just for your dog but for every human in the house.

House rules only work if every single person sticks to them 100 percent of the time. Otherwise, your Brittany will be confused and will not know what is expected of him. For example, it will be impossible to tell your pooch that he is not allowed upstairs if your children occasionally let him come upstairs and sit on the bed while munching on doggy treats.

Britts are very easy to train, but once they get away with something, they will have a hard time accepting being told "No" the next time. Everybody has to be on the same page when it comes to house rules –

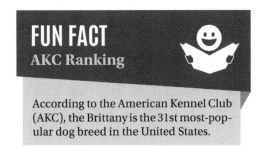

FUN FACT
AKC Ranking

According to the American Kennel Club (AKC), the Brittany is the 31st most-popular dog breed in the United States.

no exception ever! Below are a few topics to discuss with your family before bringing your new dog home:

SHOULD YOU LET YOUR BRITTANY UP ON THE FURNITURE?

There are a few things to consider when deciding whether or not your Brittany will be allowed on the furniture.

- Brittanys are a medium-sized breed and take up a fair bit of space; in other words, they are not lap dogs, even though they will try to cuddle up on your lap.

- Britts love water, rolling in mud, and other smelly unmentionables whenever they get the chance. So, there is a high probability your pooch will jump on the furniture when he is wet and dirty.

- Brittanys are a low-shedding breed, and if your dog is allowed on the furniture, there will be at least some hair transfer onto your clothes when you sit down.

It may be cute to have your Brittany puppy snuggling up with you on the sofa. However, if you allow this when he is a puppy, it will be extremely hard to change this habit when he becomes a 35-to-40-pound adult dog.

Your options are to never allow your Brittany on the furniture or always let him on the furniture. Instead of banning your dog from all furniture, you may decide to let him up on a certain chair or couch.

WHERE IN THE HOUSE IS YOUR BRITTANY ALLOWED?

Most pet owners prefer that their dogs do not roam freely about the house, especially if their puppy is not potty trained yet. Some restrict their dogs to the ground level only and do not allow them to go upstairs. Others block off access to the kitchen, pantry, laundry room, baby's room, or any rooms where delicate items may be.

If you decide to establish rules like this, you will need to use baby gates to restrict your Britt's access and make sure the entire family is consistent in never letting him into those areas. Personally, I restrict a puppy and gradually open up the house as he learns proper in-house etiquette.

WILL YOU FEED HIM TABLE SCRAPS FROM UNDER THE DINNER TABLE?

Brittanys love to eat. Even if you give your dog a treat just once in a blue moon, then he will learn to stare, drool, and beg constantly. Even though this might not be a problem for you and your family, many of your guests may find it disturbing.

Begging is one of the hardest bad habits to break, so it is best to avoid it completely. If you decide to give your Brittany table scraps or treats, the best option is to take them to your dog's food dish and never feed him from the table.

WHO WILL BE RESPONSIBLE FOR HIM THROUGHOUT THE DAY?

Before you bring your Brittany home, you will need to decide who will take care of the different tasks involved in caring for your dog, such as what needs to be done, when, by whom and how often.

Here are a few things you will need to consider:

- Who will take your Brittany for exercise and when?
- Who is responsible for feeding your bundle of energy?
- Who will brush your Brittany, brush his teeth, trim his nails? When and how often?
- Who will take the lead in the obedience sessions and how often?
- Who will be on clean up duty for your dog's toilet area in the back yard?

To avoid forgetting and/or potential arguments about who has not done what, once you agree, draw up a schedule of who is responsible for what and when. Try to get the entire family involved in caring for your Brittany, as it builds a stronger bond and relationship between each family member and your dog.

Establishing a routine and house rules are essential for your Brittany. Your pooch will be eager to adapt to his new family and to understand what is expected of him. The more consistent the entire household is at following rules, the sooner your dog will figure everything out.

Preparing Your Current Pets and Children

If you have any pets who freely move about the house, be sure to ensure them of your love. Before leaving to pick up the new dog, take your pet(s) for a walk and give them a few yummy treats. Allow them to have access to all of the areas where they were previously allowed; otherwise, they will think you are punishing them. If you have a cat, ensure he will have access to high areas so as to observe the new dog from a comfortable distance.

Create a new puppy sanctuary which includes a crate and an enclosed puppy pen. Allow the resident pets to explore the area freely before bringing home the new dog. If possible, ask the breeder to give you a piece of cloth that has the new puppy's scent. Let your present pets smell the scent as this will help them embrace your Brittany quicker.

Nothing excites children more than a cute, lovable little puppy. They just want to hug him and squeeze the bejesus out of the little bundle of fur. For this very reason, it is vital that you sit down with your children before you bring home your puppy and teach them how to pet, hold and pick up your new puppy.

First impressions have never been more important, so plan ahead for a smooth transition.

One of the best ways to teach younger children how to pick up and pat a puppy is by doing a few practice sessions using a stuffed toy. Explain to younger children that even though your Brittany looks like a stuffed bear, he isn't a toy. Even though they will want to play constantly with the new dog, tell them that he will need time to explore his new surroundings and rest.

Children tend to yell when they get excited, which can frighten the new puppy. Do practice sessions with your children, helping them to use softer, indoor voices to avoid startling the Brittany.

Golden rule: Never leave your puppy and the child alone together, even if it's only for a short period of time. Their relationship needs to develop under supervision, rewarding calm and gentle behavior.

The Ride Home

The ride home is all about safety, reducing stress, and catering to your new best friend's needs.

The first car ride home should not be taken lightly. It is an opportunity to get off on the right paw and start bonding. For the journey home, there are a few things you should consider. This includes such things as safety inside of the car, water and toilet breaks, and the possibility of car sickness.

Before heading out to pick up your Brittany, you will want to bring along some doggy treats, a chew toy, a blanket, a leash and collar, poop baggies, and pet-friendly cleaning supplies (in case there is an accident). Make sure you bring along some bottled water, portable food, and a water dish, if the trip is longer than two hours. Also, do not forget to bring any paperwork pertaining to the breeder or shelter contract.

You should expect some whining and crying from your Brittany on the drive home as he was abruptly taken away from everything he ever knew and loved. To reduce the chance of travel sickness, ask the breeder to make sure your puppy has an empty stomach for the trip home.

No food should be given to your pooch two to three hours prior to traveling to prevent car sickness. If the trip home is longer than three hours, be sure to bring along a food dish to give the dog a handful of food in case he

Photo Courtesy of Samantha Choffel

gets hungry. Brittanys love to eat, and your dog will be no exception; he will clearly let you know he is hungry by whining or barking.

Before hopping in the car and driving off with your new Brittany, take him on a short walk away from the breeder, his mother, and littermates so he can get used to being with you. An added bonus to taking him for a short stroll is that you give your pooch an opportunity to relieve himself before getting into the car.

Let your new Brittany explore the car at his own pace by letting him crawl around the car with the engine turned off. Once he is inside the car, leave the doors open and turn the car on so he gets used to the sound of the engine. Show him his crate and blanket, and when he goes inside, give him a doggy treat.

But how should you transport your new dog home? Should he be placed inside a cardboard box on the floor or in a traveling crate? Or should he sit on your lap and be allowed to roam about the car freely? Is it better for him to sit in the back seat versus the front seat? Here are some common concerns:

YOUR SAFETY – Having a loose puppy roaming about the car presents a very real danger of causing an accident. All puppies are curious by nature, and if they are not secured inside of a crate, they can easily and dangerously become wedged under the pedals while you are driving.

YOUR BRITTANY'S SAFETY – Younger pups lack coordination, and if allowed to wander around on the seats while the car is moving, they could possibly fall to the floor and hurt themselves. In addition, if you have to come to a sudden stop or swerve around a corner, your Brittany could be thrown off balance and be seriously injured.

FRONT OR BACK SEAT – In the United States, children who are seven years and younger are not permitted to sit in the front seat. In the case of an accident, the air-bag is instantly activated, releasing a punch that could seriously injure or kill a child. In the case of a baby Brittany, the force would, without a doubt, be fatal.

CRATE OR CARDBOARD BOX – Placing your Brittany in a box is a recipe for disaster, as he could easily climb over the edges and start gallivanting around your car. Your best choice is your only choice – using a crate.

If the crate is small enough, you can place it on the floor in the rear passenger seating. If not, you can place it on the back seat and secure it with the seat-belt harness. Fully line the crate with absorbent paper in case of accidents; this will facilitate clean-up and keep the mess off your pooch. Place a chew toy or two inside of the crate to keep your dog preoccupied. He most likely will ignore it and cry, but it is worth a shot!

Points to consider when choosing a travel carrier:

- **FIND THE CORRECT SIZE** - A 12-week-old Brittany weighs approximately 12 to 14 pounds. A full-grown Brittany will weigh between 35 to 42 pounds and range from 17 to 20 inches in height. The carrier or crate should be big enough for your pup to stand up in and to turn around.

- **DESIGN MATTERS** – Look for a dog carrier that has passed third-party crash tests and comes highly reviewed. A poorly designed dog carrier can be hazardous in an accident.

- **CHOOSE A STYLE** – There are two basic styles of travel carriers for dogs – hard and soft. Hard covers offer superior protection for your dog and are preferable if traveling long distances. Soft covers offer less protection for your dog but are easier to carry.

TWO IS BETTER THAN ONE. If you have company on the ride home, you can take turns sitting in the back of the crate beside your Brittany. Brittanys tend to bond quickly with people they encounter early on. Plus, remember that this is the first time he has been on a car ride and separated from his family, so being alone can be a terrifying experience.

THE NEED FOR WATER AND TOILET BREAKS. If it is a long trip home, your pup will need to stop for water and toilet breaks approximately every thirty minutes or so. It is best to combine these two events, as your pooch will need to urinate a few minutes after drinking water.

Whenever you stop for a water and toilet break, make sure your Brittany is on his leash and tightly held before you even open the door. A nervous puppy could easily bolt in panic, as he will not understand what is happening and may be scared.

AVOID SPOTS THAT ARE FREQUENTLY VISITED BY OTHER DOGS. This is because your Brittany puppy hasn't received all of his vaccinations yet, and you do not want to risk him picking up a disease. As an extra precaution, carry your Brittany, only put him down to do his business, and then carry him back to the car.

YOUR PUPPY MAY GET CAR SICKNESS. It is normal for puppies and older dogs to suffer from motion sickness on their first car trip. Be prepared by bringing along some paper towels, baby wipes, plastic bags, and deodorizer to clean up after any accidents. Watch for your dog pointing his nose towards the floor, lips wrinkled up, drooling, and heaving.

Go straight home with no unnecessary stops! Your new Brittany is having the most stressful day in his life, so do not make it harder than it already is by taking him to strange places and passing him around to strangers to meet him. You want to get him home quickly so he can start the process of settling into his new forever home. This is not a time to stop and grab some groceries or stop off for a quick visit with friends.

Additional considerations. Cover the pup's crate with a blanket to help him feel more secure, or open the window a crack to let in fresh air. Puppies have a difficult time regulating their body temperature and are prone to hypothermia and hyperthermia. Make sure the inside temperature of your car is comfortable, and never leave your dog alone in the car.

Make your Britt's first journey together with you a memorable one. Avoid creating emotional scars that could resurface later on in life, such as separation anxiety. Talk to your dog in a soft, calming voice throughout the trip home to make him feel safe. If you decide to play music in the car, choose relaxing tones that transmit tranquility.

The First Day

> Brittanys are extremely intelligent, clever, and fast. They can grab something and run quicker than you can catch them. It is important to have plenty of safe, interactive toys that will occupy your puppy and discourage them from playing or chewing on items that are off limits in your home.
>
> JESSIE SCHULZ
> *Credit Brittanys*

Even though you are over-joyed at the prospect of finally having your new Brittany at home, remember he is overwhelmed and exhausted.

Before introductions to your family, the very first thing you want to do is take your new dog straight to his designated bathroom spot, whether it is inside on potty pads or a spot outside. As soon as you arrive home, take him there, place him on the ground and wait for your Brittany to do his business. This may take thirty seconds or even as long as ten minutes. Be patient, and when your pooch finally goes, praise him profusely.

Keep your Britt's home coming low-key and stress-free. Be sure to phone your friends and family ahead of time to let them know you will not be having a meet-and-greet the first day your pup comes home. The fewer new people your dog has to meet on his first day, the better.

A dog from a shelter might arrive sleep deprived or stressed, so do not be surprised if the first thing he does after exploring his surroundings is fall into a deep slumber. Your adopted Brittany will need a short period of time to adjust to his new routine and structure, no matter if he was in the shelter for a few days or a couple of months. He will need to learn new habits and rules as he settles into his new, forever home.

If you have other pets, now is not the time for first introductions. Shut them in another room, away from your new dog, as things are stressful enough. Of course, your entire family will be excited to say hello to your new dog, but make sure you have instructed everyone to remain calm and avoid loud voices. It is especially important to instruct your children on how to act in advance, as their excitement can easily startle your puppy. Explain that they need to stay calm and gentle during the first impression.

After getting out of the car and giving your pooch his first bathroom break, play with your puppy in an enclosed safe area, preferably near to his crate and food and water dishes. Let your Britt take his time sniffing his surroundings and getting used to his new little world.

Everyone can take a turn stepping into your pup's enclosed space and getting down to the puppy's level by sitting on the floor so they are less intimidating. Let your Brittany come to them instead of having them chase after the dog and scooping him up, as this may frighten your little pup.

All of this stress, excitement, and mental stimulation most likely has exhausted your dog. As soon as the first introductions have ended, put him to bed for a short while. Trust me; he is going to need it. You may have to coax him into his crate with a treat or two.

As for your pup's behavior on his first day, he may run around like a little hurricane, smelling anything he can stick his nose into, barking, and bouncing from one spot to another. On the other hand, your pooch may be completely overwhelmed and retreat into his crate. Give your dog the space he needs to accept his new world on his terms. Never force your dog to do something he does not feel comfortable doing.

It takes an average of two to three days for your Brittany to embrace his new home, love his new family, and recognize his name.

If you normally work on the day you plan to bring your Brittany home, make sure you request time off, so you can spend as much time with the puppy as possible. After all, it is the first day that you embark on an incredibly special friendship!

Introducing Your Brittany to Your Resident Dog

Brittanys are social animals who tend to love the company of other dogs. However, it can still be tricky when introducing the new dog to current family pets. First impressions have never been more crucial, especially if your resident pooch is used to being the only dog contending for your attention.

Your older resident dog has already declared your house his territory and may feel the need to defend what he rightfully considers to be his property. Depending on your new Brittany's energy level and personality, your old dog may be submissive, act fearful, or worst-case scenario, fight back.

According to the Humane Society, more than 40 percent of US households that have pet dogs have more than one dog. The majority of those dogs in a multiple-pet household did not arrive at the same time. So, if you are bringing your Brittany into your pack, what are the dos and don'ts of the first introduction?

DO'S

Prepare your house beforehand – Prior to bringing your new Brittany home, put away anything your resident dog may be protective of such as his food bowls, bones, beds and toys. Make sure your new puppy has his own designated area for his items. Even if your resident dog has never been possessive in the past, it is best to be vigilant.

Use a leash – Introduce your new Brittany to your current dog while on the leash. This will allow the older dog to feel as if he is in control of the situation. Also, if there are altercations, you can quickly pull your puppy out of harm's way without causing a huge commotion. Keep the leash slack so your dogs do not feel as if they are being held back.

Choose a neutral area – The initial meeting should occur in a neutral environment such as a park or a walking trail. It is preferable to avoid first encounters in your house, or even in your front yard, as your resident dog may become territorial. Ask a family member to meet you at the meeting spot. Expect your dogs to sniff, circle, play, urinate, or even ignore each other. Keep the first introduction short, followed by the next step.

Go for a walk together – Once the dogs walk together side by side, tolerating each other, then you can go home. First, enter the house with your current dog, and then bring in the new dog inside of your house. By doing this, your resident dog is essentially inviting the new dog into his territory as his guest.

DON'TS

Do not force interactions – One of the biggest mistakes pet owners make when introducing their new dog to their older resident dog is simply tossing them together and hoping for the best. Also, do not place the dogs in the same crate. This is a recipe for disaster, as both dogs could end up seriously hurt.

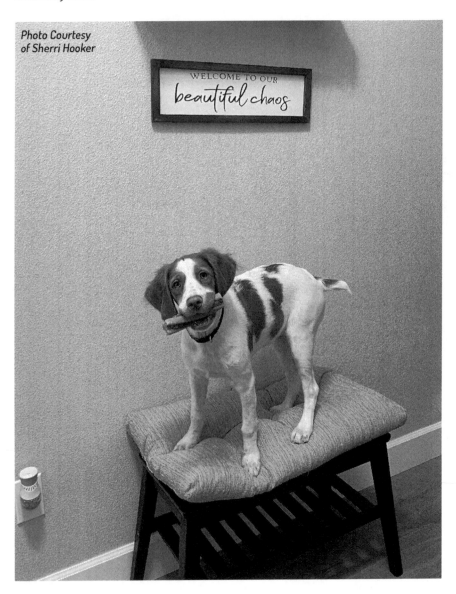

Photo Courtesy of Sherri Hooker

WELCOME TO OUR
beautiful chaos

Do not get involved – Once your dogs are both inside the house together, there may be altercations between the two of them, but do not become irritated or annoyed with your older dog. It is natural that the older dog will try to put the new dog in his place. Stay calm and let them establish hierarchy among themselves.

If your older pooch is being a bit of a bully to your puppy or even vice versa, place them in separate areas and do not give them toys when they are spending time together. Teach your younger pup to respect the older dog's personal space. Establish a quiet retreat for your older dog where he will not be disturbed or harassed by a puppy demanding attention.

Do not forget to show affection to your older dog – Small puppies can be quite annoying for older dogs, and older dogs can feel a tad bit jealous of the attention you are giving the new dog. Do not forget to cuddle your older dog with extra love and attention to reconfirm that you still love him. Do not expect the dogs to embrace each other instantly; often, it can take up to six months before a new addition to the household is accepted or tolerated.

Don't get two puppies at the same time – Dog behaviorists, trainers, and breeders discourage adopting siblings as their deep bond impedes their individual ability to learn basic obedience skills and form a connection with their human family. Often this is referred to as littermate syndrome, as the sibling dogs assume their interactions with each other are adequate. Littermate syndrome causes intense separation anxiety when separated from each other and fearfulness of unfamiliar people, situations, and other dogs.

Helpful suggestions to ease the tension between your dogs:

- Confine your Brittany to an established part of the house that is far away from the older dog's crate and feeding area. Be sure to make any changes at least a week before bringing home your new dog and allow your older dog to sniff out the new dog's area.

- After your dogs have finished eating or play time, place your new puppy inside his crate and close the door. Ask your older dog to come over and investigate the new dog on his own terms.

- Give your older dog the royal treatment! This will prevent his feelings from being hurt. Never let the new dog push past him for your affection or praise. Your older pet deserves and needs to feel he is still loved as much as he was before.

First Night

> "
>
> *For your Brittany puppy's first few nights with you, it is important to ease his/her transition into your home. Have them stay overnight in a small crate next to your bed. Also, having a toy for your pup with the scent of its littermates is always a good idea, many times your breeder will provide you one should you ask.*
>
> **STEVE ROGERS**
> *Winding Branch Kennel*
> "

If you have raised a puppy before, then you know this is when the real challenge begins as you will be sleep deprived for the first few nights at home with your new Brittany. At night, your pooch may feel lonely and may vocally demonstrate this by whining.

Your Brittany is still a baby. Up until today, he has spent his entire life near his mother and littermates. All the sights, noises, and smells that once comforted him are gone and replaced with strange new ones. To help your puppy settle into his new home quicker, ask the breeder to give you a piece of bedding or a snuggle toy that smells like the pup's mother and littermates.

Puppies tend to sleep between 16 to 20 hours a day, but they have near-hourly bathroom needs. When your Brittany wakes up, he will start whining or crying to let you know that he has to go to the bathroom. You will not have much time to get him to his designated potty spot. So, have a spot close by and run!

Some pet owners prefer to place their pup's crate inside of their bedroom or close by so they can hear him wake up. Once you pick a sleeping spot for your Brittany, do not move it until your dog is fully trained.

Place your Britt's crate in a draft-free area and put a blanket over it to make it seem cozier. Try placing an old-fashioned alarm clock under his bedding. The constant tick-tock sound resembles the sound and vibration of his mother's heartbeat. Another option is to place a hot water bottle under the dog's blanket to keep him toasty warm at night.

Do not be fooled by those big brown eyes! Your Britany needs to learn nighttime is for sleeping and not playtime. If he barks, take him on his leash to his designated bathroom area. After he relieves himself, praise him and take him back to his crate. Do not give him any treats or playtime. Put him back in his crate, and he should go back to sleep almost immediately.

Your new pup's bladder has not built up enough control to get through the entire night without needing to go to the bathroom. It will take a number of weeks before you will be able to sleep through the night without having to rush him to his bathroom spot. Expect to get up at least five to six times, the first few nights to take him to the bathroom.

Under no circumstances should you take your puppy to bed with you. Brittanys are Velcro dogs and love to be as close as possible to you. Once your pooch starts sleeping beside you in your bed, it will be almost impossible to break this habit. It may be difficult to avoid cuddling with him when he starts whining at night, but it is important to leave him in his crate.

Choosing a Vet

How do you know what type of veterinarian is best for your Brittany? Once you choose a vet, how do you know if you made the right choice?

Whether you are a new or veteran dog owner, unsure where to begin, or are looking for a refresher on finding a new veterinarian for your bundle of energy, this section will help you find the perfect vet. Choosing the right vet for your Brittany is something you should consider carefully.

ASK FOR RECOMMENDATIONS

Word of mouth is one of the best ways to find a reputable veterinarian in your locality. Be sure to ask fellow dog lovers for advice on different options in your area.

FIND A VETERINARIAN WITH EXPERTISE TREATING DOGS

Not all veterinarians are created equal. Some veterinarians specialize in certain types of animals, such as cows, horses, pigs, and other non-canine pets. You definitely want a veterinarian whose expertise is in treating and caring for dogs. Be sure to ask the vet how much experience he has treating dogs like your Brittany.

LOOK FOR LICENSED PERSONNEL

Most of us just assume that all veterinarians are licensed professionals, but that is not always the case. Make sure the vet is licensed in your state as a veterinarian and not just as a registered veterinary technician. On the American Animal Hospital Association (AAHA) website, you will find a list of accredited and licensed veterinarians in your locality, as well as an evaluation of the facility, staff, patient care, and equipment.

CONSIDER COST AND LOCATION

If an emergency occurs, will you be able to get to the vet's office quickly? Choose a veterinarian whose office is less than one hour drive from your house, and ask if they do house calls to your area. Costs can vary from vet to vet, so be sure to inquire about their prices to make sure they are a good fit for your budget.

LOOK FOR A CLEAN FACILITY

Ask to have a look around the office to check the level of cleanliness. If the place seems dirty, dingy, or foul-smelling, then that is a sign to move on. A veterinarian's office is a medical facility, so it should be just as clean as a hospital or clinic for humans.

INQUIRE ABOUT THEIR APPROACH TO MEDICINE AND PETS

Most vets have different approaches when it comes to pets and medication. Be sure to have a brief discussion with the potential vet to see if his philosophies about wellness and prevention match with yours. If they are not on the same page as you, then you should move on.

BOTH YOU AND YOUR DOG SHOULD FEEL COMFORTABLE

Being comfortable around your vet is vital as you should feel comfortable talking to him about your dog's health and other concerns. The same applies for your Brittany because he needs to feel at ease around the vet, especially since the vet will need to touch your dog to examine him. Some signs your dog is uncomfortable around the potential vet are uncontrolled shaking, anxiety, fear, and aggressiveness when the vet draws close to your dog.

Personal referrals are a great start, but you should still take time to research the veterinary clinic and its staff. The vet you finally choose will play a significant role in your Brittany's life, so take your time looking for the right one.

If you have any problems with the vet you chose, do not hesitate to switch facilities. Veterinary clinics expect clients to come and go. However, before you depart, be sure to request a complete copy of your Brittany's medical file. You can ask that your dog's health records be faxed or mailed to either you or your new vet.

First Vet Visit

Once you have found a veterinarian whom you feel comfortable working with, book an appointment for a meet-and-greet for your Brittany before his actual visit for his vaccines. Any reputable veterinarian will be extremely busy and will not have time for drop-ins unless it is an emergency. Therefore, make an appointment and arrive early, so your Brittany can get used to the clinic's scents, noises, and surroundings.

This will allow your puppy to associate positive memories with the veterinarian's office. The employees may slip your Brittany a treat or two. Many pet owners who skip this step end up with dogs who are absolutely petrified of going to the vet's office.

When you go in for your Brittany's actual first real vet's visit, be sure to take along any paperwork regarding your dog, such as his vaccination and health records from the breeder or shelter. Most likely, this paperwork will stay in your Brittany's personal file at the veterinarian's office. If you want copies for yourself, make photocopies before going to the vet's office.

WHAT SHOULD YOU EXPECT DURING THE FIRST VET'S VISIT?

You will be allowed into the examination room with your Brittany. Be sure to bring along some of his favorite treats. Be calm and relaxed. While talking to your pooch, use an upbeat, happy voice, praising his good behavior.

If your shelter dog or puppy has not yet been microchipped yet, ask the veterinarian if it would be possible to do it on your dog's first visit. You can find more information on microchipping in chapter 12 of this book.

The veterinarian will weigh your Brittany, check his temperature through his rectum, examine his eyes, ears, mouth, paws, teeth, genital region, and fur. Then the vet will listen to your dog's heartbeat and lungs using a stethoscope. The veterinarian will palpate your dog's lymph nodes and abdominal areas. Once the general examination is finished, the vet will administer any vaccinations and de-wormers required. In chapter 12, you can find more information about why you need to de-worm your dog.

The vet will most likely discuss any future medical procedures your Brittany might need, such as spaying or neutering and microchipping. If you have any questions regarding your pup's general health, now would be a good time to ask. Your veterinarian will give you a vaccine schedule for your Brittany. Be sure to place future dates on your calendar so you don't forget.

CHAPTER 4

Laying a Solid Foundation for Training Your Brittany

Ah, the pitter patter of your puppy's paws, topped off with the oh-so-sweet new puppy smell and the gentle sound of puppy snores. These are some of the moments that melt any new puppy parents' hearts. Unfortunately, those sweet moments come with challenges.

There are as many different methods to rear a Brittany as there are to raise a child. However, the majority of us will agree that when it comes to

Photo Courtesy of Sophia McDonald

children, there are a few hard and fast methods. Similarly, with rearing your Brittany, there are universal and indisputable techniques.

Your goal as a puppy parent is to introduce your Brittany to his new world in a positive way. In this chapter, we will discuss how to avoid common training mistakes and how to nip bad behavior in the bud.

Common Puppy-Parenting Mistakes

> *Brittanys love being with other dogs, but should always be introduced carefully. Most dog parks are not ideal for Brittanys as they are intense but small, and can get hurt or intimidated by dogs who don't like their rough play or dogs that are not well-trained. When introducing 2 dogs, always start with them on leashes in a neutral location and watch for any signs of aggression. Once it seems that your Brittany is respecting the other dog, and they both show signs of wanting to play or non-concern, you can let them off-leash (if in a safe place) and keep an eye on them as they interact.*
>
> **DARLENE VANHOEVE**
> *Shamrock Brittanys*

Your Brittany will chew on shoes. He will destroy things. He will pee on the most expensive rug in the house. He will dig up your prized flower garden. He will ignore your commands. He will sit down and refuse to walk any further. You may think your dog is trying to be dominant, rebellious, bad, dumb, or even trying to get even. But none of that is true. Your Brittany is just being a puppy, and puppies make mistakes.

However, your Brittany is not the only one who will be making mistakes. Surely, you have heard the old English saying, "To err is human." This saying could not be truer than when it comes to puppy training. You are going to make more than your fair share of mistakes.

These training errors are not life-threatening, and they can easily be amended. Mistakes are just that – mistakes. But they definitely will slow down the entire training process, causing irritation on both ends of the leash.

Here are some of the most common mistakes people make while training their puppy:

GIVING TOO MUCH FREEDOM

First-time puppy owners often make the mistake of giving their new pooch too much freedom by letting them run around and have fun. All of that extra freedom leads to unwanted accidents on the floor or chasing your puppy around the house to retrieve the headphones he just stole. Not only is this frustrating, but you are teaching your puppy bad habits that will have to be corrected later on down the road.

Puppies need structure and diligent supervision. Whenever you let your Brittany wander around freely, someone should be watching him 100 percent of the time. It helps to let your dog wander with the leash attached to his collar or harness. Your pooch can drag the leash behind him, and you can quickly grab it if you need to gently redirect your pup's attention.

NOT ENOUGH PRACTICE

Many dog owners make the big mistake of assuming their dog has learned everything in his obedience classes. But fast forward a few weeks, even a few months, and the dog has forgotten everything he has learned. What happened? Dogs, just like us, get rusty. Be sure to reinforce your dog's skills daily; all you need is a few minutes each day.

There is an old Russian proverb – "repetition is the mother of learning," which means repetition is the key element in learning. Through repetition, a skill is practiced and rehearsed until it becomes easier. Remember, when it comes to your Brittany, practice makes perfect!

GIVING ATTENTION FOR THE WRONG BEHAVIOR

Your Brittany will repeat behavior that results in praise or treats. This may seem like a simple concept, but many first-time pet owners totally get it wrong, as they forget to reward their dog's good behavior and instead give him loads of attention only when he does do something wrong.

For example, your Brittany is quietly playing with his chew toy inside of his crate, but you are busy sending a text message. When you look up, your pup has started chewing on your shoes. Suddenly your Brittany is getting all sorts of attention from you to make him stop chewing on the shoes. What did you just teach your puppy? When he plays with his chew toy, he gets ignored, but when he chews on your shoes, he gets a whole bunch of attention!

You need to be proactive in rewarding your Brittany when he is doing the right thing. Is your pooch walking calmly on the leash? Good boy! Is he sitting patiently while you serve his breakfast? Good boy! Look for opportunities to praise good behavior. If your dog's behavior is undesirable, like jumping up, barking, whining, or begging, then the best thing you can do is to completely ignore your dog until the behavior stops.

INCONSISTENCY

Inconsistent training will confuse your Brittany. For example, let's say your pooch is not allowed on the couch. Occasionally you make the exception for your dog to come cuddle with you on the couch. But then you turn around and discipline your pup for sitting on the couch. He will not understand what he did wrong.

Strive to be constantly consistent with your Brittany. For example, every time you come home, do not give your fuzzy ball of fur any attention until he is sitting on the floor and not jumping up. This can be difficult, but consistency will prevent your Brittany from becoming confused and, in the long run, will make the training process easier for both of you.

LACK OF PATIENCE

Training your Brittany takes time, and you need to remember that every dog learns at a different pace. Avoid getting frustrated while training your dog, as he will pick up on your negative vibes. Training sessions should be upbeat and positive, so make sure your attitude is in the right frame of mind first.

If your Brittany is struggling to learn something, instead of becoming frustrated with him, stop and consider whether this is a good time or if the session has gone on for too long. Remember, training sessions should be short and sweet (about five to ten minutes) and end on a positive note. If you are impatient and getting irritated with your pup, stop the training session by requesting an easy action that your puppy already knows, such as "sit," and end with a reward.

Just a word of caution: never, ever train your Brittany when you are in a bad mood. This is a recipe for disaster. You could easily take your frustration and anger out on your poor, defenseless dog if he makes a mistake. Instead, make a cup of tea and snuggle up with your Brittany on the couch until your mood improves.

HARSH DISCIPLINE

Brittanys are very sensitive dogs. They do not respond well to harsh discipline or punishment. A Brittany who is scolded or physically hit can become very timid, fearful, and over time, may become aggressive. Harsh discipline involves yelling, hitting, use of physical force, leash-jerking, grabbing at the scruff of the neck, and staring down.

Punishing your Brittany is counterproductive as he will become less responsive to training. Fear of being punished will prevent him from even trying to learn a new command as he will be confused and worried about what you will get mad at him for next. Rather than punishing your Brittany, reward him for positive behavior.

Brittanys thrive on affection, so praise your dog generously and give him treats whenever he does something that pleases you. When you hit or yell at your dog, you are teaching him to fear you; you break his trust and weaken his confidence. There is no place for any type of harsh discipline in training your dog.

Brittanys are independent dogs meaning they will feel free to break the rules over and over again if they think they can get away with it. It is vital you establish your dog's boundaries to reinforce your role as pack leader and prevent your dog from developing dominance-related behavior such as aggression. But being the "alpha" does not give you the license to treat your dog cruelly or domineering. It simply means to lead the pack. Reward your Brittany for obeying the rules, and he will happily continue to do so.

Photo Courtesy of Tyler Toporowski

How to Teach an Old Dog New Tricks

The saying, *"you can't teach an old dog new tricks,"* has been around for decades. The truth is, you can teach an old dog new tricks, and it is not that much different from teaching a puppy.

Congratulations, if you just adopted a Brittany from a shelter or rescue group! No matter the reason why your Brittany landed in a shelter, with a large dose of love, time, and patience, he will become a happy, well-adjusted member of your family in no time.

Your newly adopted Brittany most likely already has some level of obedience training; he simply needs a refresher course on what is expected of him in a family environment. There is a small possibility that something from his past may trigger bad behavior, which is why it is vital you take your time to socialize and train your older Brittany.

GIVE YOUR BRITTANY TIME TO ADJUST

All older dogs come with a prior history, either positive or negative – not to mention the trauma of being relinquished to a noisy shelter. Keep in mind that the stress of all of this upheaval, along with whatever your pooch has experienced in the past, can cause him to be wary of new surroundings.

Give your adopted Brittany time to adjust to his new home, surroundings, and family. Some dogs instantly adjust to their new life, while others may take several months before they fully embrace their forever home. If you notice your Brittany is having a hard time adapting, make him feel safe and comfortable. Do not expect him to warm up to his new home immediately; instead, be patient and keep day-to-day activities consistent and predictable.

ESTABLISH BOUNDARIES

Training your older Brittany starts from the very first day you bring him home. Avoid the temptation of coddling him the first few weeks to make up for time spent in the shelter.

If you let your older Brittany get away with bad behavior the first few days, you will have a much harder time trying to break these unwanted habits later on. This includes letting him beg while you eat dinner at the kitchen table, climbing up on the sofa, or eliminating on the carpet. Be sure to establish your dog's boundaries from day one, and make sure the entire family knows how to enforce them.

SET A SCHEDULE

Brittanys thrive on a strict schedule. If your older Britt has spent the last few weeks or even months in a shelter, he probably is very stressed out as life in the shelter can be very unpredictable. Provide much-needed stability for your Brittany by setting up a daily routine for walking, feeding, playing, and sleeping. In most cases, a well-established routine will help your dog embrace his new life faster.

ASSUME YOUR BRITTANY HAS NO TRAINING

Treat your older Brittany just as you would treat a puppy coming into your home. Assume your Brittany has no training, even if the shelter assures you that your dog is well-behaved and had obedience training in the past. Most likely, your pooch will need a few reminders about proper indoor and outdoor etiquette. For more information on how to potty train your Brittany, see chapter five of this book.

Your best choice is to assume your Brittany does not know anything at all. This way you will be pleasantly surprised when you discover he already knows basic commands such as sit, come and stay. Be sure to use loads of positive reinforcement methods while training your older pup, and keep training sessions short and sweet.

START WITH CRATE TRAINING

Just as with a puppy, you will want to introduce your shelter dog to crate training from the very first day. This way, you can instantly start working on housebreaking and have peace of mind knowing your new dog will not get into mischief when you are unable to supervise him. In chapter 5 of this book, you can find more information regarding how to crate train your dog.

Your Brittany will embrace his crate as it will give him a place to call his own. Between being relinquished at the shelter, living in the shelter, and now coming to your new home, your Brittany may feel extremely stressed out. Your pooch will thank you for having a place to retreat to whenever he is feeling overwhelmed.

A word of caution: crate training may be difficult for some dogs, especially if the previous owner used a crate as a place of punishment or the dog had to spend long periods of time confined to one. Never force your Brittany into a crate.

ENROLL IN AN OBEDIENCE CLASS

Just because your shelter Britt may be having a hard time adjusting to his new home does not mean you should put off joining an obedience program.

These regular training sessions will help you and your dog bond and help him adapt to his new routine. Brittanys crave structure and predictability, so obedience classes are one of the best gifts you can give your shelter dog.

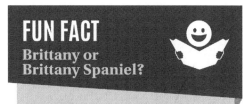

FUN FACT

Brittany or Brittany Spaniel?

The AKC deleted the word "spaniel" from the breed name in 1982 because the dogs point more than flush. While simply called "Brittany" in the United States, some countries still refer to the breed as "Brittany Spaniel."

Socialization is another important factor to teach your older shelter dog, as it is important to get him familiar with his new environments, people, and other animals. Socializing an older dog should be taken slowly and within your dog's comfort level.

CONSIDERATIONS WITH TRAINING AN OLDER SHELTER DOG

Actually, there are quite a few advantages to teaching older dogs compared to puppies, due to their longer attention span. However, your older Brittany might need a little more motivation than a puppy, especially if his previous owner mistreated him. Even though your Brittany might not be as agile or mentally sharp as a puppy, he still has a built-in desire to please you.

While your Brittany is adjusting to his new home, be sure to supervise him at all times, including inside and outside. Even if your yard is completely fenced in, your shelter dog could become startled by strange noises or smells, causing him to escape. If your dog escapes, he will have a difficult time finding his way home because he is still not familiar with his new surroundings.

Here are some suggestions to consider when training an older dog:

- Keep training sessions upbeat and positive. If you or your Brittany become agitated, anxious, or nervous, then it is best to take a break.
- Old joints do not like doing the same movement over and over again. Avoid asking you Britany to "sit" twenty times in a row without taking a break. Doing so may cause your pooch pain and may make him slow to respond.
- Keep training sessions short and sweet.
- Recognize and take into consideration your Brittany's limitations.
- Use verbal and hand signals. Older dogs may be hard of hearing, so the hand signals will help.

- Positive reinforcement is your secret weapon, especially treats. If you are worried about weight gain, chop unsalted, boiled, skinless chicken breast into small pieces.

- Be aware of the temperature. Older dogs are more sensitive to heat and cold than younger dogs.

- Train on soft surfaces. Choose soft surfaces such as carpet, grass, or a yoga mat to make training sessions more comfortable for your elderly Brittany.

- Practice one trick at a time, as multiple tricks may be confusing and frustrating for your elderly dog.

Remember that training sessions should be fun and give you moments to bond with your Brittany. If your dog's health and age prevent him from learning a new trick, concentrate on making him feel comfortable, loved, and cared for.

Why Socialize Your Brittany?

> If your new Brittany is an only dog, you will need to provide plenty of human contact. They are very social dogs and love being with other members of their pack. They don't do as well being alone for hours and hours a day.
>
> **DARLENE VANHOEVE**
> *Shamrock Brittanys*

Socializing your Brittany teaches him to be well-behaved around other humans and animals. Socialization helps your dog feel comfortable within a wide variety of situations and helps them feel confident in new situations.

Adult dogs who have not been properly socialized during their younger years often will be aggressive, fearful, and stressed when exposed to something new.

The idea behind socializing your Brittany is to help him become acclimated to different types of sights, sounds, and smells in a positive, memorable manner. Proper socialization will prevent your pooch from being fearful of the mailman, children, car rides, etc., and help him develop into a well-mannered, happy companion.

In general, well-socialized dogs are more enjoyable to be around. This is because they feel more comfortable in a wide variety of situations than a poorly socialized dog. They are less likely to be aggressive or fearful when presented with something new. Poorly socialized dogs can be a headache, as they often react with fear or aggression when they meet unfamiliar people, animals, dogs, or new experiences.

WHAT AGE IS BEST FOR SOCIALIZING YOUR BRITTANY?

Puppies handle new experiences best between three to 16 weeks of age; after that, they become more cautious of new situations. Even if your dog is older than 16 weeks, though, continued socialization and introduction to new situations and people are essential as they will reinforce good behavior.

However, socializing your Brittany before the age of 16 weeks can be a challenge as he has not received all of his vaccines. You will need to be extra cautious when exposing your puppy to unknown animals or even walking in an area that is frequented by other animals. Unfortunately, if you wait to socialize your Britt until he is old enough to be completely vaccinated, you are missing out on vital training opportunities.

If you adopted an older Brittany, you may have missed out on crucial puppy socialization, but remember, it is never too late to teach an old dog new tricks. The key is slowly reintroducing your older Brittany to sights, sounds, smells, people, and animals with careful supervision and a huge dose of positivity in the form of praise and treats. With patience, you can help your Britt overcome all of his fears.

Socializing your Brittany is a necessity and requires planning. The more positive experiences your pup is exposed to, the better!

Try not to stress out when exposing your Brittany to other dogs, people, or situations, as your puppy can pick up on that. Take baby steps and try to avoid doing too much at once. Stop socializing if you notice your dog feels overwhelmed.

Take into consideration the type of lifestyle you plan to give your Brittany and make a list of any sights or sounds he might encounter on a regular day. For example, consider some experiences such as trains, garbage trucks, crowds, cats, crying infants, a schoolyard full of screaming children, and more. While it might be impossible to expose your pooch to everything he might encounter in his lifetime, the more bases you cover, the better.

When socializing your Brittany, try the following:

- Introduce your Brittany to one new situation at a time. This will help to avoid overwhelming him. For example, if you plan a puppy play date, organize it in your backyard or a park that your dog is already familiar with.

- Immediately, after a new experience or meeting a new person, reward your Brittany with a few treats and generous praise.

- If your Brittany seems uncomfortable or wary of the new experience, such as hearing a group of children playing in the playground, move further away and distract him by playing catch, moving gradually closer each time.

- Always follow any new socialization experiences with praise, patting, a fun game of catch and, of course, a special treat.

Socializing your Brittany is not optional. It is an essential part of your Brittany training. It will help him grow up into a relaxed and happy companion. The more well-adjusted your dog is to his surroundings, the easier it will be for you to share your life with him.

Socializing your Brittany is a life-long process that will need to be reinforced throughout the years. Never ever force interactions with strangers, other dogs, or animals, or children. Always let your dog establish his own terms for discovering and accepting new situations, environments, and people.

Cats and Dogs

Here are suggestions to help your Brittany and your cat get along:

Use positive reinforcement – Never ever yell, hit, or throw something at your cat or dog to stop them from fighting as this will make the situation more uncomfortable and stressful. Instead, look for opportunities to reinforce good behavior, such as tolerating each other from different sides of the room. Offer treats for any type of good behavior around each other to teach them that good things come when they tolerate each other peacefully.

Play games together – Never under-estimate the power of playtime, especially if it encourages your beloved pets to play together. Play games with each pet separately, with the other pet observing within close proximity. Once your cat and dog appear to tolerate each other, even if it is from a distance, play games with each one simultaneously such as playing with a string, hide-and-seek, or scavenging games. Just a word of caution: be careful not to play any games that may get either pet overly excited or hyper.

Give them their space – Even though you want your Brittany and cat to be best buds, it is never a good idea to force them together. Instead, keep your cat and dog separated if there is any sign of aggression, fighting, or stress. Cats and dogs need some time and space apart from each other during an argument.

Keep them safe – While teaching your Brittany and cat to like each other, you need to take into consideration their physical safety. For first introductions, you will want to play it safe instead of sorry, as you do not really know how either of your pets will react. Provide high places for your cat, so he can run to. For your dog use two levels of safety, such as a leash and a baby gate. If your pup gets too excited, ask him to lie down or distract him with his chew toy.

Use sensory cues – Cats and dogs are both highly scent-oriented. Swap out beds, blankets, or towels to help your dog and cat get used to each other's scent without the pressure of seeing one another. Another helpful sensory cue is to let them listen to each other's sounds from a safe, comfortable distance, so when they are closer together, a bark, growl, or hiss will not frighten the other pet.

GIVE YOUR CAT HIS OWN TERRITORY

Cats like to feel safe and protected. Set up a "sanctuary" for your cat that cannot be accessed by your Brittany. Create several safe spots for your cat around the entire house to allow your cat to confidently navigate the shared space without crossing paths with his canine roommate.

Most cats are natural climbers, so take advantage of your home's vertical space to create an easy and quick escape route for your cat. Install shelves, buy tall cat trees, or place a cat bed on top of a bookcase. By doing this, you give your cat an opportunity to observe your Brittany from a safe distance of his choice.

Make sure your Brittany cannot access your cat's litter box. Cats enjoy privacy while doing their business, plus some dogs enjoy snacking on cat feces, which is a bad habit for your Brittany because he can contract intestinal parasites. These parasites can cause a long list of health problems, such as vomiting, diarrhea, anemia, and weight loss.

Baby gates are an excellent option to keep your Brittany out of your cat's base camp, but since Brittanys are known for being escape artists, keep the litter box in an open space and use an uncovered box. This way, your cat will not be surprised and cornered mid-squat.

To prevent disastrous mealtime encounters, schedule regular mealtimes for your cat and dog; in other words – no free feeding. Place bowls at separate ends of the house or place your cat's food dish up high on a table or countertop where your Brittany cannot find it.

Keep a close eye on your cat's toys. Dogs tend to love the scent of catnip even more than cats, which can prompt competitive fighting and bickering.

The following steps will maximize the chances for success:

- Before you bring home your Brittany, make sure your cat is up-to-date with her vaccinations and is parasite-free. Plan to keep your pets separated for at least three days after the new arrival. The goal is for your cat to get used to your dog's presence without face-to-face contact. Even though they cannot see each other, they can smell and hear each other.

- Feed your cat and dog on opposite sides of a closed door. This will help your cat to associate the presence of the new dog with something pleasant, such as eating. If your cat seems skittish about eating close to the door, then place her food dish a few feet away and slowly move it closer each day or until your cat is comfortable eating next to the door.

- Begin face-to-face meetings in the common area of your house. Keep your Brittany on a leash and distracted with a chew toy, and let your cat come and go as she wishes. Do not restrain either pet as that could result in injury. Reward your cat with treats and praise, then do the same with your dog. If either pet shows signs of aggression, redirect your pet's attention by tossing a play toy, etc.

- Be prepared to supervise your pets' interactions for at least the next few weeks, perhaps even longer.

There is no need to be alarmed if there are altercations. If your cat bats her paw or growls at the dog, she is simply communicating her boundaries to your new dog. With time, your cat will learn to co-exist with your Brittany, and your dog will learn to respect your cat's space.

Just as you would with an older resident, reassure your cat that you love him by giving him extra attention and treats. Cats like to do things on their own terms, so never force your cat to meet-and-greet the new dog, especially if he is still a puppy, as it will not end well.

Recognize your cat has a definite personality. If your cat acts like she barely tolerates the new dog, then it means she has accepted your Brittany. Remain watchful to ensure all of their interactions go smoothly – especially when your Brittany hits his rambunctious "teenager" stage.

Options if Your Pets Don't Get Along

Every pet owner's secret dream is to come home and find their pets cuddled up together on the couch. Unfortunately, pets do not always get along, especially if they are different species. If you find your pets cannot be friendly, keep them separated for a few days, then reintroduce them to each other.

Reasons why pets may not get along:

HORMONAL – Many disagreements between pets often are related to hormonal changes. An easy fix for this problem is to make sure that all of your resident pets are neutered or spayed, as this will keep any aggression at bay.

FOOD – All animals, no matter their species have a built-in instinct to protect their food. If your pets tend to become aggressive around mealtimes, place your pets' food dishes in separate parts of the house and feed them at the same time.

JEALOUSY – All pets need to feel loved and cherished. An easy solution for this problem is to designate quality time with each of your pets alone, without the other pets watching. This will ensure each pet that you love it and will never replace them.

DOMINANCE – Rivalry among pets is normal, especially if you bring a new pet into the household. Only one pet can be the leader of the pack, and this is something they need to figure out on their own terms and time schedule. Once your pets have established which pet is the leader, respect their decision by feeding the boss first.

A good relationship between your pets may take a few days to establish, or it may take a couple of years. Fights will happen, especially during the first few weeks, as they determine who will be the dominant leader in your house. One method to make your animals back off from fighting is to douse them in water – trust me, they will back off immediately.

If you fear your pets' behavior towards each other may cause harm to each other, you, or even another person, it is not unreasonable to think about giving up one of your pets. Some pets cannot and will not tolerate other pets and are happier living in an "only child" environment.

But, before you consider such a drastic decision, there are lots of behavior specialists out there who are willing to extend you a helping hand to encourage your pets to get along. A certified dog or cat trainer or a board-certified veterinary behaviorist will be able to diagnose and treat your pets' stress, anxiety, phobias, aggression, and reactivity towards each other. Often extreme misbehavior occurs because the pet is suffering from an underlying medical condition, so be sure to check with your vet.

ASK AROUND

Perhaps you have come to the difficult decision to give up one of your pets. If so, first ask a friend or family member if they would like to adopt your pet. If you ask around, you will be pleasantly surprised how many people would be thrilled to give your pet a new forever home. Just make sure the home is suitable for your pet by visiting ahead of time.

If you did not have luck with the above alternatives, then think outside of the box and contact dog trainers or your veterinarian to see if they know of any good homes who are searching for a good pet.

SEEK OUT RESCUE GROUPS

Most localities have active rescue groups dedicated to "fostering" pets in a caring home until they can find them their forever home. One of the main advantages to a rescue group is you are assured that your pet is going into the home of someone who not only loves pets but understands how to take care of them. There is also the option of looking for rescue breed-specific groups. If you are considering surrendering your pet to a shelter, you need to make sure it is a no-kill facility.

Socializing with Other Animals

> *Early socialization is critical for any breed but especially important for a Brittany. Socialization establishes the future development of the pup.*
>
> ROBERT FLEURY
> *Birch Hill Brittanys*

Do you have smaller pets, such as hamsters, rabbits, guinea pigs, gerbils, geckos, etc.?

Brittanys have a high prey drive and usually consider small animals as prey rather than buddies, but the two species can live together peacefully. Before you introduce your Brittany to your small critters, it would be helpful if your dog has previously learned some basic commands such as *sit, come, and stay*. These commands will guarantee your Brittany will be well-mannered and make a good first impression with your small critter.

Before a meet-and-greet with your smaller pets, take your Brittany out for an invigorating run or hike to tire him out. A hyperactive dog will not make a good impression on your smaller pet.

Make sure your tiny critter is confined to his cage. Bring your Brittany close while on a leash. Command him to sit and stay next to the cage and reward your dog for any calm, non-aggressive behavior. Allow him to sniff at your small critter through the cage, then reward him once again for any good behavior. If your dog tries to snap or bark at the small critter moving freely in his cage, walk away with your dog and try again later.

After the initial introduction, continue having your pets meet for a few minutes at a time, lengthening the time of each meeting. Always keep your Brittany on a leash and your small critter confined until your dog shows no sign of aggression. Once this happens, let your small critter run about its enclosure freely while your Brittany observes on his leash. When your dog neither shows any interest in chasing after the critter nor displays any signs of aggression, then you can try letting him off his leash. Never forget to praise and reward your dog's good behavior.

Brittanys are bred to hunt small animals, so a small rodent such as a rabbit, guinea pig, or hamster is an almost irresistible temptation. Even if your dog shows no signs of aggression or prey drive around your small critter for an extended period of time, he could still harm it, even by accident. Never ever leave your Brittany unsupervised with your small critter.

Socializing with Strangers

"

Dog parks are all the rage, but not the place for a puppy. Once your Britt is used to your household and has immunity to diseases you can begin taking it for walks, training classes, visiting friends with dogs; keeping in mind to be watchful that it's a great experience for your dog. Do not allow growling or fighting of any kind.

DIANA L KUBITZ
Renegade Brittanys

"

According to the AKC, the Brittany rates four out of five on the scale of breeds that are considered the friendliest dogs to strangers.

However, even the friendliest dog can become aggressive if not properly socialized. To avoid this happening to your Brittany, it is vital you expose him to a number of different types of people such as men, women, children, men with beards, people in a wheelchair, and so on. But the quantity of those experiences is not as crucial as the quality of each of these encounters.

If your Brittany only spends time with you and your immediate family, over time, he can become wary of anyone who is NOT his family. For this very reason, it is crucial you diversify your pup's social calendar and organize a meet-and-greet.

If your Brittany has not received all of his vaccines, have a plan-and-greet party at your house for him by inviting friends and family over. Ask them to dress up wearing a wide variety of clothes such as uniforms, rain jackets, face masks, hats and gloves, etc. Before introducing your Brittany to someone new, tell them ahead of time so they can pamper him with love and affection, and be sure to slip them a treat or two for your pooch.

Remember Rome was not built in a day – take your time introducing your Brittany to everyone on your list. Start off slow, first with friends and family, then integrate a stranger, such as the postman. Avoid taking your dog to busy public areas too soon, as he may become overly excited or fearful of strangers in general.

Start off with meeting people in neutral, familiar environments, not a beer garden with a live band playing, as it can be overwhelming for your pooch. Instead, plan your meet-and-greet while on your walk together, in your yard, at a dog-friendly café, or in a small store. Once your Brittany has acclimatized to these situations, you can try standing outside of a busy supermarket with more people.

Here are some helpful suggestions to help your Brittany become acclimated to all sorts of people:

- Stay calm and confident during meet-and-greets, even more so if your Brittany is frightened. If your dog is skittish or agitated, don't make a big deal about his behavior as it will cause him to become more upset.

- When asking strangers to pat your Brittany, ask them to pat him where their hands can be seen, such as his chest or under his chin.

- Use treats and praise to give your Brittany a positive association with meeting strangers and experiencing new situations.

- Enlist a different dog-walker or dog-sitter each week to expose your Brittany to a variety of caregivers during the day.

Your Brittany should be exposed to the following people within his first few months with you:

- Neighbors
- Family and friends
- Groomer and vet
- Unfamiliar people wearing different styles of clothes (hoods, jackets, face masks, sunglasses, uniform, hats, and so on)
- Postman
- Anyone who regularly comes to your house

Follow your Brittany's cues. Interactions should be long enough to make a positive impression, but not so long that you wear your buddy out. Even simple new experiences can be overwhelming for your puppy, so keep them short and sweet!

Socializing with Children

Even though Brittanys are noted gundogs, they are also exceptional family dogs because of their love of children. Your Britt's high energy means he can keep up with children's hyper-activity. However, as mentioned earlier, the first impressions make long-lasting impressions, and this statement could not be truer when introducing your dog to small children.

Brittanys are very gentle with children, but with their exuberant personality, they may accidentally knock over a small child while playing. Attentive supervision and training can prevent mishaps.

Dogs and children need to be properly prepared for first introductions and taught proper manners. If adequate training and supervision do not take place, it may create a dangerous situation for both the dog and child. An overly enthusiastic child can easily injure your tiny Brittany. Likewise, a scared or overly excited puppy could bite, scratch, or seriously hurt a child. These tragedies can be easily avoided if you are willing to put in the time to properly socialize your Brittany with children.

How to educate children on how to behave around your Brittany:

- They should pat the dog gently.
- Never force attention on the dogs, instead let the dog come to them.
- The dog's crate is not a play toy or a place for hide-and-seek. It is strictly off-limits. If the dog goes inside, leave him alone.

- Do not approach the dog while he is eating or chewing a bone.
- Leave the puppy alone while he is sleeping.

Make sure there always is an adult around to supervise interactions. Young children should never be left unattended with your Brittany.

Children can often mistake your puppy for a cuddly, stuffed toy, so it is important to remind them how to properly handle your dog. A general rule of thumb is to teach them to treat the puppy as they would another child; do not pull the dog's ears or tail, climb on the dog or engage in rough play. Here are some suggestions to consider when socializing your dog with children:

CREATE A CALM ENVIRONMENT – Before the meet-and-greet, make sure everyone is in a good mood. Never encourage a grumpy, cranky child to meet your Brittany or vice versa. A boisterous, rowdy child will also frighten your dog.

Photo Courtesy
of Andy and Abby Buckner

TAKE IT SLOWLY – Children tend to have jerky movements and high-pitched voices when they get excited, which can easily frighten your Britt. Before first introductions, show the children how to walk, talk, and approach your puppy. Tell them to use their inside voices and use gentle hands while patting the dog. No poking, grabbing, pulling, or squeezing the puppy. Keep introductions short and sweet!

SUPERVISE – No matter how well your Brittany and children get along, never ever leave small children alone without proper supervision. Accidents happen within seconds, and the only way to prevent them is by regularly supervising them.

LET YOUR BRITTANY SET THE PACE – If your Brittany is nervous around children, let him set the pace. Instead of handing your puppy to the child to hold, ask the child to sit on the ground and place your Brittany nearby. Ask the child to play with something, and let your curious puppy come and investigate. As your Brittany's confidence grows, let the child pat him and eventually hold him.

KEEP IT POSITIVE – When your pooch is behaving properly around small children, generously praise him and give him a treat or two. Positive reinforcement will teach your dog that good things happen whenever children are around. Soon he will seek out children and be on his best behavior.

For the best success with his first encounter with a small child, choose a moment when your Brittany is tired, perhaps after a walk or playtime.

Suggestions for a smooth first encounter with small children:

1. Ask the child to sit on the floor with his legs crossed. Place your Brittany nearby and have the child place his hand out with a treat for the puppy.

2. Once the puppy sniffs out the little person, you can gently pick up your puppy and place him on the child's lap. Remind the child to use his inside voice and to talk softly. Generously praise your Brittany and give him a reward. Instruct the child to gently pat the puppy using soft, gentle strokes.

3. Your Brittany most likely will curl up and go to sleep. If not, he will decide to move on and explore his surroundings. If the latter happens, tell the child not to grab or pull the puppy back to his lap. Doing so could frighten and maybe even hurt your small Brittany.

4. If your puppy decides to explore his surroundings, let him do so for a minute or two, then direct his attention to the child by repeating steps one and two. If the dog runs away again, be sure to reassure the child that the puppy likes him, but he is very curious.

(5) Do not forget to praise and reward your puppy every time he sits and plays with the child. Positive reinforcement is the key to laying a healthy foundation for a healthy relationship between your Brittany and children of all sizes.

Socializing Your Dog During a Pandemic

During the recent pandemic, we were encouraged to stay home and to socially distance ourselves. However, the lack of exposure to different situations can hamper your Brittany's physical, emotional, and behavioral development.

As mentioned previously, there is a relatively short window to socialize your Brittany – between three to fourteen weeks of age. Insufficient or lack of socialization may cause your puppy to grow up fearful, anxious, or even aggressive when faced with new situations later in life.

For obvious reason, you will want to follow government and state advice regarding social distancing at all times. Below are a few tips to minimize the disruption of your puppy's socialization and prevent any future behavioral issues.

ROUTINE

During a pandemic, most pet owners are working from home, which is ideal for your new puppy but not so much for teaching him independence. Even though your life may be less structured than previously, your Brittany still needs a regular schedule to feel safe and secure. Your pooch will need to play, eat, and sleep at the same time every day. This schedule should resemble your "normal life" and not the schedule you currently have.

Teach your Brittany independence by placing him in his playpen/crate area for at least two hours a day while you and the rest of the family go about your day-to-day activities. This exercise will teach your Brittany that being alone is not scary, which will prevent social anxiety later on in life. If you find your Brittany gets agitated when left alone, give him an extra special chew toy or bone that he can only chew on when he is alone.

HANDLING

During the pandemic many services that were deemed nonessential, such as groomers or obedience classes had to temporarily close their doors to the public, and vet visits were kept to a bare minimum.

Since your Brittany will not be handled by strangers as often as normal, it is up to you to get him used to being handled. Touch and closely examine his paws, nails, teeth, eyes, and underneath his tail at least three to four times a week. Get the entire family involved in brushing your Britt for about 5 to 10 minutes a day. Be sure to praise your little puppy throughout the process and give him a treat or two.

People tend to pat dogs in many different ways, so get your Brittany used to a number of different ways of being handled by scratching him under the chin, patting his head, or by going against the grain of his hair. If he gets nervous at any point, stop, and try again later on.

SOCIALIZE

Make it your goal to expose your Brittany to new experiences in or near your house every day. For example, wear a large oversized hat, stand outside and watch the garbage truck, open an umbrella, or walk on a street with heavy traffic (with your dog on a leash, of course).

Due to the pandemic, it may be impossible to take your puppy to obedience classes. Practice the different training techniques provided in this book in different environments, such as different rooms, the garden, or in a parking lot. Some trainers provide online classes, but your dog will still be missing out on the most important aspect of the classes – socializing with other dogs.

You can take your dog outside, but puppies can be people magnets. One of the simplest ways to prevent people from approaching you and cuddling with your dog is to avoid eye contact or cross the road. While walking your Brittany, be sure to praise him and give him a treat every time you walk by someone on the street and keep doing this until the person passes. This exercise will teach your pup that people coming toward him is a positive experience.

Unacceptable Behavior from Day One

"

One thing that is very important for new owners to remember is to not coddle scared behavior or reward spastic behavior (such as over excitement when you get home and jumping up). As hard as that sounds, if you do reward those things, you will be teaching your pup bad behaviors. Instead, just carry on like nothing happened and your pup will key off you. By coddling the scared and the over spastic behaviors, you also set the foundation for separation anxiety.

ARLETTE HENNESSEY
K Nine Birddog Brittanys

"

Many dog behaviors that we consider to be inappropriate are actually an instinctive part of their canine personality, such as digging, barking or rolling on a dead animal. For your pooch, these activities are innate behaviors, but you can train your Brittany to at least minimize these habits.

Chewing

Chewing is a natural instinct for your Brittany. Puppies chew to relieve teething pain, and older dogs chew on bones to keep their jaw strong and their teeth clean. However, excessive chewing can quickly become a bad habit if you do not teach a dog what objects are appropriate for chewing and what is not.

SIMPLE SOLUTION: *If you catch your Brittany chewing on your shoes or your furniture, do not scold him. Instead, quickly distract him by clapping your hands, then replace the object with an appropriate chew toy. Never give your Brittany an old sock or shoe to chew on, as he cannot tell the difference between new or old ones.*

Excessive Barking

Brittanys love to vocalize in one way or another. Your dog may bark, howl, whine, or cry. Barking out of excitement may be acceptable, but excessive barking is an extremely annoying behavior issue. Before correcting this behavior problem, determine why your Britt feels the need to vocalize himself in the first place. Your dog may be barking out of excitement, boredom, attention-seeking, anxiety, fright, or in response to other dogs.

SIMPLE SOLUTION: *If you determine your Brittany is barking for your attention, simply ignore him until he stops barking, then be sure to praise him for being quiet. Do not even look at your Brittany while he is barking, as he will assume you are encouraging his behavior and will bark even more loudly. If your pooch is barking at a stranger such as the delivery guy, assure your pooch everything is okay and introduce him to the new person, reassuring him there is no reason to be frightened.*

Digging

If given the chance, your Brittany will have a ball digging up your flower garden, as it is part of his natural hunting instinct. In general, most dogs dig out of boredom or to burn off excess energy, fear, hunting instinct, trying to cool off, or desire to conceal their most precious possessions (like bones or toys).

 SIMPLE SOLUTION: *Nobody wants a dog who is constantly digging up the backyard. But before you decide to lay down cement, determine why your Brittany is digging, then work to eliminate the source. Perhaps, your high-energy pooch needs more exercise or more quality time with you by playing fetch or by practicing obedience training. If digging seems inevitable, establish an area where your pup can freely dig, such as a sand box. Train your Britt that it is only allowed to dig in this area.*

Separation Anxiety

Separation anxiety is one of the most common behavioral issues for Brittanys and occurs when your dog is left alone for long periods of time. Separation anxiety can be manifested by barking, whining, chewing, inappropriate urination, and even defecation. Often a dog who suffers from separation anxiety will have the tendency to follow his owner around constantly.

SIMPLE SOLUTION: *True separation anxiety can be extremely difficult to break as it involves dedicated training with professional help. Here are a few simple steps to prevent separation anxiety from developing in the first place:*

- Ask a family member to hide near your Brittany's crate, but out of sight.
- Place your Brittany inside his crate with a chew toy and few treats. Avoid making a big show about leaving.
- Before entering the house, ask the family member who is hiding, how your pup behaved via text message. If he behaved, calmly greet him and reward his good behavior.
- Each time that you leave, slowly increase the time away until your Brittany learns how he is supposed to act when he is left home alone.

Running Away

Your Brittany's desire to chase after moving things or follow a scent is simply a display of his predatory instinct. However, your pup's little nose can lead to devastating and dangerous outcomes. You may not be able to prevent your Britt from sniffing out a small rodent or animal, but you can take direct steps to avoid disaster.

SIMPLE SOLUTION: *If you have a fenced-in backyard, get down on your knees to make sure there are no small holes or spaces that your Brittany can squeeze under and escape. If you don't have a fenced-in backyard then keep him tied up when left outside unsupervised. Keep your dog on a leash until he is trained to come when called, and watch out for potential triggers such as joggers. Have a dog whistle on hand to get your Britt's attention when he starts to get too far away.*

Jumping Up

Jumping up is another common behavior for Brittanys. Puppies learn to jump up to greet their mother; later, they repeat the same behavior when meeting people. Your dog may jump up out of emotion to see you or when he is seeking an item in your hand. A jumping dog may be cute when he is still a puppy, but a full-grown jumping dog is not only annoying but also dangerous.

SIMPLE SOLUTION: *There are a handful of different methods to teach your pooch not to jump up when greeting you; however, not many of them are successful. For example, lifting the knee or grabbing his paws and pushing him away often sends the wrong message to your dog. Jumping up is an attention-seeking behavior, so any type of acknowledgment (whether positive or negative) of your dog's actions means you approve of his behavior. The best way to teach your Brittany not to jump up is to simply turn around and ignore your dog. Once he has all four paws on the ground and has ceased jumping up, praise his good behavior. Trust me; it will not take too long before your pooch understands what you expect of him.*

Begging

Begging is a habit that your dog learns from you and it is extremely difficult to break. Most Britts love to eat; however, table scraps are not doggy treats and can cause a long list of digestive issues and obesity. It may seem almost impossible to resist those soft brown eyes but giving in just once will create a problematic behavior in the long run.

Photo Courtesy of Desmond & Lori Perez

SIMPLE SOLUTION: *Before you sit down for dinner or chow down on some pizza on the sofa, tell your Brittany to go to his place. If necessary, confine your pooch to his crate or another room. If he behaves, be sure to give him a treat or two after your family has completely finished eating.*

Mounting

Mounting and humping are normal behaviors for both male and female dogs. Your Brittany may attempt to mount moving and inert objects, such as people, other animals, dog beds, and toys, or he will just lick himself. Neutered and spayed dogs may continue mounting or humping because this behavior feels good.

SIMPLE SOLUTION: *If you notice that your Brittany is trying to mount or hump, quickly try to distract him. Play a game, toss him a chew toy, or ask him to perform a trick such as give a paw. Over time, your dog will forget about this behavior, but only if you nip it in time.*

CHAPTER 5
Basic Training

Dog training can seem pretty overwhelming, especially if you are a first-time pet owner. Training your Brittany is a long-term project. Remember that Rome was not built in a day. However, if you take it step by step, you will find the task far less daunting. In this chapter, you will learn everything you need to help you get started, such as house and crate training.

Photo Courtesy
of Brittany Lorenzo

Crate Training Basics

Some first-time pet owners may shy away from crate training, believing it is cruel and will isolate their new four-pawed best friend. However, your Brittany's crate is his own private bedroom for resting and sleeping. Dogs instinctively seek out small places to shelter themselves. Your dog's crate is more than an essential tool in house breaking your puppy; it will also be your Brittany's safe haven.

Crate training is widely accepted by professional trainers and veterinarians to be one of the most effective methods to teach your dog desirable behaviors and help to prevent separation anxiety.

When properly and humanely used, crate training provides many advantages for you and your Brittany.

ADVANTAGES FOR YOU:

- If you need to travel with your fur baby, many hotels will permit you to stay with your dog if he is in a crate. You will be able to travel with your Brittany safely and be assured that your dog will quickly adapt to any new situations or strange surroundings, as long as he has his familiar "security blanket" – his crate.
- If you are unable to take your Brittany on a holiday, friends and family may be more willing to watch him if he is crate trained.
- You will have peace of mind when you have to temporarily leave your Brittany home alone, knowing your pup is comfortable and safe in his private bedroom, instead of running unrestrained throughout your house and, destroying who-knows-what.
- By temporarily confining your Brittany to his crate, you can effectively establish a regular bathroom schedule and prevent unwanted accidents during the night or when your pooch is left alone.
- If you ever need to leave your pooch overnight at the vet or a kennel, you will be at ease knowing he will be comfortable and safe inside a crate.
- Crate training will allow you to confine your Brittany when he becomes overly excited by guests or children.
- Another advantage is that you can place your dog inside his crate during dinnertime, which helps to prevent him from begging.

ADVANTAGES FOR YOUR BRITTANY:

- Your Brittany will love having a den of his own where he can retreat whenever he is tired, not feeling well, or is stressed out.

- Your Brittany can be included in different family activities such as picnics, camping trips, etc., instead of being left at home alone.

- Since your Brittany will avoid soiling himself inside his crate, he will learn to control his bowels faster and associate elimination only within a specified location.

- Your dog's crate will spare your Brittany from feeling isolated, lonely, and frustrated by being placed alone in the basement or laundry room. The crate will only restrict him from certain things for his own safety and will not keep him away from his family.

Your Brittany is very social and does not like being left alone. One of the main benefits of a crate is that you can bring your dog with you wherever you go, even if you are busy and cannot interact with him. Your Brittany needs to feel that he is part of your family, and this comes from being with you as much as possible.

Crate training is a fantastic training tool, but it can be abused. Never leave your Brittany locked in the crate all day long, as it is inhumane and cruel. Plus, this can cause emotional distress or promote problematic behaviors, such as barking, chewing, and jumping.

If your schedule requires you to spend the majority of time away from home and your Brittany, you will need to hire a dog sitter to drop by every two to three hours to let your dog out of his crate. This will give your pooch a chance to stretch his legs, relieve himself, and burn off excess energy.

 A WORD OF CAUTION: *Brittanys do not do well in a working household. They prefer being around their family, and when left alone regularly, they often develop separation anxiety.*

Your Brittany is a high-energy dog who will run through mud puddles, bushes, and shrubs, and may even roll in a pile of bear poop or two. For this very reason, your dog's crate can become soiled very quickly. Do not forget that your Brittany's crate requires regular maintenance. If not maintained, it can become a breeding ground for bacteria. To avoid this from happening, regularly wash your pup's bedding in hot, soapy water and disinfect his crate using dog-friendly cleaning supplies.

If your Brittany is under twelve months of age, he should never stay inside of his crate for more than two to three hours at a time. This is because your puppy cannot control his bladder and bowels for long periods at a time.

Be sure to remove any dangling ID tags, harnesses, collars, etc., as these items can easily get caught on the crate doors causing injury or accidental strangulation.

DOES MY BRITTANY NEED A BED IN HIS CRATE?

Generally, I start using old towels or blankets. It is not wise to put an expensive new dog bed in the crate until your Brittany is house trained and past the teething stage as it most likely will get mauled. One advantage to using towels is they are easy to wash and dry.

DOES IT MATTER WHERE I PLACE THE CRATE?

Whenever possible, place your Brittany's crate in a location that is close to the main "people area," such as the kitchen, living room, or family room. Your Brittany will feel more safe and secure if he can see you.

In addition, choose a place inside your house that is draft-free and does not receive direct sunlight. To create a den-like environment for your Brittany, place the crate in a corner or drape a sheet over the sides.

How to Crate Train

66

Brittanys are very intelligent and love to please you. They have a high food drive making them very easy to train. When house-training your puppy, be consistent and establish a schedule. There is no need to set an alarm during the night, if your puppy wakes up and starts to whine always take them outside. Don't ever ignore them. Once they go to the bathroom bring them right back inside and put them back in their crate. Don't give the puppy any treats or play with any toys during these nightly outings. Your puppy will learn to wake you up because they want a treat or want to play. They will have you trained.

JESSIE SCHULZ
Credit Brittanys

99

Make sure your attitude toward crate training your Brittany is one hundred percent positive. If not, your dog will pick up on your negative feelings about his crate and feel the same way. Even though you may occasionally use your dog's crate as a "time out," it should never be used as a disciplinary tool or a jail. Your Brittany needs to view his crate as his bedroom or a safe place to retreat to when he is overwhelmed.

One of the best ways to start crate training is simply to start using the crate. Avoid making the common mistake of only using the crate when you have to go out, as this can cause your Brittany to develop a fear of being inside his crate. Introduce the crate when you will be home and use it while you are in the room with him.

If you do not handle crate training properly, your Brittany may come to fear his crate. First introductions have never been more important!

If you follow the suggestions below, your Brittany will love his crate and may even start to go into it on his own whenever he needs some quiet time or rest.

FIRST INTRODUCTIONS

Make your Britt's first introduction to his crate as pleasant as possible. Be sure to place a soft, fluffy blanket inside with a couple of chew toys and leave the door wide open or if possible, remove the door. If you have a piece of blanket with the scent of your Brittany's mother, place it inside the crate to reassure your puppy that the crate is a safe place.

While your puppy is watching, throw in a few treats, then back off and give your Brittany the space he needs to explore his crate on his own. Most

Photo Courtesy of Dave Fowler

Brittanys will immediately go into the crate after the treats and start sniffing around.

Some Brittanys may be wary of their crate and may need additional enticing such as placing his food and water dishes inside. Your goal is to make your pooch feel comfortable with being inside of his crate. This may take a few days. If your dog is claustrophobic, try taking the top off the crate until he gets used to the feeling of an open crate, then try placing the top back on. However long the process takes, be patient with your pooch throughout the entire process.

> ## HELPFUL TIP
> ### Crate Training
>
> Many people hate the idea of keeping their dog in a crate all day. However, it's still a good idea to use crate training as part of house-training. Not only can crate training make house-training a little easier, but you never know when your dog will encounter a kennel in the future. It could be at the groomer, the vet, or a boarding facility. Your dog should be comfortable in a kennel rather than terrified. Once your puppy is house-trained, there's no need to lock him up all day, but he should still feel comfortable in a crate.

USE DURING MEALTIMES

Once your Brittany freely enters and leaves his crate, your next goal is to get your dog comfortable with staying in the crate for longer periods of time. Use your Britt's love of food to your advantage by creating a positive association with the crate by feeding him inside the crate.

Try placing the food dish far back in the crate so your Brittany has to go all the way inside. If your puppy is not willing to go all the way back, place his food dish toward the front of the crate. Each time you feed him, slowly move the dish back.

CLOSING THE CRATE

Once your Brittany is happy to be sitting inside his crate, then it is time to practice closing the door. Throw in a few treats, and while he has his back to the door and is munching down on his treats, close the door without locking it. Once your pup is finished eating, quickly open the door. Repeat this a dozen or so times, each time leaving your puppy inside with the door closed a minute or two longer.

EXTENDING CRATE TIME

Once your Brittany goes in and out of his crate of his own accord, then it is time to start lengthening his time inside. Start with enticing him inside with a few of his favorite treats and a chew toy or two. Once he is inside the crate, close the door. Spend a few minutes hanging out near the crate then move out of sight by going into another room. This will get your Brittany used to being alone inside the crate with the door shut.

When you return, do not open the crate immediately; instead, sit beside the crate for a few minutes more. Slowly increase your dog's time inside the crate, being sure to reward him after each crate training session.

LEAVING AND RETURNING

Once your Brittany has mastered all of the above steps without whining, then he is ready for you to leave him for a short period of time. For this stage, it is vital that you do not show any emotion or excitement.

Entice your dog into the crate with a treat and a favorite chew toy. Once he is inside, quickly praise him for being such a good boy and close the door. Go about your business in the house, then go outside, shutting the door to the house behind you. When you come back inside, let your dog out and keep a low-key attitude and ignore any excited behavior your dog may be displaying.

USING THE CRATE AT NIGHTTIME

Before bedtime, take your Brittany to his designated bathroom spot outside and do not come back inside until he has relieved himself. Place the crate near to where you are sleeping, so you can hear him when he wakes up to go to the bathroom. If your Britt is still a puppy, he will need to go to the bathroom approximately every two to three hours.

If your Brittany cries from inside his crate during the night, it might be difficult to discern if he is whining to go to the bathroom or whether he wants to be let out of the crate. Ignore him for a minute or two and, if he continues whining, use the word or phrase your dog associates with eliminating himself. If he gets excited, then take him to his designated bathroom spot.

If your Brittany is older, place the crate close to you, so your dog doesn't associate his crate with being socially isolated. Once, your Brittany sleeps through the entire night without disturbances, then you can move the crate to another location.

If you think your Brittany is only whining to play with you, resist the urge to give in. Simply ignore him until he stops crying, otherwise you are basically teaching your pooch that by whining loudly, he can get you to do what he wants. Never yell at your Brittany or pound on the crate, as any type of attention, especially negative, will make things worse.

Once your dog is comfortable with being left in the crate for fifteen minutes at a time, you can start leaving him inside for longer periods. If he is still a puppy and not housebroken, never leave him inside his crate for more than thirty minutes at a time. A full-grown dog that is house-trained should never be left inside of his crate for more than four hours at a time.

DO'S AND DON'TS OF CRATE TRAINING:

- Do not punish your dog while he is inside the crate; otherwise, he will associate his crate with negative experiences.

- Do not leave your dog inside the crate for more than four hours at a time. Crates are NOT substitute dog sitters. Leaving your dog locked inside for an extended period of time can cause separation anxiety and depression.

- Do not make a big show over your departure. Place your dog inside the crate a few minutes before leaving, and make sure he is occupied with a toy or treat before you leave.

- Do let your dog out as soon as you get home and take him to the bathroom, as this will help your dog realize potty time comes after crate time.

House Training Basics

> "
>
> *We have one magic word for house-training: consistency! It is very important you take your Brittany to potty in the same area outside at the same times each day. This helps build the habit of using the bathroom outside in your dog's brain, and allows them to stay on a proper potty schedule.*
>
> **STEVE ROGERS**
> *Winding Branch Kennel*
>
> "

House training your Brittany takes time, patience, commitment, and vigilance. Accidents in the house are a normal part of bringing home a puppy. It may take several weeks to a few months to successfully train your Brittany. However, by following the suggestions below, you will learn how to minimize potty accidents.

Try to maintain the routine below for two to three weeks. If your dog stops having accidents in the house, you can start giving him a little more freedom each week. Reinforce good behavior by continually rewarding your Brittany for going in his designated spot.

Establish a routine and be consistent in sticking to the following suggestions:

TAKE YOUR PUPPY OUTSIDE FREQUENTLY – Plan on taking your Brittany outside at least every two hours, including right after he wakes up from a nap, during and after playing, and after eating and drinking.

PICK A BATHROOM SPOT OUTSIDE – Choose a convenient location inside your house or outside to be your Brittany's bathroom spot. If you clean-up an accident inside of the house, after disinfecting the area correctly (as discussed later in this chapter), take the soiled paper towels and rags to the bathroom spot. The scent will help your Brittany recognize the area where you want him to eliminate.

REWARD YOUR BRITTANY EVERY TIME HE ELIMINATES OUTDOORS – Generously praise or give treats to your Brittany every time he eliminates outdoors, but remember to do this immediately after he has finished. Do not skip this step as it is vital in reinforcing proper bathroom etiquette and the only way to teach your dog what you expect of him.

 JUST A WORD OF CAUTION: *Before rewarding him, be sure your pooch is finished going potty. Puppies are easily distracted; your Brittany may forget to finish his business until he goes back into the house.*

PUT YOUR PUPPY ON A REGULAR FEEDING SCHEDULE – What goes into your Brittany on a schedule also comes out of him on a schedule. Depending on the age of your puppy, he may need to be fed three to four times a day. By putting your puppy on a regular feeding schedule, it will be more likely he will eliminate at consistent times, making house training easier on both of you.

USE A VERBAL CUE – Before and while your dog is relieving himself, be sure to say the command word for bathroom – go potty – to remind him of the task at hand. Do not play with your dog until after he has relieved himself, as puppies get easily distracted and may forget they had to go to the bathroom until they go back inside the house and have an accident.

BEDTIME – Bedtime does not mean you can take a break from house training. Take turns with a family member to get up every hour or two to take your puppy outside to the bathroom. Your dog's bladder is not fully developed yet, and he will not be able to hold it all night.

SUPERVISE, SUPERVISE, SUPERVISE – Until your Brittany is fully house-trained, avoid letting him roam about your house freely, as it will reduce any opportunities to have an accident inside. Use baby gates or tether him with a long leash to prevent him from wandering around unsupervised.

DO NOT ACKNOWLEDGE BAD BEHAVIOR – If your Brittany has an accident, simply take him to his pad or litter box. Never yell at him or tell him he is a bad dog or give him another type of punishment. Clean up his mess using an enzyme-based cleaner. Remind yourself that the reason your dog had an accident is because you were not paying attention to his signs when he needed to go to the bathroom.

> *Consistency on your part is the key. Puppies cannot control the muscles that prevent them from peeing until closer to 4 months of age. It is your job to keep them from soiling in the house as much as possible by using a consistent routine. Also, restrict their access to the entire house until they are trained. You should always be able to watch them for signs of needing to go outside.*
>
> DARLENE VANHOEVE
> *Shamrock Brittanys*

Mistakes happen

Be mentally prepared for your puppy to have accidents inside the house; it is a part of house training. Here are some suggestions when it does happen:

- Interrupt your Brittany when you catch him in the act.
- Make a startling noise or say in a firm voice, "Outside!" and take him outside right away. Praise and give your pup a treat for finishing up his business outside.
- Clean the soiled area thoroughly. Puppies and dogs will be enticed to return to areas that smell like urine and fecal matter.
- Never punish your Brittany for eliminating inside your house. Just clean it up. Do not rub your dog's nose in it or scold him for his accident. This will only make your dog afraid of you or afraid to relieve himself in your presence. Punishing will do more harm than good.

Cleaning up after doggy accidents

Puppy accidents can be a pain in the neck, but they can easily be prevented if you clean up quickly, efficiently, and correctly. Contrary to common belief, your dog is not relieving himself inside the house out of spite or because he is impossible. The majority of potty accidents happen for one of the following reasons:

- Your puppy does not quite understand where his designated bathroom spot is.
- You are not giving your puppy frequent opportunities to go outside in his designated spot.
- Your pup suffers from a medical condition, which will be discussed below.

If you do not thoroughly clean and deodorize where your puppy had an accident, it will lead to more accidents in the same area. Simply wiping up the mess might satisfy your eyes and nose, but there is an enzymatic scent only your dog can smell that will lure him back to the same spot later on.

Follow this three-step cleaning process to deter any future potty accidents:

(1) Protect your own paws: Before cleaning up your dog's mess, make sure to wear gloves to protect yourself from potential urine and fecal pathogens, especially if your Brittany is not fully vaccinated yet.

(2) Remove the mess: For any type of accident, pick up any solids with a paper towel or baggy and blot up (do not rub) any excess liquid. Once you have removed the bulk of the mess, follow up by using damp towels or rags to gently blot away the rest of the smaller residue.

(3) Use a good enzymatic neutralizer for doggy accidents: Avoid using any ammonia-based cleaning products as it may enhance the urine smell, which will make the spot irresistible for your puppy. The best cleaning products will not mask the scent or simply clean up the accident, but they will neutralize the enzymes that entice your dog to pee or poop in that same spot. Look for products that are specifically designed for cleaning up after dogs.

WHEN HOUSE TRAINING RELAPSES

Nothing can be more disheartening than to discover your well-behaved Brittany regressing to bad bathroom manners. The good news is if your Brittany is suddenly relieving himself indoors again, there's probably a good reason.

- **Medical problems** – Bathroom accidents may be a sign of medical conditions, such as urinary tract infections or parasites. Your veterinarian will be able to rule out any possible medical issues.

- **Submissive/excitement urination** – Some Brittanys, especially younger ones, may temporarily lose bladder control when they become overly excited. Often, this occurs during greetings or playtime. Involuntary urination or defecation is not a house-training issue, as your dog simply has no control over it and is unaware that he just soiled himself.

- **Hormonal behavior** - As your Brittany matures, he will undergo hormonal changes. Marking territory is a common behavior trait for both male and female dogs. If your dog is marking inside the house, then return to the first steps of house-training. If the problems persist, you can consider using a belly-band designed to prevent him from marking.

  A belly band for dogs looks like a big Band-aid or diaper that wraps around your Brittany's rear girth. Often, the belly band has a waterproof shell with an absorbent liner which prevents any unwanted accidents in your house. Most styles are reusable and machine washable.

- **Climate changes** – During the warmer summer months, your pooch may spend more time outside and, therefore, be able to go potty whenever and wherever he pleases. But on the other hand, during the colder winter months, your dog may need to be reminded of inside bathroom etiquette.

- **New environment** – Just because your dog is housebroken in your house does not guarantee that he will know how to act when placed in a new setting. If you are traveling or visiting a friend's house, go back to the basic house-training methods until you can trust your Brittany again.

- **Fear or anxiety** – If your Brittany is afraid of loud noises such as fireworks or thunderstorms, he may lose control of his bladder and/or bowels. If this happens, try to isolate the sounds that frightened him and help him learn to associate good memories with those noises.

Tell-tale signs your Brittany needs to go to the bathroom

Puppies under the age of four months do not have enough muscular control to hold the urine or feces. The instant they have to go to the bathroom, they go. If you wait for any tell-tale signs that your little Brittany has to go, you will be too late. Instead, you need to anticipate your puppy's needs.

As mentioned before, your baby Brittany will need a bathroom break as soon as he wakes up, or after munching a few treats. Puppies also need to relieve themselves after a few minutes of playtime. You are much better off giving your Brittany too many potty breaks than too few, because the more often he has accidents inside, the harder it will be to house train your puppy.

There are some tell-tale signs that indicate a dog of any age has to go to the bathroom. By learning to read your dog's body language, you can learn to tell when he needs to relieve himself. Watch for the following telltale signs to prevent accidents:

- **Sniffing the floor** – Dogs will sniff out an area to go potty. If your Brittany starts sniffing the floor or around your furniture, immediately take him to his designated area and praise him for going potty there.

- **Turning in circles while sniffing the floor** – Sniffing the floor might just mean your pup is searching for something to eat. If he starts turning around in circles while sniffing, however, then he probably has to poop. Pick him up as fast as you can and get him to his bathroom spot. Again, praise him for a job well done.

- **Barking, scratching, or standing at the door** – Puppies generally are very vocal about when they need to go. If your Brittany starts barking and staring in the direction of the door or his pee pads, then take him to his spot immediately.

- **Whining** – If whining is combined with any of the above behaviors, your dog most likely needs to go potty. Younger dogs who still have not mastered housebreaking will often just sit and cry to tell you they need to go really badly.

Understanding Doggy Language

Since your Brittany does not speak your language, the only way to truly understand what he is trying to tell you is through body language. For example, determining what your dog's wagging tail or exposed tummy really means can sometimes be the difference between a belly rub or a bite.

Canine communication consists of whining, barking, and growling, but more often, dogs rely on nonverbal body language to express what they are thinking or feeling. Deciphering your pup's body language is no easy feat as none of his signals act alone and work more as a package. So, be sure to look for every signal from your Brittany's soft brown eyes to his tail's height. Your dog is trying to communicate with you constantly.

Understanding what your dog is trying to tell you will help you develop a deeper bond of trust and respect. Plus, it will help you predict your pup's behavior and prevent issues before they even occur. To communicate better with your Brittany, here are some tips on reading dog body language.

TAIL WAGGING – Tail wagging is frequently misinterpreted. Pet owners believe a wagging tail means their dog is happy, which is often true, but it can also mean a dog is in pain, aroused, nervous, or overstimulated. To decipher your Brittany's emotions, look at the wag speed and direction as well as the position.

> **EXAMPLE** *A fast, twitch-like wag generally, means your Brittany is aroused, alert, and possibly irritated. A long, slow, side-to-side tail wag shows your pooch relaxed and happy to see you.*

TAIL POSITION – Even though your Brittany's tail may be stubbed, it still holds clues about his emotional state. If you get to know your dog's neutral tail position, it will be easier to recognize when his emotions have shifted.

> **EXAMPLE** *If your dog's tail is pointing to the ground or tucked between his legs, he may be stressed or scared. If your dog's tail is pointed upwards, it means he is assertive, confident, perhaps even aggressive. If your Brittany is relaxed, he will hold his tail in a neutral position.*

POSTURE – Your dog's posture can tell you a lot about his mood and intentions. A common behavior in Brittanys and other gundogs is a raised paw, which is a pointing behavior, that indicates nearby prey. But it can also indicate your dog is uncertain about a situation.

> **EXAMPLE** *If your dog shifts all of his weight forward as if he is going to lurch, it is a clear indication something has captivated his interest. Or if he is in the same position but growling, it could mean he is being protective or even aggressive. If your dog is cowering and hunched towards the ground, he is trying to look smaller and submissive.*

FACIAL EXPRESSIONS – Your Brittany has some very expressive facial expressions, but they can be easy to misinterpret. For example, humans tend to yawn when tired or bored, but dogs yawn when they are stressed out.

EXAMPLE *Lip-licking may be an indication your dog thoroughly enjoyed his meal, but it can also be an indication he is anxious. Ever notice your Brittany smiling? If your pup's smile is accompanied with a loose and wiggly posture, then he is trying to tell you he is happy. On the other hand, if his smile is more of a snarl with teeth and growling, then your pooch is not a happy camper.*

How Do You Become the Alpha?

Wolves operate as a social hierarchy, with one leader and his or her followers. The alpha or pack leader is often the strongest and establishes the rules for the rest of the pack. Just because your Brittany is domesticated and docile does not mean he has lost his hierarchical instinct. Trust me; your innocent looking dog will push the boundaries to see who is the boss.

Brittanys may be easy to train, but they will attempt to be the alpha dog. Your Brittany will not do it by fighting or snarling his way to the top, but he will do it by charming you into doing things his way. If you want your Britt to be a joy to live with, you need to be the one in charge.

If you have more than one dog in your house, you may have noticed how one of the dogs seems to set the tone over the rest. Regardless of how many dogs you have in your house, there should only be one alpha in the house – YOU!

HELPFUL TIP
Crate Training

Many people hate the idea of keeping their dog in a crate all day. However, it's still a good idea to use crate training as part of house-training. Not only can crate training make house-training a little easier, but you never know when your dog will encounter a kennel in the future. It could be at the groomer, the vet, or a boarding facility. Your dog should be comfortable in a kennel rather than terrified. Once your puppy is house-trained, there's no need to lock him up all day, but he should still feel comfortable in a crate.

Your Brittany has to know that you are in charge, and he must obey your commands. Being the alpha leader does not give you or anyone the right to punish or physically hurt your dog. By being the leader, you are simply establishing that your rules protect your dog. A word of caution: if you lose your patience and get visibly upset with your dog, in the eyes of your Brittany, you have lost your position as the alpha leader.

You will discover that your Britt will gravitate toward

whoever is in charge. However, maintaining dominance is easier said than done. During your dog's adolescent years, he will test your dominant position before deciding to be a submissive, obedient dog.

If you are wondering if your dog sees you as the boss or alpha dog, ask yourself if you relate to any of these situations:

- Your dog walks over to the treat jar and starts to whine.
- Your Brittany does not move off the couch or floor when asked to move.
- Your pooch does not come when repeatedly called.
- Your pup defends his possessions and will not let you near them.
- Your Britt drops a toy at your feet when he wants to play.

If you answered yes to any one of these questions, then your Brittany is giving you commands and does not see you as his boss.

ESTABLISH THE RULES AND LIMITATIONS

Brittanys are extremely intelligent, which means your dog will challenge your authority. Never physically punish your dog; instead, firmly correct any bad behavior by redirecting his attention to appropriate behavior such as chewing on a chew toy instead of your furniture.

EXAMPLE *The moment your dog is allowed to come and go as he pleases; he is basically telling you that he is the boss. This even applies to lying on the floor. Alpha dogs will never walk around members of the pack. If your Brittany is in your way, gently tap him with your foot and remind him where his spot for napping is.*

BE CONSISTENT

A good alpha leader is fair and makes the rules clear through consistent communication. Have a family meeting with everyone in your household to decide on the ground rules for your Brittany and make sure everyone is diligent in enforcing them. Your dog can be submissive to two or more humans, but he will favor one over the other when listening to commands.

Remember that being an alpha leader is not about punishing your dog with excessive force. If you are not consistent and fair, you will never see the results you want.

> **EXAMPLE** *If your Brittany is going to understand what is expected of him, the entire family needs to be on the same page. If one person says, "Sit," and another says, "Sit down," your puppy is going to be very confused, and it will take twice as long to teach him this command.*

ESTABLISH A ROUTINE

Your Brittany loves routine! The structure of a well-established routine is the best gift you can give your dog as it teaches him what to expect each day. Be consistent with feeding times, daily walks, naps, and bathroom breaks. Your Brittany will thrive with a daily routine, as he will not need to worry or wonder what is or is not about to happen next.

> **EXAMPLE** *Sticking to a regular bathroom schedule while house-training will prevent accidents in the house. If a dog feels a certain urgency to go to the bathroom, he is more likely to "hold it" if he knows and trusts that you are going to be giving him an opportunity soon to relieve himself.*

STAY CALM YET ASSERTIVE

In nature, the alpha dog takes charge of every situation by taking the lead. He is not nervous or doubtful. Remember your Brittany is a highly sensitive dog and picks up on your emotions. If you are uncertain or fearful, your dog will interpret it as a sign of weakness. He will think he needs to protect you and become your leader.

> **EXAMPLE** *If your Brittany starts chewing on your furniture, say a firm NO. Then distract him with a more appropriate chew toy. Once he is chewing on the toy, praise and reward him.*

Rewarding Positive Behavior

In the 1980s, a dog trainer named Ian Dunbar developed a reward-based obedience training program. Ian Dunbar is considered by many to be the "Father of Positive Reinforcement Training." Dunbar's training methods revolutionized the dog training industry without the need to use force, cruelty, or punishment. Positive reinforcement focuses on rewarding right behavior and ignoring bad behaviors.

Fear aggression often results from force/punishment-based training. This fear aggression is even more common in dogs that have a soft personality, such as your Brittany. A fearful dog may lash out at the first sign of fear, which often means biting, as that is your dog's only real option for self-defense.

Positive reinforcement is one of the most effective ways to train your Brittany. When using this method, you give your pooch a reward to reinforce good behavior. For example, you ask your Brittany to "Sit," and he immediately does it, so you give him a treat. You are rewarding his good behavior.

Positive reinforcement teaches your dog that positive actions equal rewards. This reward can be in the form of verbal praise, scratching behind his ears, a game of fetch, or a delicious treat. Your dog's brain observes the cause and effect. Your dog's brain says, "If I sit, I get spoiled! Wow, I need to sit every time they ask me!" And practice makes perfect.

It might take a few practice sessions for your Brittany to notice the pattern of COMMAND + OBEDIENCE = REWARD. If you want to get the most out of positive reinforcement training, there are a few Dos and Don'ts to follow:

DO

Immediately reward your Brittany's good behavior

Despite the fact that your Brittany is highly intelligent, he has a short attention span and lives in the moment. This means you will need to reward your pup's good behaviors immediately. For example, if you are house-training your Brittany, be sure to reward him every time he does his business outside.

Keep training sessions short and fun

Your goal is to teach your Brittany that good things happen when he obeys you. Make training sessions short, fun, and positive – leaving each class on a good note. For example, if your Britt has difficulty learning a new command, end the session by asking him to perform a command he already has mastered.

Wean from treats

Treats are an excellent tool to motivate your Brittany in the beginning, but you will eventually want to wean him off all of those extra treats and switch to more praise and affection. Over time, your dog will forget about those high calorie treats and just want to please you.

DON'T

Make it complicated

Keep commands simple and clear. Instead of teaching your Brittany to "Sit down here," simply say "Sit." Choose specific and simple commands.

Be inconsistent

It is useless to reward your dog for staying off the couch but then later let him come on the couch for a cuddle. This type of behavior will confuse your Brittany and he will not be able to decipher what you actually want. Additionally, everyone in your household needs to understand and abide by the rules for your dog; otherwise, he may run himself ragged trying to figure out how to behave with each member of your family.

Stop correcting your Brittany

Many pet parents assume that positive reinforcement means they cannot say no to their dogs. This is not true. If your Brittany is acting out of sorts, a firm NO is one of the best ways to correct his bad behavior. Of course, you should never yell, scold, hit, grab, or hurt your Brittany in any way.

How to Reward your Brittany

Positive reinforcement creates the ideal environment for your Brittany to learn. Since there is no verbal or physical punishment involved, he can relax. Studies have shown that relaxed dogs learn faster and perform better. Positive reinforcement focuses on building a bond between you and your dog based on mutual respect. Your Brittany wants to do the right thing so he gets a reward or two.

Knowing which rewards to give your Brittany can make training sessions more stimulating and fun for both you and your dog. Here are several ways to reward your pup's good behavior:

PRAISE AND ATTENTION

There is nothing your Brittany loves more than being praised and getting attention from you. A pat on the chest or a scratch under his ears is just as rewarding for your dog as a handful of treats. Instead of giving him your undivided attention, make him work for it first.

 Ask your Brittany to sit down. Once he does what you have requested, then give him some cuddle time. If he does not do what you requested, then walk away

and when you return, try again. This exercise teaches your pooch that certain actions do or do not generate attention.

GAMES

Often, pet owners forget that games are another fun way to reward their pups. Initiate a game your dog enjoys immediately after your dog does something which pleases you. Games stimulate your dog's brain in the same way as yummy treats.

> **EXAMPLE** *Ask your pooch to sit, and once he sits, offer him the ball and start playing fetch. During the game, you can teach him the command Leave It or Drop It. Once he drops the ball, tell him to sit down again and when he does, start playing fetch again. Your Brittany will love this method, and it will reinforce proper behavior.*

TREATS

Treats are one of the most popular rewards for positive reinforcement, as they are fast and easy to dispense. Plus, it is gratifying to see our little four-pawed companion happily devour their snacks. However, the downside to treats is they are high in calories, which can be an issue if your Brittany has a weight problem.

> **EXAMPLE** *Treats are ideal for training sessions with your Brittany when you are teaching him to learn a new behavior or command.*

Picking the Right Treats

Food is a powerful motivator for your Brittany, which is why it is an essential element for obedience training.

With obedience training, you are asking your Britt to understand a verbal or visual cue and then perform the desired behavior. This may seem pretty straightforward to you, but for your pooch, it can seem extremely complicated. This is because dogs do not communicate this way naturally. However, by harnessing the power of something very primal for your Brittany – food – you will be able to make learning a new command much easier for him.

Picking the right treat to motivate and encourage your Brittany is essential. Enticing treats for dogs come in a wide assortment of flavors, sizes, textures, and shapes. Some training sessions require a more appetizing reward with a stronger scent, such as meat and cheese.

However, many treats your Brittany loves are often high in fats and sugars. These fats and sugars may be a hidden cause of weight gain, health issues, or dental problems.

It can be easy to lose track of the number of treats you hand out throughout the course of the day. Depending on your Brittany's activity level, a 10-pound dog may burn only 300 calories each day. If one medium-sized doggy biscuit contains roughly 20 to 30 calories, just two or three of these can quickly become an overindulgence.

- Choose treats which are especially formulated for dogs to avoid tummy upset.
- Choose treats which have added nutrients or benefit your dog's teeth.
- Keep track of the calories you give your dog each day in treats and subtract these from his total daily caloric intake.
- Try to keep treats under 10 percent of your dog's daily intake.

Remember, your goal is to reinforce whatever type of behavior preceded the treat, so be careful not to unintentionally reward hyperactive behavior. Wait until your Brittany is calm and in the right frame of mind to reward him.

Reward each step toward the desired behavior. Many new pet owners make the mistake of waiting until their dog performs the entire command before giving the treat. You want to reward progress, no matter how insignificant it seems.

EXAMPLE *If you are trying to teach your Brittany to sit, but he only lowers his butt partially, still give him a treat and generous praise. When he does it again, give him another treat. Eventually, your Brittany will associate the cue word with sitting and then getting a yummy treat.*

Due to the wide variety of treats available, try to make wise choices. Be sure to read the ingredient label and check for fat content. Ask your veterinarian for recommendations about the best type of treats to use for rewards for your Brittany. Here are some useful tips to help you choose the best reward for different training situations:

- **Small-sized treats** – Smaller-sized treats can quickly be gobbled up, making them ideal for keeping your Brittany motivated and attentive during training sessions. If your dog spends too long chewing a treat between repetitions, cut the treat in half.

- **Soft and smelly treats** – Soft, smelly treats will be your Brittany's favorite treats. These treats are better suited for training your dog to do more complex commands, such as "roll over" or "leave it." Or perhaps you have stepped up your pup's training sessions to a public area with more distractions; this type of treat will keep him motivated.

- **Chewy treats** – Some training sessions will need the treat to last a little longer, such as crate training or learning to stay still on the couch. For these occasions, a chewy treat is ideal as it keeps your dog distracted for a longer period of time.

- **Switch it up** – Dogs can become bored with the same old treat. For training, mix a bunch of different treats together in a baggie to keep your Brittany intrigued, especially if he is struggling to learn a new command.

Clicker Training – It Really Works

In the late 1990s, clicker training began to gain popularity as an effective alternative to cruel and negative training methods that relied heavily on pain, fear, and intimidation. Unlike traditional training techniques, clicker training is an easy and effective training method that works on dogs of all ages, including older dogs.

Clickers and markers are some of the fastest ways to create a common language with your Brittany. A clicker (or a marker) is often combined with other positive reinforcement methods. Your Brittany does not know what you want him to do, so you need to mark his behavior. A clicker marks the exact behavior you approve of and want the dog to repeat.

WHAT IS A CLICKER?

A clicker is a small, handheld device that you hold in your hand. It has a thin metal strip inside that makes a distinctive clicking sound whenever you push down on the button. You can find a good-quality clicker at most pet supply stores;

an added bonus is that they are quite inexpensive. If you prefer, you can download an app on your phone that duplicates the clicking sound.

In positive reinforcement, we use a short marker word to show our approval. A common marker word used by many trainers is "Yes!" So, when you ask your Brittany to sit, the second his butt hits the ground, you would say "Yes!" The clicking noise takes the place of a "marker word." The clicking sound is faster than you can say "Yes," much more effective than training with treats, and healthier for your dog's waist line.

The clicker allows you to communicate effectively with your dog by showing him exactly what you liked about his behavior and solves the problem of having to dig a treat out of your pocket in time to reward him. In clicker training, the clicking sound over time will replace your "Yes" of approval. When you ask your Brittany to sit down, the instant his butt hits the ground, you activate the clicker, followed with a reward as quickly as possible.

How to use a clicker:

(1) Choose a calm and quiet place to help your Brittany stay focused without any distractions, such as your backyard. Choose a moment when your dog is hungry, preferably before mealtime. Do not forget to have a handful of treats in your hand or pocket.

(2) Teach your Brittany the meaning of the click. Click the device, immediately say the marking word, and give him a treat or two. Repeat two or three times each day until he associates the sound with a treat.

(3) Start using the clicker in training sessions to reinforce good behavior. Once your Brittany learns the positive effects of the clicking sound, the noise starts acting as a reward in itself.

(4) Once you and your dog have mastered clicker training, you can move on to more complicated commands and even tricks.

A clicker creates an unmistakable, distinct sound that only occurs when you are actually holding the clicker and training your dog.

A further advantage to using a clicker over a marker word is that neutral sounds such as the clicker eliminate the stress or confusion your Brittany may feel around trying to figure out your mood.

How to use the clicker for basic and advanced commands:

(1) At the exact moment your Brittany completes the desired action, press the clicker. Then, reward him with a treat and with praise.

(2) Be aware that if you do not click at the exact moment your dog performed the new behavior, he might not associate the new action with the treat.

(3) For more complicated commands or tricks, you can click and reward for small steps toward the desired behavior. For example, if you are teaching him to fetch the ball and bring it back to you, click for fetching, then click again when your Brittany brings the ball back.

A clicker will not replace high-calorie treats, but with time you will be able to wean your Britt off them, as the sound of the clicker is an award in itself. However, this does not mean you can stop using treats. You will still need to give him an occasional treat; otherwise, the clicker will stop being as effective.

If you have an older Brittany with teeth or weight issues, a healthier option to doggy treats is to give him a few pieces of unseasoned cooked chicken or turkey breast during the clicker training sessions. Remember, your dog lives in the moment, so when you click the clicker, immediately give him a treat, so he can learn to associate the clicking sound with a treat.

Test your Brittany when he is playing or distracted by clicking the clicker. If he immediately stops whatever he is doing and looks at you, then you know he is ready to start being weaned off treats. If your pooch does not acknowledge the sound, then you know you need to spend extra time training with the click-treat combination.

One of the most common mistakes with clicker training is that pet owners forget to give their dog verbal praise. Your Britt will associate the clicker sound with a yummy reward, but he still needs your verbal approval.

Tips for successful clicker training:

- Try using a clicker with a wristband, as it will stay tethered to you and prevent you from accidentally dropping it.
- Place the treats in a baggie. You only have two hands, and a baggie allows you to keep the treats close at hand yet still hands-free.
- Keep all of your clicker-training sessions short and sweet. Brittanys learn better in bursts of five to seven minutes instead of longer sessions.
- The clicker is not a remote control to cue your Brittany into doing something. The clicker only marks the moment your dog does something worth rewarding.
- Keep the clicker in a safe place, out of reach of mischievous children who will think it is a toy.

GUN DOGS AND CLICKER TRAINING

There is some debate about gun dogs and clicker training. Some trainers believe clicker training is a betrayal of traditional training methods. On

Photo Courtesy
of Avery Woodmansee

the other hand, other force-free trainers consider clicker training to be a valuable tool when training your gun dog.

More and more hunters prefer using a clicker while training their Brittanys, as this gets them predisposed to the sound of the safety pin of the shotgun. When the dog hears the click, he will instantly become alert and focuses on the direction of the gun barrel.

Clicker training is based on a scientific principle called operant conditioning, which means that the animal's actions can reliably be predicted by the chance of those actions being repeated over and over again. Undesired behaviors are essentially ignored and never rewarded, naturally extinguishing bad habits.

There are some challenges involved in clicker training your gun dog, but it is not impossible. Successful clicker training has to be combined with rewards. For example, if you want to train your Brittany for "off lead" walks in the woods with lots of gamey scents such as rabbits and other things to chase, you will need to have an even more attractive treat prepared for your dog than the ones he could catch for himself.

Many hunters start off by using a "long line" for the first several weeks before letting their dog off the lead. However, a long line can be difficult to manage for a novice trainer in certain terrains and can easily become tangled up in bushes and shrubs.

There are many opportunities in the field for distractions; therefore, clicker training must be introduced before field training and carefully monitored to maintain high standards.

Mental Stimulation

Your Britt is extremely intelligent, which means he will get bored easily. A bored Brittany may develop destructive behaviors such as barking, chewing on furniture, digging up the garden, or trying to escape from the yard.

Brittanys often start exhibiting boredom barking when their daily physical and mental stimulation needs are not being met. In other words, your dog barks constantly because he does not have anything better to do than bark. One of the best ways to eliminate boredom barking is by increasing your dog's stimulation.

Here are some creative ways to keep your Brittany mentally stimulated and keep misbehavior at bay.

Teach him a trick or two – Your Brittany will love to learn a new command or two as it will give him a mental challenge and a chance to bond with you. Once you move past the basic commands, then move on to more advanced commands. Even older dogs will benefit from training sessions, often helping them become less anxious and calmer around other dogs.

Play together – Play an interactive game together to challenge your Brittany. Keep your dog engaged with a game of Doggy Dominos or Dog Memory. If you cannot play with your dog then give him a chew toy that lets you hide a treat inside.

Run errands with your Brittany Even a quick errand to the mailbox, grocery store, or friend's house will leave your Brittany feeling quite stimulated. (Remember, you should never leave your dog alone in the car, even if it's just for a few minutes.) Your Britt will absorb the new sounds, scents, and situations. By the time you get home, your pup will fall right asleep, even though the outing was not physically taxing.

Give him a task to do – Your Brittany was originally bred for hunting, herding, and retrieving. It's in his blood. A hearty game of fetch or Frisbee will leave your Brittany feeling satisfied. Take a tennis racket and a few balls to the park and hit the ball as far as possible; your Brittany will bring your ball back again and again, like it's his job.

Socialize your pooch – Every time your pooch meets a new person or fellow canine, he is being exposed to new butts to sniff, new faces, and new sights. Taking your Brittany to a dog park gives him an excellent opportunity to engage his senses. Or take your dog for a walk down main street; he will love all the attention from everyone wanting to stop and pet him.

Rotate your dog's toy collection – You would not enjoy playing with the same toy day after day. So, why should you expect your dog to love the same toy he has been chewing on for months? Give your Brittany a toy to play with, and when he becomes bored of it, replace it with another one. Keep all of his toys in a box and rotate them out. Your pup will love it when you switch up his toys, just as if he is getting a brand-new toy.

CHAPTER 6
Expanding on Basic Training

> *Brittanys are active dogs. They were bred to be a hunting companion dog, and have a need for a great deal of exercise. While they are fine not being hunted, owners need to substitute other forms of exercise and stimulation for them to be happy.*
>
> **DARLENE VANHOEVE**
> *Shamrock Brittanys*

Training your Brittany will teach him basic good manners, such as politely greeting guests when they arrive, walking properly on the leash, and coming when called. By teaching your dog these basic commands, you are setting him up for a happy and safe life. Plus, a well-mannered dog is loved by all!

Many of the misunderstandings between dogs and humans are related to a communication gap. However, obedience training takes time; think of it as a marathon and not a short sprint. Some commands your pooch may learn in a day or two, and others may take a few weeks to master.

Benefits of Proper Training

If your dog is constantly disobedient or exhibits serious behavioral issues, it can become a source of stress and discouragement for both you and your Brittany. Training your dog is your responsibility, not just for your peace of mind but for your dog's best interests.

Your Brittany's behavior reflects directly on you as his owner. No matter your dog's age or temperament, he can benefit from a little extra instruction.

Here are five reasons why you need to train your Brittany:

Training benefits both you and your Brittany – When you train your dog, he is not the only one reaping the benefits. Regular training sessions with your pooch help you to understand your dog's needs and personality, making you an even better owner.

Training keeps your Brittany safe – The more easily you can control your Brittany by using basic commands, the better you can protect him when unrestrained. A dog who bolts when he is off the leash is likely to run in front of a car and get hit or even escape out the front door before you are ready to leave.

Training helps your Brittany to be more sociable – Obedience training teaches your Brittany his limits, boundaries, and how to behave in social situations. As a result, other people and dogs will enjoy being around your dog.

Training makes traveling a breeze – Nobody enjoys being around a disobedient dog. A well-trained dog will obey your commands but also those of others. Training will make boarding easier, either at the kennel, a close friend's house, or a relative's home.

Because you can teach an old dog new tricks – Old dogs can learn new tricks. It is never too late to improve your Brittany's education. With a little extra patience, an older dog can learn just as well as younger dogs.

*Photo Courtesy
of Bridgette Shaw*

A well-behaved dog experiences less stress and anxiety, interacts better with others, and over time, will form a stronger bond with you. One of the best gifts you can give your dog is your time and energy to train him, which will make him a happier and healthier dog in the long run.

Basic Commands

Your Brittany will love the chance to bond with you while learning these basic commands. It is fundamental you begin teaching your dog these commands as soon as possible, as it will help him grow up into a well-behaved dog wherever you go together.

If your Brittany is older, most likely he has already learned these commands in the past but may need a refresher course. Be more patient with your older pooch as he may be dealing with mobility or hearing issues. Remember training your Brittany, no matter his age, is an excellent way to spend time together and have fun!

Brittanys are very intelligent and are eager to please you, so use that to your advantage. With a large dose of love and patience and a couple of dozen doggy treats you should be able to teach your pooch to sit, come, stay, etc. in a few weeks.

Avoid training your dog when you are grumpy, upset, or irritable, as your Brittany will only pick up on your foul mood. Start training your Brittany in an enclosed area with zero distractions; as he masters different commands, move to a new environment, such as a park or a spot along your walking route.

The following commands can be combined with clicker training, as discussed in the previous chapter.

HELPFUL TIP

Be Careful with Small Pets

Since Brittanys are such intense hunting dogs, they may see any small pets as prey that should be chased. Early socialization and introduction to a variety of animals and pet types may help your Brittany understand the difference between a friend and prey.

As we noted earlier, keep commands simple. Say "Sit" instead of "Sit down here."

When training your Brittany, pay close attention to the tone of your voice. Never yell at your dog as he has exceptionally good ears and can hear you very well. A loud, angry voice is not going to teach him anything except the fact that you are upset.

Patiently show your dog what you expect of him; speak in a soft, kind voice, and praise him affectionally.

Sit

It's worth noting that many experts recommend NOT teaching the sit command to any bird dog until they are at least two years old. The reason for this is that they may get nervous and resort to sitting instead of pointing when they spot a bird in the field. If you plan on using your Brittany as a hunting dog, I recommend waiting to teach this command until after you have a strong foundation in field work training.

Once your dog knows this command, he will be much calmer and easier to control. Plus, the sit command is the foundation for other commands, such as stay and come.

1. Hold a treat near to your dog's nose.
2. Slowly move your hand upward, allowing his head to follow the treat, which will cause his bottom to lower to the ground.
3. Once your Brittany is in a sitting position, say "Sit," and give him the treat and affectionately praise him.

Repeat this sequence a few times a day until your Brittany has mastered it. Then start asking your dog to sit before dinnertime, while going for walks, or in any other situation you want to teach him to be calm.

Stay

The stay command is similar to the sit command as it makes your dog easier to control in certain situations. This command is handy for moments when you need your pooch to stay out of the way as you clean your house or if you do not want him to overwhelm your houseguests.

1. Tell your Brittany to sit.
2. Once he is sitting, then open the palm of your hand in front of you and say, "Stay."
3. Take a few steps back. Reward him with a yummy treat and affection if he stays sitting.
4. Gradually increase the number of steps you take backward each time before rewarding your dog.

(5) Always reward your Brittany for staying still, even if it is only for a few seconds.

This command teaches your dog self-control, so do not be discouraged if it takes a little longer than you thought. Most dogs, especially Brittanys prefer to be on the move, exploring their surroundings instead of simply sitting still and waiting.

Down

This can be a challenging command to teach your Brittany, as it requires him to get into a submissive posture. Be sure to keep the training sessions for this command fun, upbeat, and positive. Also, never forget to praise and reward your dog once he successfully follows through on the command.

(1) Tell your dog to sit.

(2) Use a particularly delicious-smelling treat and hold it out in front of you in a closed fist.

(3) Place your closed fist in front of your Brittany's snout. When he sniffs it, slowly move your hand toward the floor, so he follows the treat.

(4) Slide your hand along the ground in a vertical line toward you to encourage the dog's head to follow.

(5) Once your Brittany is in the down position or lying down, say "Down," give him the treat in your hand, and generously praise him.

You will need to practice this command daily until your dog has mastered it. If your pooch tries to lunge toward your hand, say a firm "No" and take your hand away. Never push the dog into a down position; instead, encourage him every step of the way until he figures out how to please you.

Come

This command is a godsend for times when you lose grip on the leash or when your dog catches the scent of something and runs off before you can say stop. This command is quite easy to teach and will keep your Brittany out of trouble.

(1) Put a leash and collar on your Brittany.

(2) Get down to your dog's level and say, "Come," while gently tugging on the leash.

③ When your pup comes to you, be sure to reward him with treats and affection.

Once your Brittany has mastered coming to you with the leash on, then attempt the same sequence without the leash and in a safe enclosed space.

Off

Off can easily become confused with "Down." The Off command is used to teach your Brittany not to jump on people or to climb on certain furniture. The goal is for your dog to keep all four paws on the ground.

① When your dog jumps up, say a firm "Off" and point to the floor. Once he is standing with all four paws on the ground, reward his good behavior.

Photo Courtesy of Marissa Bassette

② If you found your Brittany on the couch, and he is not allowed to be there, say a firm "Off," and encourage him to come to you. When he comes, reward him with a treat and praise.

Another way to avoid this bad behavior is by simply ignoring it. When the dog jumps up on you, turn around and act like you are leaving. Wait a few seconds, and then try again. Reward your dog when he does not jump up on you.

Leave it

This command can keep your Brittany safe when his curiosity gets the better of him, such as when he smells something on the ground that may be potentially dangerous for his health if he eats it. The goal of this command is to teach your dog that he will get something even yummier if he ignores the other item.

(1) Place a treat in each of your hands.

(2) Open one of your hands with the treat inside and say, "Leave it."

(3) Close your fist again; ignore any behaviors such as licking, sniffing, pawing or barking at your hand to get the treat.

(4) Once the dog stops these behaviors, give him the treat from the other hand.

(5) Repeat until your Brittany moves away from the fist when you say, "Leave it."

(6) Next, give your Brittany the treat in the other hand only when he looks up at you and away from your closed fist.

It is vital to maintain constant eye contact with your Brittany during this command session. Make sure you always have a smelly, yummy treat in your second hand, and in the other hand, just an ordinary piece of kibble.

How to Teach Your Dog to Walk on the Leash

> "
>
> *The Brittany's strong natural prey drive makes it very unique in the field; they follow their nose. A new owner can expect their Brittany to be very interested in bird watching and tracking down scents. You should be extra careful to keep an eye on your dog at all times!*
>
> **STEVE ROGERS**
> *Winding Branch Kennel*
>
> "

Some Brittanys are quick to embrace their collar and leash, while others tend to shy away from them.

Whether you live in an urban or rural setting, your Brittany is going to need to learn to use a collar and leash. Often the breeder will introduce your Brittany to a collar when he is only a few weeks old. The first thing you need to do is make sure you have all of the right equipment for training your pooch to walk on a leash.

Below is just a short overview of the different types of collars and leashes available and their uses:

Standard collar – This is your basic collar often used to place your dog's ID tags, etc. Brittanys are expert escape artists, and they will easily slip their head out of a standard collar.

Muzzle harness – Often, this type of harness is used for training sessions for show dogs. The general idea is to keep your dog from following his nose.

Back harness – This style of harness is great for smaller breeds such as your Brittany. This style of collar prevents a dog's airway from being damaged when he pulls. Also, it prevents your four-pawed friend from sliding out of his collar.

Martingale collar – This collar option is for dogs who have the tendency to pull on the leash. It is a double-looped collar, which tightens when your dog pulls on the leash. There is no need to worry about choking, as the collar only tightens enough to be uncomfortable.

Standard leash – The classic leash comes in a variety of styles and lengths. It can be a rope style or a flat band.

Retractable leash – A retractable leash has a coiled-up compartment, allowing you to let out as much length as desired or lock it so your Brittany cannot go any further.

The following steps will help you train your pup to use a collar and a leash:

Go to a neutral space, such as your living room or backyard, and let him sniff the collar. Put the collar on your dog when he is distracted. Once he is used to the collar, attach the leash and let him run around with it behind him while in the house. Just keep an eye on him to make sure he doesn't get the leash caught on anything and possibly hurt himself.

Take your Brittany for a walk around the block or to a neighbor's house. This will allow your pooch to get used to the leash and collar while in a safe environment. If your Brittany walks without pulling, give him praise and treats.

Now you are ready for a real walk. When you start walking, if your Brittany pulls or tugs on the leash, do not painfully pull back on the leash. Just stop walking and say, "No." When your dog stops pulling on the leash, give him a reward and affection.

How to Teach Your Dog to Walk Off the Leash

> *They are generally not good off leash, if they saw a bird, squirrel, rabbit, snake, etc they would not hesitate to cross a street. Brittanys are sporting dogs at heart and it doesn't matter how much training they have, their instincts take over. An owner of a Brittany must understand the characteristics of this breed and be willing to do what is necessary to keep them safe.*
>
> **JESSIE SCHULZ**
> *Credit Brittanys*

Brittanys love to run, play, and explore their surroundings without feeling hindered by their leash. However, letting your energetic dog off the leash can quickly turn into a massive headache for you, not to mention dangerous for him.

Your dog must be properly trained to behave on the leash before you even attempt training your Brittany to walk off the leash.

CONSIDER THE RISKS

Before you let your Brittany off the leash, you should consider some factors that may jeopardize the safety of your dog and others. For example, many cities and towns have leash laws in place to keep everyone safe. If you choose to break the law, be prepared to pay expensive fines and maybe even get a citation.

Even the best trained dog can get distracted. A loose dog may act out of sheer instinct if he encounters another dog, cat, or a prey animal. An unleashed dog may end up getting lost, be hit by a car, ingest toxins, get in a dog fight, or be attacked by a wild animal, among other things.

Also, it is important to remember that not everybody likes dogs, and some people may be terrified of a loose dog. Some dogs may sense this fear and react unexpectedly.

MASTER BASIC COMMANDS

There is no way you can completely guarantee your dog's safety when he is off the lead. However, advanced obedience training can decrease any chances of your Brittany getting hurt. You need to teach your Britt that freedom comes with obeying the rules. You need to trust that your off-leash dog will stay right by your side or can easily be called to your side.

Here is a checklist of basic commands your Brittany should have mastered before being left off the leash:

- Loose leash walking
- Leave it
- Drop it
- Look
- Stay
- A reliable recall
- Come

POTENTIAL DISTRACTIONS

As your Brittany becomes more comfortable and obedient being off-leash, you can start to work your way up to more challenging environments, such as a hiking trail. Before letting your dog off the leash, make sure he is allowed to be, as many public parks or state parks have regulations for dogs. For your pup's safety, never let him off the leash in a crowded public area or around traffic, regardless of the leash laws in that area.

No matter how well trained your Brittany is, always carry a leash with you for the unexpected, such as a surprise encounter with a wild animal. Remember that your Britt has a very high prey drive, and it may be almost impossible for him to resist the temptation of following a scent.

Here are some tendencies that put your dog in danger when off the leash:

Squirrel chaser – Does your Brittany love chasing small animals such as rabbits, cats, squirrels, or grouse? Chasing after animals could cause your dog to get separated from you and perhaps even get lost.

Car chaser – Dogs that chase cars, motorcycles, or bicycles are at risk of being hit or causing a car accident.

Aggressive or hyperactive around other dogs – Dogs who are aggressive or get excited when other dogs are around can cause unwanted dog fights.

Wanderlust – Some Brittanys love to explore their surroundings, and your dog's sniffer can quickly get him excited so that he runs away and completely ignore anything you say or do.

Afraid of noises – Some dogs are frightened by loud noises such as thunder, fireworks, or even a car backfiring, which may cause the dog to run off.

Training can help to minimize these tendencies, but they may never completely vanish. If you know your Brittany cannot resist a certain situation, then you will need to keep him on the leash. Remember, always put your dog's safety first.

Obedience Classes

> Once your puppy has received all their puppy shots it is safe to begin socialization. There are wonderful dog clubs that offer plenty of classes based on age, experience level, and type of class. These classes will provide safe, positive interactions between your dog and others along with an instructor to help monitor and provide advice in a safe environment. You might just discover an activity that brings out the best in your Brittany. Don't ever try to socialize your puppy outside of a class, with another dog you don't know. Your puppy could have a bad experience, leaving an impact on their confidence and personality.
>
> **JESSIE SCHULZ**
> *Credit Brittanys*

Whether you have a puppy or a shelter dog, obedience classes can help your Brittany learn to behave correctly at home or while out and about. Typically, obedience classes teach the pet owners how to teach their dog basic commands, such as lie down and sit. Also, your Brittany will learn the socialization skills required to interact with different people and other dogs.

Puppies between the ages of 8-12 weeks make the best students as they have not developed bad habits yet. But since puppies under 12-weeks of age are not fully vaccinated, many pet owners put off obedience classes until their pooch begins to annoy them. Before your Brittany begins any type of obedience or socialization classes, be sure your pup has received all of his vaccinations at least seven days prior.

Professional trainers recommend attending obedience classes with your pooch every year or two at the most, and of course, you should practice the lessons at home. The more classes you and your Brittany attend, the better you and your dog will get.

Beginner obedience classes for dogs are often divided into age groups and will teach your Brittany the following:

- Basic commands, such as sit, lie down, come, and roll over
- Not to pull on the leash while going for a walk
- Not to jump up on other people or dogs

- Not to chew on your furniture
- Socializing with new people, dogs, and places

Obedience classes are designed to teach basic training and socialization skills. Socialization with other dogs, as well as humans, is essential for your Brittany's development into becoming a positive member of the family and a good canine citizen. So do not expect them to resolve any major issues such as aggression, separation anxiety, depression, and excessive barking.

The majority of obedience classes will meet for approximately one hour each week for a period of eight to ten weeks, depending on the program. The success of each course will depend entirely on pet owners having daily training sessions with their dog, putting into practice what they learn each week.

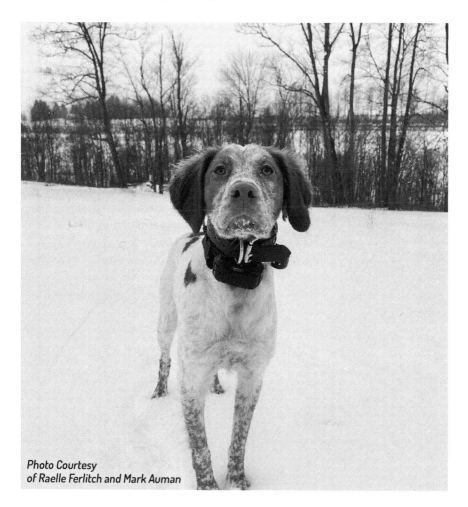

Photo Courtesy
of Raelle Ferlitch and Mark Auman

Here are some suggestions to consider when choosing the right obedience course for your Brittany.

ASK FOR REFERRALS

The best place to start is by asking fellow dog lovers, friends, and family, and of course, your veterinarian for recommendations about obedience classes in your locality. In addition, you can also look online for reviews on the obedience course you are interested in.

CHECK THEIR CREDENTIALS

Look for an instructor who has credentials from one or more of the following associations: National Association of Dog Obedience, Association of Pet Dog Trainers, National K-9 Dog Trainers Association, and the International Association of Canine Professionals.

VISIT A FREE CLASS

The majority of obedience classes will let you observe a class or two before signing up for the entire course. If they do not allow you to sit in on a class for free, even without your dog, then that is a warning sign to look for another course. Transparency is essential for the well-being of you and your dog. Be patient in searching for the best choice for you and your Brittany.

WATCH OUT FOR RED FLAGS

Obedience classes are not only about teaching your Brittany new commands, but also about socializing your dog with other people and dogs. The class should also be fun and enjoyable for your dog. Never accept an instructor who encourages pet owners to yell or hit their dogs or use potentially harmful techniques or devices. Dogs are very intuitive. If you notice your Brittany is uncomfortable around the instructor, there probably is a good reason.

PICK THE RIGHT FIT

The best dog obedience course should be a good fit for your budget, driving distance, quality, content, and of course your overall first impression of the instructor. Be sure to take into consideration any referrals you received to help choose the best obedience course for you and your Brittany.

When to Call a Professional

Besides obedience school, there are other options such as hiring a personal dog trainer for private classes.

A personalized trainer will work on issues specific to your Brittany. An advantage to personalized trainers is they can go with your dog to a specific location where he typically misbehaves, such as at the dog park. You are not limited to a restricted classroom setting as in conventional obedience classes.

While Brittanys tend to be easily trained, as they are attuned to paying attention to people and picking up on their trainer's signals, sometimes Brittanys may develop behavioral issues that are difficult to break. If your dog does have a behavioral problem, normal training tactics may not be enough. There are a few extreme cases where you might need extra support:

BITING

All puppies typically go through a biting stage while they are teething. However, when a dog viciously bites and snaps, that is unacceptable behavior. Aggressive behavior cannot be fixed by common obedience classes. In this case, the dog will need professional help by a dog trainer who specializes in behavioral issues.

Photo Courtesy of Rowan Folske

SEPARATION ANXIETY

Brittanys often suffer from separation anxiety. If you have unsuccessfully tried to correct your Britt's destructive behavior when he is left alone even for short periods of time, then he may need specialized training.

CHAPTER 7
Introduction to Training for Field Work

> "
>
> *Britts are enthusiastic about all game birds and love doing what they were bred to do! I raised Brittanys for 45 years and it never ceased to amaze me that you could see a 6 week old puppy point a quail in a cage, first try! I would have the litter playing in their play yard and casually throw a two litter bottle into their area to see who would point first, who would back that pup first, and how long it took the other pups to back. This is entirely instinctual, no training involved!*
>
> DIANA L KUBITZ
> *Renegade Brittanys*
>
> "

As long as anyone can recall, man has always fared better in his pursuit of game with the help of a canine.

Brittanys - A Versatile Gun Dog

Brittanys are not headstrong, have good manners around other dogs, and naturally understand what a gun range is. They are considered to be one of the most versatile show and field dogs.

POINTING

Pointing Britts tend to roam around, often out of the shotgun range of the hunter. When the dog finds a bird, he will lock up and point toward it, often with one of his front paws lifted and his head pointing toward the bird. The hunter will walk toward the area the dog is pointing to flush out the bird.

Many hunters prefer to keep their Brittany within gun range, as the dog may spook the birds causing errant flushes of a certain area. Even if the Brittany does not retrieve, he will sniff out the downed bird and re-point the bird's location, and will run down any crippled birds.

FLUSHING

Flushing Britts work next to the hunter, often within shotgun range and are taught to flush the birds out into the air so they can be shot. The Brittany will locate pheasants, quail, doves, grouse, ducks, etc., and flush the birds out of hiding.

Often the Brittany will establish a tight zig-zag pattern that covers the immediate ground within the range of the gun and will check in with his handler frequently. Many Brittanys are natural retrievers and can easily be taught to retrieve the bird.

> **"**
>
> *A well field-bred Brittany, like other pointing breeds, should have a desire to explore. But don't panic if they don't show interest right away, some lines are much slower to mature then others. I always tell people the first step to failure is putting a time limit on what you expect. Instead grow with your pup and do not force them to do anything it is not ready for. Your pup, with good timing and the desire bred into them, should eventually be a dog that enjoys hunting.*
>
> **ARLETTE HENNESSEY**
> *K Nine Birddog Brittanys*
>
> **"**

Choosing a Hunting Puppy

If you are planning on buying a Brittany, you are mostly paying for natural instinct. But before taking the plunge and getting a hunting dog, there are a few things to watch out for. Your goal should be to set yourself and your Brittany up for success, and the best way to do that is by finding yourself the best dog in the first place. Here are a few things to consider when considering different breeders.

BUY THE BEST QUALITY BRITTANY YOU CAN AFFORD

Well-bred Brittany Spaniels cost a pretty penny as they come from a bloodline predisposed to accomplishing a certain task. Another advantage is that they are trainable and intelligent enough to learn the necessary job and have the disposition to handle the pressure of high-stress training.

Additionally, a well-bred Brittany comes with a health screening, which often costs the breeder money but ensures that puppies will live long and healthy lives.

The cost of the well-bred Brittany will be only a small portion of the money you will invest on your dog. Good quality food, shelter, vet visits, training (if you go the professional route), boarding, etc., will add up over the next ten to fifteen years that you own your Britt. A well-bred hunting Brittany may cost $1000 upwards, but it will save thousands of dollars in vet bills later in life.

BUY A BRITTANY FROM A PEDIGREE YOU WANT

If you want a hunting Brittany, then look for one with a field pedigree. Field-trial and hunt-test parent dogs will have been tested against other dogs by hunting standards. A field pedigree assures you that your dog will have the smarts, trainability, and natural instincts to find game.

If you are not interested in a Brittany from a bloodline of test or tria lines, look for a dog that comes from hunting stock. Ideally, the breeder will let you watch the pup's parents' hunt.

Photo Courtesy of Glenn Murphy

CHOOSE A BRITTANY WITH GENETIC TESTING

It may cost more money to buy a Brittany who comes from parents who were genetically tested before breeding, but it will eliminate a long list of genetic mutations that can cause future health issues. Many mutations will not appear until your Brittany pup is two to three years old, such as blindness, kidney failure, neurological disorders, just to mention a few. Genetic testing may cost you money but it will save you time, money and heartache in the long run.

Basic Gun Dog Training

> *We teach the word 'steady' instead of 'whoa'. Whoa and No sound so much alike that it can confuse a started dog sometimes. It's called blinking the bird. You said whoa and the dog thinks you said no. He walks away from his pointing. He loses interest in birds now because he thinks he's in trouble for pointing them. Now you have to teach him a new word and get him interested in birds again.*
>
> **KEVIN GILMORE**
> *Gilmore Brittanys*

Whether you are new to hunting or an experienced hunter, it can be overwhelming to raise a working Brittany, but getting started is not as challenging as it sounds. The key to training your Brittany to be a hunting dog is to choose one single training method and stick with it.

Basic obedience training is essential to create a perfect hunting dog, but without exposure to actual hunting, your dog will never develop into a hunter. Your young Britt must gain experience, spending ample time actually hunting during the first two years of his life. This means you will need to spend weeks in the field to ensure your Britt interacts with game as often as possible.

Your Brittany will learn to hunt in the woods, not your backyard. Running through swamps, swimming across creeks, trekking through the bushes, and being exposed to different types of elements are all aspects of being a hunting dog. As your Britt's personal trainer, you should plan on spending at least an hour in the field, two to three times each week, for your dog's first year of his life.

FUN FACT
Versatile Gun Dogs

The Brittany is known as a versatile gun dog because it points, hunts, flushes, and retrieves game for hunters. Many other gun dogs have a more specialized purpose. Brittanys are the smallest breed identified as versatile gun dogs.

Raising a hunting dog take time, energy, money, and patience. Many first-time field dog owners prefer to purchase a young, already partially trained gun dog. Many field Brittany breeders and trainers sell one- to three-year-old dogs that are already trained in obedience and have experienced one or two hunting seasons. These dogs are quite a bit more expensive than a puppy, but the initial foundation has been laid for you and you will be able to take the dog hunting with you immediately.

PUPPIES

Basic obedience training is essential, as your Brittany will need to be obedient. One of the biggest mistakes first-time gun dog owners make is trying to rush their dog through learning a bunch of complicated commands, when the dog hasn't yet mastered the basics.

Force yourself to take it slow with your Brittany pup as he will have a very short attention span. Focus on one command at a time and work your way through all of the basics such as sit, come, down, stay, and drop it. If you plan to use your Brittany as a pointer, you will also want to teach him the "whoa" command.

How to teach the "Whoa" command:

As with any training exercise, it is best to train according to your dog's temperament. If your Brittany has a bold personality, you may want to consider starting to train this command before he is four months of age. Before you take your Britt into the field, it is vital he knows this command and obeys it.

1. Place your Brittany on a bench and tell him *"Whoa."* If he moves, physically pick him up so his feet are off the ground. Put him back on the bench, repeat the command, and pick him up when he moves. Most dogs learn this step in a week.

2. Place your Brittany on a bench and say, *"Whoa."* Take a few steps back from him. The first few times, your pooch will try to follow you, but do not let him. Pick him up and place him back on the bench but do not repeat *"Whoa."* Only give the command once, and reinforce it by returning the dog to the bench. Practice this step for two weeks or until he stays in place while you walk in front or behind him.

③ Place your Brittany on a short lead and have him walk beside you. Tell him, *"Whoa,"* and then pick him up and place him on the ground when he moves or lunges.

④ Once he stays still when you pick him up after hearing *"Whoa,"* say the command but do not pick your dog up; instead, continue to walk forward or around your dog. If he stays still, then you can try the command with the leash attached in a secure, closed-in area. Every time he

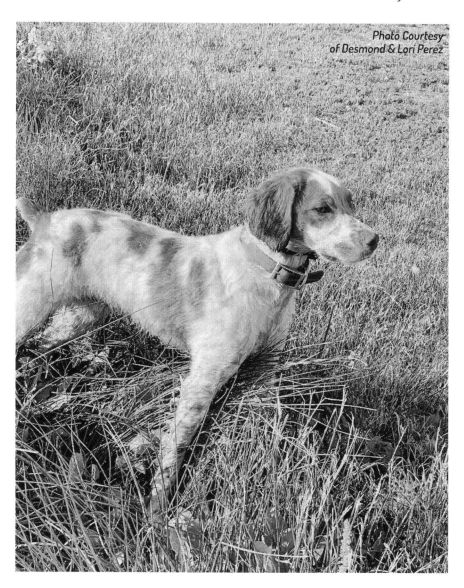

Photo Courtesy
of Desmond & Lori Perez

disobeys and moves after hearing *"Whoa,"* pick your Brittany up, place him back in the original spot, and repeat.

The purpose of the *"Whoa"* command is to teach your dog to stop moving, perhaps to avoid bumping into a bird or prevent your dog from running across the cattle grate, etc.

Before introducing a new command, backtrack to an older command that your pooch has already mastered, as this will help him be more confident, which means he will be easier to train. Do not forget to end each training session on a positive note. For your Brittany, it may involve a simple retrieve or two.

OLDER DOGS

Perhaps you have a two or three-year-old Brittany who has loads of potential but is not quite the hunting partner you desire. Often this happens because the dog was allowed to develop some bad habits when he was younger.

Bad habits are like weeds; it is difficult to keep them in check. Weeds tend to grow back unless they are uprooted by the roots, and even then, they always seem to want to grow back. Your older dog's bad habits can become a chronic issue.

If your pooch seems to fall into this category, you will need to start from the beginning. This may seem counterproductive, but you need to be one hundred percent sure that your dog has mastered everything. Otherwise, his behavior will give you a constant headache. One advantage to backtracking with obedience training is that your older Brittany's attention span will be better than a puppy's.

Whether you have a puppy or an older pooch, you need to make time to train your Brittany daily. Training your dog does not take more than fifteen minutes a day to practice different drills and commands. Short training sessions are preferable over long, once-a-week sessions.

FUN FACT
Dual Champions

More Brittanys have become AKC Dual Champions than any other breed. What's a dual champion? It's a dog that has won awards both in the show ring and in the field.

MEASURE PROGRESS

I find it helpful to keep a ledger of my weekly and monthly goals for my Brittany, as well as our daily progress. It is easy to forget where your Brittany is during the training process, and notes in the ledger will help you. If you keep a ledger, you can compare your dog's performance from one day to another.

Keeping a ledger and paying attention to your Britt's skills will help you to grasp his strengths and weaknesses. If you notice that your pup is a little slower at learning things, then it is a sign that you need to slow down. If your dog is struggling, do multiple training sessions each day with ample play breaks between drills, and your dog will eventually retain the commands he is struggling to learn.

The E-Collar Debate

An e-collar is an electric training aid, often referred to as a shock collar, zap collar, or remote training collar. The collar has a wireless receiver that the dog wears close to his neck, and the wireless remote may be controlled by you or a stationary location. The idea is to teach the dog the difference between good and bad behavior by sending the dog an electronic vibration through his collar.

E-collars use something called electronic stimulation, which is the same technology used if you have ever visited a physical therapist or chiropractor. The electronic stimulation is not an actual electronic shock but more of a pulsing wave sensation. Most e-collars have vibration and intensity settings, ranging from low to high, so you have control over what your pooch feels.

In the past, shock collars were more intensive.

E-collars have been used for decades in field-training dogs of all sorts. Some trainers are against the use of e-collars, and others swear by them. Some e-collars have GPS settings so you can track your dog and his movements.

The use of hand-held e-collars is banned in Denmark, Norway, Sweden, Switzerland, Slovenia, United Kingdom, Germany and Australia. These countries consider hand-held e-collars to be barbaric devices as they are often abused and can create fear, aggression, and anxiety in a dog. Even though shock collars may aid in suppressing unwanted behaviors, they do not teach the dog proper behavior.

E-collars are considered to be a form of negative reinforcement, as the desired behavior is enforced by a negative outcome when the dog does the opposite. Many dog trainers compare negative reinforcement to not wearing a seat belt while driving the car; the car will make an annoying ding, ding sound until you put your seatbelt on. The ding-ding sound will stop when you perform the desired behavior, which is the same principle applied to the function of e-collars.

If you are considering using an e-collar to train your Brittany to work in the field or just to prevent him from running out of the yard, I highly recommend consulting with a professional to incorporate this into your training program. It is essential you completely understand how and when it is appropriate to use the e-collar.

PROS OF E-COLLARS

Adjustable intensity – The majority of e-collars give you the flexibility of using either a warning beep or vibration intensity. This option can be comforting if you are on the fence about using a shock collar.

Fast results – Many field trainers prefer using e-collars because it only takes a few times to correct bad behavior, and after that, using only the beeping sound is warning enough. E-collars are also very effective at keeping your Brittany in the yard, which keeps him safe while having freedom. However, if your Brittany is on the stubborn side, he may take longer to train.

Affordable – One of the main reasons that gundog owners prefer using e-collars for training their dogs is because it is more affordable than paying for a professional dog trainer. E-collars range in price from $80 and up, depending on the features such as adjustable warning/vibration levels, remote controls, a range of distances, and number of collar sizes.

Off-leash – In field environments, e-collars provide the ability to communicate with your pooch, to guide him, and help him avoid potentially dangerous situations.

CONS OF E-COLLAR

The shock – In the past, e-collars were called shock collars, but due to negative marketing, companies changed the name. However, many pet owners still associate e-collars with the word shock, and you still are using aversive behavior modification. More and more field trainers are opting to use positive training methods over negative reinforcement.

Fear – There are reports that some dogs develop extreme fear of objects, people, or certain situations they associate with the electric vibration of the e-collar. One pet owner I know used a low-vibration collar on a dog to prevent him from leaving the yard, and then the dog refused to go outside and started urinating inside the house.

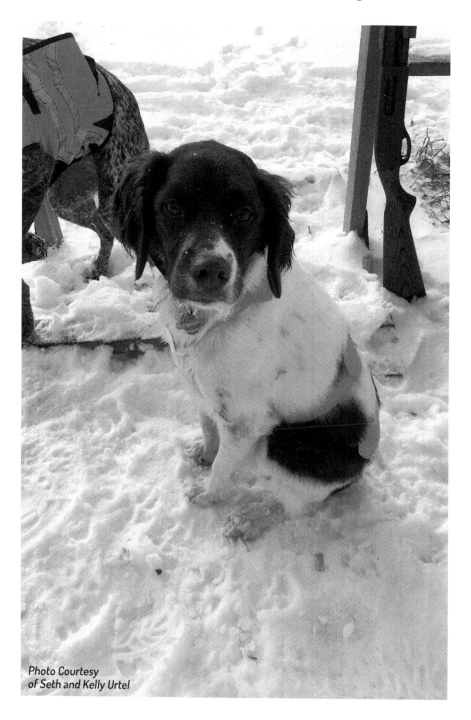

*Photo Courtesy
of Seth and Kelly Urtel*

Overcorrection – For this very reason, I do not recommend leaving your Brittany unattended while wearing an e-collar, as it could malfunction. It could unnecessarily confuse your Brittany by "correcting" a problem that was not even there.

No positive reinforcement – E-collars do not reinforce good behavior with praise, treats, and affection. Whatever training method you decide to use, never underestimate the power of a reward, verbal approval, or affection.

E-Collar Training – How to Get Started

Before you start using an e-collar to train your Brittany, he should know basic commands such as sit, come, and whoa. Your dog should immediately obey these commands without needing you to repeat them two or three times.

If your Brittany does not obey basic commands, then he is not ready for e-collar training.

COLLAR CONDITIONING

Long before you start e-collar training, you want your Brittany to recognize that the collar goes on at the beginning of his day. It is part of your dog's daily outfit – nothing more. You want your Brittany to associate the collar with going on walks, going outside, and playing. The collar is part of his everyday life.

At this stage, the power switch stays off unless you are actually training your Brittany or you are in a situation when you need to enforce a command.

One of the keys in e-collar training is selecting the correct stimulation level. Each collar will come with at least three different adjustable levels. The sensation level should be adjusted to a level that the dog understands as part of his training. It should never be painful.

When training, you will want to tighten the collar just a notch so the contact points actually touch the skin. My recommendation for Brittanys is that you should be able to slip two fingers under the collar comfortably; three fingers is too loose. Never over-tighten as the constriction may cause muscular strain.

FIRST INTRODUCTIONS

Ask your Brittany to sit in front of you. Put the stimulation level on the lowest setting. Slowly, increase the setting until you notice your Brittany seems

137

to be slightly annoyed with something, such as the buzzing sound from a fly around his head. You want to see a vibe of confusion, not a yelp or cry of pain.

If your furry companion vocalizes, his ears turn down, or if he tucks his tail between his legs, it is an obvious sign the stimulation is too high. Dogs feel pain, but their reactions to pain are different than humans. Dogs' natural instinct is to hide pain and act stoic, to protect themselves and not seem vulnerable. If you see a reaction, it is a level of discomfort that would be unacceptable to humans, making it definitely unacceptable for your best friend.

COMING WHEN CALLED

Now that you have established the baseline stimulation level for your pooch, you can start teaching him the come command using the e-collar. However, it is imperative that your Brittany already obeys the verbal command, "Come."

Put your dog on a long leash, at least twenty feet in length. Tell your Britt the "Sit" command, and once he is sitting, walk backward about ten to twenty feet. Stimulate your dog collar using the baseline stimulation level while giving the "Come" command enthusiastically. Gently nudge the dog's leash to come toward you.

When your Brittany is within arm's length, release the stimulation button on the e-collar. Generously praise your pup. Let your dog know that this is exactly the type of behavior you approve of.

The goal of this training exercise is to teach your Brittany that the annoyance will go away when he obeys your command.

You will need to do this practice training in various different situations and environments. Start off in your backyard, then move to a place with more distractions, such as the dog park or near a playground. If your Brittany does not come, be prepared to slightly increase the stimulation level. Never underestimate the power of generous praise, affection, and yummy rewards each time your dog comes when asked.

THE DO'S AND DON'TS WHEN USING AN E-COLLAR

The e-collar is a powerful tool as it gives you the ability to enforce a command at a distance. Many hunters prefer using e-collars for this reason as it improves communication between them and their dogs despite the distance.

However, this powerful tool is often abused. Never turn up the stimulation level past the point of being annoying to being painful. If your Brittany is not responding, it is more than likely your training methods have failed along the way. Take a step back and reinforce more simple commands. If your dog is having a bad day, there is no need to make it worse by using the e-collar. Give your dog a break, and do not even turn the collar on. Never take your frustrations out on your Brittany, who adores you.

If you have a professional trainer in the area, who specializes in training hunting dogs, take a few classes with them to learn how to ethically handle your Brittany. If you misuse your dog's e-collars, it can cause more behavioral problems than they can actually solve.

Introduction to the Gun

One of the important aspects of introducing your Brittany to the sound of gunfire is to take it slowly and not rush anything.

If your pup is confident and has already mastered all of his basic commands, such as sit, come, whoa, and stay, then you should be ready to introduce your dog to gunfire noises by seven to eight months of age. If your pooch is on the timid side and still needs to master basic commands, then leave things until he is at least one year of age. Also, your pup should have mastered walking by your side and be able to obey the stop command or whistle before you even think about firing a gun in the vicinity of your Brittany.

The majority of gun dog trainers prefer to wait till a dog is at least eight months old, as the dog's hearing will have fully developed by then. If you have any questions, contact a local professional gun dog trainer to evaluate your Brittany. It is better to be on the safe side than to end up with a dog who has lifelong problems with hearing gunshots.

HOW TO INTRODUCE GUNFIRE NOISES

One of the first steps is to start getting your Brittany acclimatized to loud, cracking noises without being startled.

Start by dropping empty metal food bowls on the floor near your Brittany to desensitize him to loud noises. Clap your hands when you are walking up behind him. Make loud background noises and observe your dog's reaction each time. Teach your dog to associate loud, startling noises with something he enjoys, such as being walked or fed.

Some gun dog trainers like to fire an older air gun without pellets at a considerable distance from their dog to give off a realistic "crack" sound. Over a period of weeks, the trainer will repeat the process but move a little bit closer each time to the dog. Over time, they will switch it up with an actual shotgun, again at a considerable distance, maybe starting with a starting pistol and graduating to finally a .410 with a short cartridge.

Remember the following when introducing your Brittany to gun noises:

- Do not fire a gun in the close vicinity to your dog to gauge his reaction to the loud sound.

- Take things gently, and do not rush things.

- Never introduce your Brittany to gunfire until he is at least seven months of age.

- If your pooch shows any signs of anxiety or nervousness, then you will need to take things even slower.

- Get your Brittany used to the sight of the gun by carrying around an un-cocked air rifle over your arm during training practices so when the time comes to fire it, he will not be alarmed.

Some gun dog trainers use party poppers to introduce their pups to gunfire noises and bangs. You can buy a bag of a hundred or so for about ten dollars at any supermarket or dollar store. They make a loud banging sound

Photo Courtesy of Anthony Holifield

but are still soft enough not to frighten your pooch. Pop the party poppers at a considerable distance and come a little closer each time.

Starting pistols are ideal for the next step for training your Brittany. Many professional trainers prefer to fire the pistol inside of their game bag, so it muffles the sound of the shot. Be careful of shooting a dummy launcher too close to your dog. There are numerous stories of gundogs being so badly spooked by dummy launchers too early in their training and being frightened of the sound for the rest of their lives.

The key to introducing your Brittany to gun noises is to gradually desensitize the puppy. Expose your Brittany to as many different noises as possible, such as having the radio on in the background and slowly increasing the volume. Or play gunfire noises in the background while your pooch is eating and gradually increase the volume.

Once your dog seems totally oblivious to the background sounds, then clay shoots and country fairs are in order, but at a distance. If you take your time, you should eventually have a much bolder gun dog who is not afraid of anything.

How to Prevent Common Issues with Gun Dogs

If you are a veteran gun dog owner, you know it is rare to make it through hunting season without encountering one or two badly behaved gun dogs. Here are some of the most common issues with gun dogs and how to avoid them.

WHINING AND MAKING NOISE

Whining dogs can be distracting and frustrating for both the handler and other fellow hunters while hunting. The same goes for dogs that whine or bark while inside of their crates in the car or at the camp. Dogs normally whine because they are impatient and desperately want to get something.

SOLUTION – If you notice your dog whining or making noise on shoot day, do not simply ignore it and hope it will get better. Go back to the basics and avoid taking your pooch out shooting again until he has proved himself to stay calm even when he is excited. Return to a controlled environment and practice with food, dummies, and game, only progressing to the next stage when your dog stays quiet throughout each stage.

HUNTING ON THEIR OWN ACCORD

It is common for dogs to thinks they are better hunters than their owners.

 SOLUTION: *Never allow your young Brittany to stray far away from you. Always teach hunting as a controlled exercise. For example, you may drop a dummy near to your feet when your pooch is not looking.*

RUNNING IN

Running in is when your Brittany decides to run in and flush game without a direct command. Many hunters refer to these dogs as spoiled brats, as they do not obey their parents. The key to avoiding this happening is to lay a solid foundation before you take your Brittany shooting.

 SOLUTION: *If your dog runs in without you giving the recall command, run after him. Trust me; he will be surprised to see you there. Put him on the lead, give him the recall command again, and walk with him to where you recalled it. If your dog runs in, do not start whistling or calling his name, as this will just teach him to ignore your commands, and he will only return to you when he has had his fun.*

BAD BEHAVIOR AROUND OTHER DOGS

Not only can this be embarrassing, but it can even be dangerous. On shoot day, a wide range of dogs of all breeds and temperaments will be present. It is vital that they all get along and concentrate on the job at hand instead of one another.

 SOLUTION: *Be sure to start socializing your Brittany with a wide range of dogs and other animals as soon as he is fully vaccinated. I recommend introducing young dogs to other dogs in a calm, controlled environment. If your dog is aggressive or overly excitable, then maybe you should consider visiting a professional dog trainer.*

Field Trials and Tests

The majority of gun dog owners, especially newbies, do not know the difference between field trials and hunt tests. Both activities are a fantastic way to keep you and your Brittany in shape and practice training skills during off-season; however, it can be confusing to know which activity is best suited for you and your dog.

FIELD TRIALS

Field trials are competitive events. In a typical field trial, only one dog will win, or depending on the event, one dog from each division wins.

HUNT TESTS

Hunt tests are non-competitive, and each dog is judged individually and awarded a score based on its performance. The dogs are not compared against each other as in a field trial. At the end of the hunt test, there may be several dogs with close to perfect scores and other dogs who did not pass the test. The objective of a hunt test is to evaluate each dog independently.

Field trials and hunt tests provide breeders with an opportunity to assess their dogs. Both activities serve the purpose of producing a better hunting

Photo Courtesy of Kent Baxter
Baxter's Bird Dogs

dog by fine-tuning the dog's inherent abilities and training. Field trials and hunt tests have annual events at a local, state, and national level, for both puppies and adult dogs.

Whether your dog is an amateur or an expert, you can find a program to participate in. Field trials and hunt tests provide the perfect opportunity to hook up with fellow gun dog owners. Often, they will gladly share suggestions on how to improve your dog's training program.

There are quite a few different organizations regularly running field trials. However, the format and style may vary. Some field trials use pen-raised birds and others may observe the dog flushing out wild birds. The American Kennel Club, American Field Sporting Dog Association, and the National Bird Hunters Association sponsor the majority of national field trials.

As for hunt tests, the North American Versatile Hunting Dogs Association, United Kennel Club and the North American Hunting Retriever Association are leaders in noncompetitive events such as hunt tests. One of the advantages of these programs is that they provide an excellent opportunity to train yourself and your dog for field trials without the pressure.

Field trials have the dog perform once a day. On the other hand, with the hunt tests, the dog can be performing several times each day. For example, in the utility test, each dog is required to perform a 30-minute hunt, plus a 10-minute duck search in a large body of water, a heeling sequence, a tracked field retrieve, and a combination of retrieving tasks. Both the field trials and hunt tests have complex scoring criteria to ensure the judges' evaluations are as objective as possible.

Depending on the field trial or hunt test, the dog will be required to demonstrate his ability to search for game, hold point, flush, shot and drop, and retrieve downed game. Brittanys are versatile hunting dogs, so they will be expected to search the water for game and mark and retrieve downed game, as well as flush out wild fowl on land.

If you are unsure what type of event is best suited for your Brittany, attend a couple of field trials and hunt tests. Talk to your dog's breeder for recommendations and research what activities are available in your area. Then grab your Brittany and have some fun together.

CHAPTER 8
Living with Your Brittany

> "
>
> *Brittanys need lots of mental and physical exercise. If you have an area where your dog can run off-leash, such as a field or dog park, that is optimal. Keeping thought-provoking, puzzle toys in your house for when your Brittany gets bored is an excellent thing to do as well.*
>
> **STEVE ROGERS**
> *Winding Branch Kenne*
>
> "

"The journey of life is sweeter when travelled with a dog." Unknown

Sharing your life with your Brittany involves happy moments, funny moments, sad moments, and everything in between.

Your Brittany will not only fill your heart with love, but he will make it stronger. Recent studies have shown that having a canine companion can lower your blood pressure, cholesterol, and triglyceride levels. Also, your Brittany can have a positive effect on your mental health and well-being.

Your dog will be an essential part of your life and family, so you will want to give him the best life possible in every aspect. In this chapter, we will discuss some fundamental day-to-day activities you can do with your Brittany.

Physical Exercise

> **"**
>
> *Play games that build your pup into being the dog that you want as an adult. Make games very short: get the desired response, reward, and move onto something else. Do not push games until puppy fails, quit on the small, good notes. Don't worry about how long you can get the pup to do something, quit when you are ahead.*
>
> **ARLETTE HENNESSEY**
> *K Nine Birddog Brittanys*
>
> **"**

Being a good puppy parent means providing your pup with daily physical activity. The benefits of regularly exercising your Brittany are endless. Regular physical activity helps your Brittany to sleep better at night. Just a slight case of sleep deprivation for your dog can cause all sorts of behavioral issues. You will notice your pup's overall mood will improve with daily exercise.

Another reason to regularly exercise your Brittany is that it helps keep his weight down. In the United States, more than fifty percent of dogs are considered to be overweight or obese. Like people, excess weight leads to a long list of health problems. Exercise also improves blood circulation, which decreases the risk of cardiovascular diseases.

A few health benefits for dogs derived from regular physical activity:

- Maintains and builds muscle mass, which can reduce risk of injury
- Helps to prevent canine diabetes and certain cancers
- Decreases the risk of urinary tract infections, as exercise stimulates frequent urination
- Helps to reduce the risk of arthritis
- May increase your Brittany's lifespan

There are other benefits derived from providing your Brittany with a regular exercise regime. For example, just sticking to a walking schedule can combat many common behavioral problems such as barking, aggression, and chewing.

Exercise Requirements for your Brittany

> *Britt's should be exercised in a safe environment, such as a fenced yard or while on a long lead. This is a fast breed with an excellent prey drive for hunting, which at times can put them in danger. They are BIRD dogs and whether you are a hunter or not, your Brittany is! Finding a safe environment can be a challenge. Many states have designated training areas to exercise or train dogs. Check with your states wildlife or parks division for areas near you.*
>
> DIANA L KUBITZ
> *Renegade Brittanys*

As mentioned above, exercise plays a vital role in your Brittany's overall health and may even extend his lifespan. However, providing your pooch with adequate exercise goes beyond taking him out for an occasional walk or two.

All Brittanys are considered to be high-energy dogs and require at least 60 minutes of exercise each day to keep them healthy and to keep boredom at bay.

Puppies – Puppies need several bouts of short exercise sessions throughout the day, but excessive exercise for puppies may be detrimental to their growth. Over-exercise refers to repetitive actions, such as walking briskly or running for an extended period of time, not typical playing in the yard or romping around the house.

Adults – An adult Brittany is considered to be in his prime from one year old to seven years old and requires, on average, 60 minutes of exercise per day or more. There will be days when the weather is bad, so you will need to offer other indoor alternatives.

Seniors – Do not make the mistake of assuming your elderly Brittany does not need exercise. Unless your pooch has serious health conditions that prevent him from exercising, you will want to continue with his daily walks. Regular exercise can relieve joint pain and maintain muscle mass. Plus, being out in the fresh air will put a little pep in your old pup's step.

Health exceptions – Some health conditions, such as patellar luxation (trick knee), may require strict bed rest while recovering to reduce swelling and manage pain. However, after that, a veterinarian will suggest

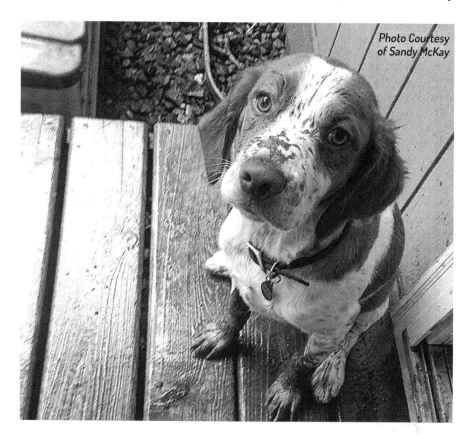

Photo Courtesy of Sandy McKay

doing strengthening exercises, such as walking uphill to build muscles around the knee.

Pregnancy – In general, pregnant Brittanys should be taken for daily walks and exercised as normal, except for the last week of pregnancy. Regular exercise will help the pregnant dog stay in shape, which will help in her labor and delivery. Exercise can gradually resume two to three weeks after the dog gives birth.

Running Partner

Running with your Brittany can bring enormous benefits for both you and your dog's physical and mental health. It will help to keep your dog's weight in check, which is particularly important as veterinarians report an increasing number of overweight dogs. Plus, running can do wonders for your Britt's mental health. The sights, smells, and sounds your dog will encounter on a run, and the change of scenery will provide him with more than enough mental stimulation to reduce anxiety and boredom.

Running is a positive outlet for dogs who exhibit destructive behaviors. Instead of tearing through your favorite pillow, he can burn off his excess energy tearing through the countryside. But before hitting the running trial with your Brittany, there are a few things you need to consider.

CONSIDER YOUR BRITT'S AGE

Take into consideration your Brittany's age and health condition. It is not advisable to start running with your puppy until he has finished growing, as he is more prone to injury. Wait until your Brittany is at least one year old before taking him on vigorous runs in the countryside. Similarly, this would apply to running with a dog who suffers with joint problems or has weight issues. If you want to help your dog to lose weight, talk first to your vet for some suggestions for an activity that is less painful on his joints.

REMEMBER, IT IS NOT A RACE

There is no denying the truth; Brittanys love to run and run. But if you are trying to break a new sprinting record, it probably is best not to take your dog with you. Remember that you will still need to stop and clean up after your dog, and all dogs can easily get distracted by sniffing their surroundings. Running with your dog needs to be a fun occasion for both of you, and your pooch should feel free to stop if he needs to. Instead of breaking records, try to see running as a healthy activity you can do leisurely with your pooch.

Photo Courtesy
of Marissa Bassette

START OFF SLOWLY

If you want to start running with your Brittany, take things slowly. Can you imagine how you would feel if someone took you on a 5M run, and you had not been running in some time? Your Brittany may be full of energy, but he still needs to build up tolerance. Start with a mile and slowly work up to a longer distance. Find a running area that both of you enjoy.

HELPFUL TIP
Dog Sports

Thanks to their high energy levels and strong drive to work, Brittanys are excellent at dog sports. You don't need to be a hunter, either—you can enjoy flyball, agility, dock diving, or other dog sports with your Brittany.

Remember never let your pooch off the lead unless he has mastered basic commands, and you can trust him to stay close to you at all times.

DO NOT PUSH YOUR BRITTANY TOO HARD

Do not be fooled by your pup's energy. Dogs do not sweat through their skin; instead, they cool their body temperature down by panting. Pushing your dog too hard for too long can lead to hyperventilation and breathing difficulties. Stop frequently to give your Brittany a break; trust me, he will appreciate it. Remember, you and your Brittany are a team, and you need to be aware of his body language as he cannot tell you when he has had enough.

HIKING PARTNER

Your Brittany is an instant companion for adventures in the great outdoors, as he is always ready, willing, and eager to hit the trail. Hiking is one of the best activities you can do with your Brittany, as it will deepen your bond of friendship though shared experiences.

Before you hit the trails with your Brittany, consider the following guidelines:

Make sure dogs are allowed on the hiking trails you will be hiking and obey any restrictions concerning off-limit areas.

Keep your Brittany on a leash at all times. Most national parks allow dogs on the hiking trails if they are always on their leash. Keeping your dog on the leash will prevent him from chasing after wildlife or tearing up the delicate forest undergrowth. Many parks have hefty fines if they find you hiking with your dog off his leash.

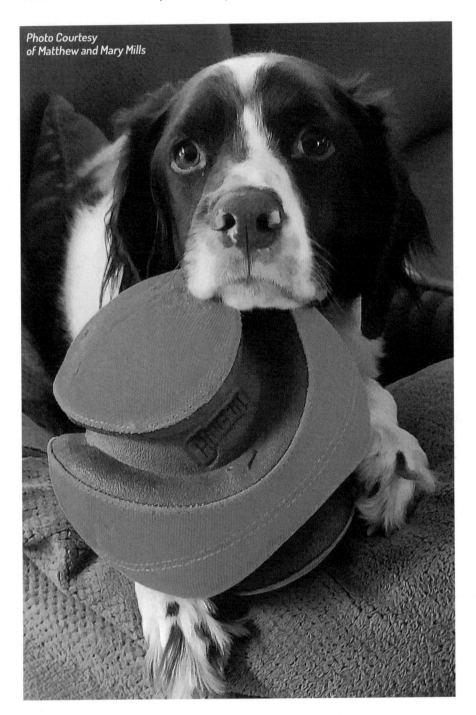

Photo Courtesy
of Matthew and Mary Mills

Another factor to consider is that your dog can leave behind his predator scent that may disrupt the local wildlife and hinder feeding and nesting activities. Unleashed dogs can quickly catch the scent of something and may disappear from your view instantly.

Never assume that other hikers will love your Brittany as much as you. Always keep your dog on a leash so other hikers do not feel frightened or threatened. This is especially important if you are hiking through bear country. Many unleashed dogs have been mistaken for wild animals and accidentally sprayed with bear spray. Also, never assume other dogs you encounter on a hiking trail will be happy to meet your Brittany.

Always clean up after your dog. Carry along a small spade and bury his waste in the ground or carry it out with you in a plastic bag. Dog waste contains fecal coliform bacteria, salmonella and giardia which can cause other animals to become sick.

Make sure your dog has mastered all of the basic commands and is completely vaccinated before hitting the trails. The following is a list of gear for hiking with your Brittany.

Collar or a harness – Never use a choke collar, as it could get caught on a twig or branch and strangle your dog. Make sure you can slip two fingers under the collar or harness to prevent your dog from hyperventilating on the trail.

Leash – Make sure you use a heavy-duty leash that can withhold the rigors of hiking. If you plan to use an expandable leash, keep the leash short enough to maintain control over your dog.

Water – Carry at least eight ounces of water per hour of hiking. If you are hiking in hot weather, freeze your dog's water bottles the night before; the ice will melt as you hike, providing your dog with a refreshing cool drink. Water found in ponds, streams, and creeks may contain harmful bacteria and parasites that cause your Brittany to become sick.

Food – Be sure to bring along enough food for your Brittany for the duration of the trip. I recommend feeding your pooch smaller quantities but more frequently to prevent the discomfort of exercising on a full tummy.

Collapsible bowl – A collapsible bowl does not weigh much and will make it easy to give your Brittany water or food along the hike. Most collapsible bowls for dogs can be attached to the outside of your bag for convenience.

Plastic bags or a small spade – Bring a small spade if you decide to bury your dog's fecal matter in the ground, or bring plastic bags if you plan to carry out his waste.

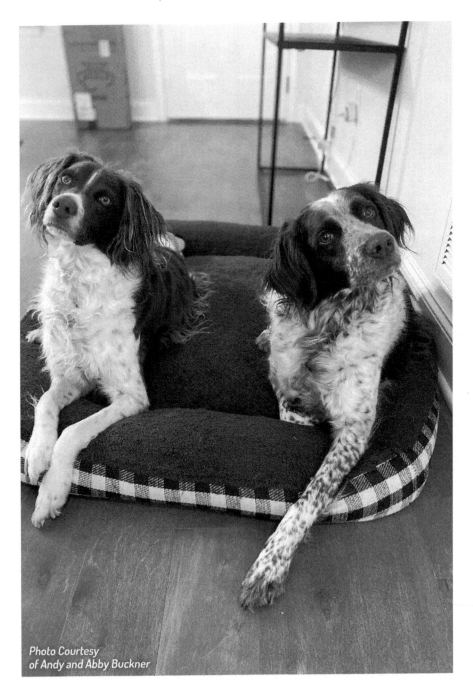

Photo Courtesy
of Andy and Abby Buckner

Canine first aid kit – Just as you would bring along a first aid kit for yourself, be sure to bring along extra items for your dog. Be sure your first aid kits have the following items: hydrogen peroxide to disinfect cuts, scissors with a rounded tip to cut back any fur around a wound, bandages and gauze, and a small sock to protect a sore or wounded foot.

Reflective lights – Reflective lights can be attached to your Brittany's harness, leash, or collar to protect him when crossing the road at night time.

Specialized clothing – For adverse weather conditions or special activities, have on hand booties, bandanas, canine flotation devices, or insulating jackets. Before heading out into the great outdoors, check the weather conditions and determine what type of clothing your Britany may require.

Fun Sport – Agility and Flyball

> "
>
> *They are highly intelligent and enjoy training. Routine training, even if you are just working on a new trick, forms a very strong bond between you and your dog. There are plenty of different activities and classes offered that will aid in your Brittany's mental stimulation. You might just discover a new sport both of you enjoy.*
>
> JESSIE SCHULZ
> *Credit Brittanys*
>
> "

Canine sports are becoming more popular with pet owners around the world. Maybe you have heard of agility, fly ball, or nose work but are unsure what they exactly are. Or maybe you are interested in trying them out but do not know which sport is best suited for your Brittany. Here is a quick rundown of the differences of each sport.

AGILITY

Agility requires your Brittany to go through an obstacle course, such as jumping through hoops or over poles, crawling through tunnels, and more as quickly as possible. Your dog will be faulted if he misses an obstacle in the course or disobeys the instructions. Agility is a fantastic way to challenge your pup's mind and body.

FLY BALL

Flyball requires your Brittany reach the ball dispenser at the end of the relay race, but before reaching the dispenser, your dog will have to pass through several obstacles, grab the dispensed ball and run back through the obstacles before the next dog is released to do the same thing. Often the dogs will work in teams of four, and the fastest team will win the race. Fly ball is exhilarating not only for your dog but also for spectators.

NOSE OR SCENT WORK

Nose or scent work involves your Brittany's exceptional sniffer. A course will be set up with hidden scent markers, and your dog's task is to find all of the different scent markers in order to get a reward. The course is quite similar to how dogs are trained for search and rescue work or police work. This

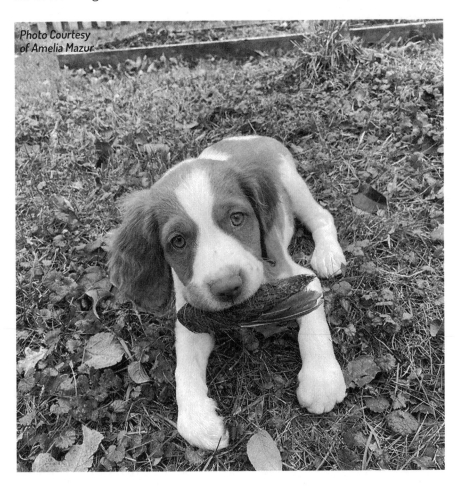

Photo Courtesy
of Amelia Mazur

option is great for a shy dog, as the course is performed by one dog at a time. Nose work may not provide as much physical exercise as the above two options, but it is great mental stimulation for your Brittany.

Which sport is the best choice for your Brittany? It will depend on your preferences and your dog's personality. For example, if your dog thrives on being active, then give agility a try. If your dog is very social and enjoys being around other dogs, then maybe flyball. If your pooch is less social and enjoys seeking out objects, then nose work may be best suited for him. No matter what you choose, agility, flyball, and nose work are all mentally stimulating sports.

HELPFUL TIP
Energy Overload

Brittanys were bred to work alongside hunters all day long. They have a tremendous amount of energy and require plenty of vigorous exercise. Whether it's in the yard, on a leash, or at the dog park, plan on running your Brittany for at least an hour every day.

Show Life

A show dog is not born a show dog. Preparing your dog to become a show dog requires a lot of time, energy, money, care, and determination. Here are some things you should know about show dogs:

Show dogs are not easy to find – Show dogs are not easy to come by, so do not expect to phone a breeder and request a show dog, especially if they have never met you. Show dogs are the cream of the crop, and not every litter produces a show-dog quality pup. Often, you will have to wait one year or more for a show dog. Some people wait years for a dog out of a specific litter.

Show dogs have to remain intact – Show dogs cannot be neutered or spayed. Often you do not have a say in the gender of your show dog. Show dogs originally were designed to show off the breeding stock of the dog's bloodline. The dog's appearance and structure are judged according to the dog's ability to produce quality pedigree puppies.

BE PREPARED FOR CO-OWNERSHIP

The majority of breeders who agree to sell you a show dog often will retain partial ownership of the dog. Perhaps the breeder will want to maintain the breeding rights to the dog or to protect the bloodline and prevent the dog from being bred irresponsibly. Be sure to read the fine print on the contract before you sign.

*Photo Courtesy
of Vicki Walsh*

Be determined to work – Show dogs do not get in the ring and automatically strut their stuff. Your Brittany will need conformation classes to learn how to have a proper gait, be properly socialized, and travel well.

Do not expect to get rich – Dog shows are not money makers; instead, they are quite expensive. However, if your dog places first place, you will get the bragging rights.

HOW DOG SHOWS WORK

Each dog registered at the dog show will be presented to a judge by its owner or breeder. However, some pet owners prefer to hire a professional handler or exhibitor.

The sole purpose of a dog show is to evaluate the dog's breeding stock. Your Brittany will start off in classes competing for points toward his American Kennel Club championship. Your dog will win points according to the number of dogs he defeats in the dog show. The more dogs of the same breed who enter a competition, the more points a dog will win. Your dog will need fifteen points that have been awarded by three different judges to become an AKC champion.

Dog shows are a process of elimination, and only the Best of Breed winners will be able to compete. There are seven different groups: Sporting, Hunting, Working, Terrier, Toy, Non-Sporting, and Herding. Brittanys are allowed to participate in the Sporting Group. The judges will select the Best in Show winner.

The judges will judge each dog against a written standard describing the ideal dog of the specified breed. The standards for Brittanys are established by the American Brittany Club. Each judge will give his or her own opinion as to which dog represents the breed's standard appropriately.

CHAPTER 9
Traveling

A recent survey discovered that more than 95 percent of dog owners plan at least one overnight trip each year with their dogs. Most Brittanys love to travel, but it can be stressful on your dog and you if you are not well-prepared.

Before hitting the road with your pooch, take the time to choose the safest and most comfortable option for your Brittany. Ask yourself how much time you will be spending with your dog on your vacation. If he will be spending the majority of time alone, then he will most likely be happier left at home than tagging along with you on your journey.

By planning ahead, you can have a safe, stress-free trip.

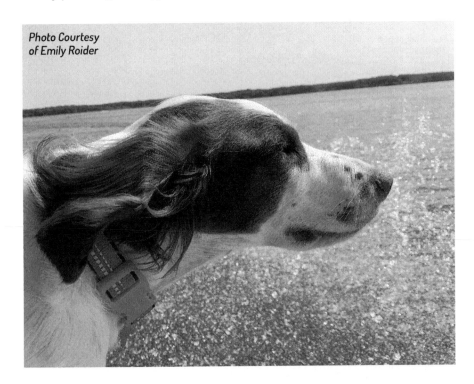

Photo Courtesy of Emily Roider

Preparing to Travel with Your Brittany

Whether you are planning to travel with your Brittany for necessity or pleasure, you will need to take some definite steps to prepare for your dog's needs along the way. Car travel and air travel, especially longer trips, require some forethought. Never assume you will be able to find everything you need for your pooch during the journey.

- **Food** – Be sure to pack enough dog food for the duration of the entire trip, as switching your dog's food may cause him to have an upset tummy. If you are planning on traveling for a longer period of time, research ahead of time whether your Brittany's regular dog food will be available at your final destination.

- **Water** – Throw in a bottle or two of clean drinking water to keep your dog hydrated throughout the journey. Never allow your dog to drink water from an unfamiliar source such as a creek, puddle, or pond.

- **Food and water dishes** – Do not forget to bring your pup's food and water dishes along. Be sure to place them in an area where you can easily reach them throughout the trip. If you are tight on space, look for a set of pop-off food dishes.

- **Crate or carrier** – Depending on your method of travel, you might need either a hard-cover crate or a soft-cover carrier. Make sure to choose a comfortable traveling case, as it will most likely be used as your dog's personal bedroom when you reach the final destination. How to choose an appropriate crate is discussed in the following pages.

- **Toys** – Be sure to bring along a few of your Brittany's favorite toys for the journey, as this will keep him distracted during long-haul trips and also help to relieve stress.

- **Blankets and doggy beds** – A nice, fluffy blanket will keep your Brittany warm during the journey, plus the familiar scent will keep him calm. If you have space in your luggage, bring along a doggy bed so your dog can use it at the final destination.

- **Collar, leash, and ID tags** – Be sure to place your dog's collar and ID tags on him before leaving the house, and do not remove them until you return home. If your Brittany is an adventure-seeker, he may suddenly escape to explore his new surroundings, so you may also want to invest in a GPS-dog tracker tag.

- **Cleaning supplies** – Traveling with dogs can get messy. Be prepared by bringing along potty pads, baby wipes, paper towels, disposable garbage bags, and of course, a pet-friendly stain remover.

- **Medications** – If your Brittany is taking any type of medicine or supplements, make sure you have enough for the duration of your trip.
- **Health and vaccination certificates** – Do not forget to bring along your Brittany's medical information when traveling, in case of an emergency.

Photo Courtesy
of Emily Roider

Traveling by Car

Whether you are taking your Brittany on a short trip or a long journey, you will want to ensure your pup is comfortable and safe.

Avoid the temptation to let your Brittany sit in the front seat or roam freely about the vehicle while it is in motion. If you have a car accident due to being distracted by your dog, you could be held accountable. Even worse, you or your pooch or other parties could be seriously injured.

DO

- Secure your Brittany inside of a hard-cover crate that has been anchored to the vehicle by using a seat belt or other secure means or placed on the floor.
- Bring along plenty of clean drinking water to keep your pooch hydrated, especially during summer months.
- Give your dog plenty of rest stops, not only for your Brittany to relieve himself but also so he can stretch his legs and drink some water.
- If you have the air conditioner on or a window open, make sure it is not directly blowing on your Brittany. If the window is open, make sure your dog cannot stick his head out or accidentally jump out.
- If your pooch suffers from motion sickness, ask your vet to prescribe a mild medication and follow the vet's instructions for administering it.
- Make your Brittany feel at home inside of his crate by bringing along some familiar items such as his blanket, chew toys, etc.
- Bring along a human buddy. Whenever possible, share the driving and dog caretaking duties with a friend or family member. You will be able to use the facilities or grab a quick bite to eat, knowing someone you trust is keeping a watchful eye on your Brittany.

DON'T

- Never transport your Brittany in the back of an open pickup truck.
- Do not allow your dog to sit in the front seat and hang his head out of the vehicle while it is in motion. He could be injured by particles of debris or get sick from breathing cold air forced into his lungs.
- Never leave your Brittany alone inside of a hot car. It only takes a few minutes for your dog to become overheated. This may cause irreversible organ damage or even death.
- Do not feed your Brittany at least two hours prior to traveling in order to prevent motion sickness.

*Photo Courtesy
of Billie Gandara*

A year-round hazard is leaving your Brittany unattended in your car. In addition to the dangers of heat and cold, anytime you leave a dog alone inside the car, you are making an unspoken invitation to pet thieves.

Choosing the Right Crate for Long Distance Car Travel

Whether your Brittany loves long road trips or quivers at the very thought of getting into the car, you will want to make the journey as comfortable and pleasant for him as possible. Dog travel crates are designed to provide a safe, enclosed place for your pooch to travel in comfort. These crates differ from your Brittany's home crate, as they come with extra security features such as fasteners to keep the crate secure while traveling.

Here are the factors to consider when choosing a travel crate for your Brittany:

Size – The crate should be big enough for your Brittany to sit, stand, lie down, and turn around in, but small enough to keep him secure. A general rule of thumb is that travel crates should be no more than six inches longer than your pooch. A bigger crate may give your dog more space to move about, but this also means he may involuntarily slide around inside of the crate while the vehicle is in motion.

Soft vs. hard-cover – A soft carrier may be more comfortable for your Brittany. However, for car travel, a hard crate provides your dog with more protection if you get into an accident. Another advantage to hard-cover crates is that they are easier to clean up if your dog has an accident or gets carsick.

Harness – Due to new state laws, many car crates come with a built-in harness, which allows the crate to be securely fastened to the seatbelt for extra stability. By fastening the crate to the seat belt, you are creating a more secure ride for your Brittany, as the crate will not slide around on sharp corners or fly forward if you come to a sudden stop.

Visibility – Brittanys are very curious by nature and love to observe their surroundings. Choose a crate that will give your dog an unhindered view and lots of fresh air. If your dog is nervous about car travel, then the more visibility, the better.

Traveling by Plane

Traveling by plane with your Brittany can be complicated and more expensive than flying solo, but it is possible with a little extra research ahead of time.

Generally, veterinarians and breeders do not recommend flying with your pet unless absolutely necessary. Ideally, dogs should not fly unless their owner is permanently moving to a new location or taking a long trip of two to three weeks minimum. This is because flying can be extremely stressful for your Brittany.

Air travel removes your pooch from his comfortable home and familiar surroundings, forcing him into a strange environment with loud noises, bright lights, changes in air pressures and cabin temperature, and to make matters worse, few opportunities to use the bathroom.

CARGO OR CARRY-ON?

If you must fly with your Brittany, ideally, the best place for him would be in the cabin under the seat in front of you. However, each airline has different rules and regulations as to where your pooch will be allowed to spend his time during the flight, depending on his size.

Typically, your dog will be allowed to fly in the cabin, as a carry-on if he is small enough to fit in a carrier under the seat in front of you. Most airlines have a weight limit of twenty pounds for dogs flying in the cabin, though there are some exceptions. Any larger than that, and your dog will usually have to travel in the cargo hold, along with the luggage and freight.

Every year, hundreds of thousands of dogs fly in the cargo without incident, but there are many unknown variables that you have no control over once you hand your Brittany over to airline personnel.

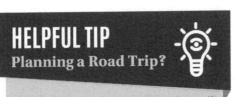

HELPFUL TIP
Planning a Road Trip?

Brittanys want to be by your side at all times and are definitely always up for a road trip. However, you need to plan ahead and make sure you still give your dog plenty of exercise and water while traveling. A long day in the car without a good run first could make your Brittany restless.

Airlines do their best to make your dog comfortable in the cargo hold. However, baggage handlers are often just trying to get the plane loaded or unloaded on time. They are not paid to give your dog extra attention inside of his kennel. Unfortunately, many pet owners have horror stories of their pets being injured, becoming seriously ill, getting lost, or even dying after flying in the cargo hold.

Unfortunately, for many airlines, a full-grown Brittany is too big to fit under the seat in the cabin, so the only option will be to place him in the cargo hold.

Familiarize your Brittany with his carrier or crate well in advance of the actual flight. If possible, take your dog to the airport's departure area several times so he becomes more comfortable with this noisy, strange place.

HOW MUCH DOES IT COST?

Prices may vary airline to airline, but the average price for your Brittany to travel in the cargo hold is approximately $75 each way. Of course, the price will vary depending on the traveling distance, as well as the combined weight of your dog and his crate. The majority of airlines will provide you access to an online calculator to estimate the cost.

RESEARCH

As mentioned above, each airline has different rules and regulations, and these are constantly changing. It is important to read through these rules thoroughly before traveling so your Brittany is not turned away before boarding the plane. To avoid this, a few days before flying, phone the airline company to double check that you have all the required documents for traveling with your Brittany.

Look for non-stop flights with no transfers. Avoid traveling with your Brittany during the holiday season when airports are busy and flights are packed. This is to minimize the risks of any unexpected changes or cancellations.

Consider the weather in your final destination. If you are traveling somewhere cooler, choose flights in the middle of the day when the temperature is not as cold. If you are traveling somewhere warmer, choose flights later in the evening or early mornings before the temperature rises. Keep in mind, most airlines will not let your pet travel in the cargo hold if the temperatures are too extreme at the final destination.

The majority of airlines allow only a certain number of dogs each flight, so always call the airline and make sure they have space for both you and your Brittany. Always make reservations for you and your dog at the same time to avoid unwanted last-minute surprises at the airport.

CONSIDER YOUR DESTINATION

If you are planning on traveling internationally or even to some U.S. states such as Hawaii or Puerto Rico, be sure to check local animal transportation regulations before purchasing your ticket. Many international destinations have a complicated process and/or lengthy quarantine periods, which may mean you will be separated from your Brittany for part or most of your trip.

The CDC has recently suspended dogs coming in from high-risk countries for dog rabies. American citizens and lawful citizens can request an import permit, but these permits will be issued on an extremely limited basis. If you are planning to travel to one of these countries with your dog, be aware that your dog may not be permitted to reenter the United States.

Before traveling, research the departing and destination airport so you know exactly where any pet-relief areas are located inside the airport. If you have flight transfers, your Brittany will thank you for letting him relieve himself and stretch his legs. Consult the terminal, so once your flight lands, you will know where to head with your dog.

CONSULT WITH YOUR VET

Before planning any flight with your Brittany, be sure to consult with your veterinarian about food, water, and medication. The American Veterinary Medical Association does not recommend sedating dogs prior to flying. There are health risks with sedating dogs, and certain airlines prohibit sedating pets without a certified note from the dog's veterinarian.

If your Brittany is slightly overweight, your vet can formulate a weight loss plan to help the dog lose those extra pounds before the big journey. This is important, as obese dogs are at a higher risk of having their airways collapse while traveling.

Many airlines require that your Brittany have a clean bill of health before flying. Your veterinarian can issue a health certificate stating that your dog is healthy enough to fly and is up-to-date on his vaccinations. If the duration of your trip is longer than the certificate's validity, then you will need to get another certificate from a veterinarian while on vacation in order to meet the requirements of your Brittany's return flight.

AT THE AIRPORT

Make sure to arrive at the airport with plenty of extra time to avoid being stressed.

IF YOUR DOG IS TRAVELING IN THE CARGO HOLD

Most airlines require you to arrive at least three hours before domestic flights and at least five hours before international flights. You may have to take your Brittany to a separate cargo drop-off section in the terminal, so review your departure and arrival airport maps ahead of time to avoid confusion.

Be sure to paste a current picture of your dog on the crate along with his name. Also, you can tape a bag of food to the outside of the crate in case of a long delay. Be sure to have a current picture of your Brittany on your phone and a picture of his crate, in case the airline accidentally misplaces your dog, which is not likely to happen, but it is better to be prepared than sorry.

IF YOUR DOG IS TRAVELING IN THE CABIN

Go directly to the passenger check-in desk, where the agent will request to see your dog's health certification and proof of immunizations.

Once you pay the pet carry-on fee, head directly to security. Deal with your personal items such as computers, jackets, shoes, etc., before tending to your dog. Remove your Brittany from his carrier case and carry him through security, while his carrier goes through the X-ray machine. To speed things up, do not forget to remove your dog's harness or collar so it does not set off the metal detector.

IN THE PLANE

Once you and your Brittany are on the plane, he cannot leave his carrier for the entire duration of the flight unless your dog has special certification such as an emotional-support dog or guide dog, etc.

Keep your Brittany well hydrated throughout the flight by using an attachable water dispenser. Your dog's ears can pop due to the pressurization upon take-off and landing. To avoid this, give your Brittany a few pieces of chewy jerky to munch on during this portion of the flight, but be careful not to give him too much as he could get airsick.

IN THE CARGO HOLD

Make sure you invest in a good quality hard-cover crate with adequate ventilation, waterproof bottom, spring-locked door, and no handles. Your Brittany should be able to completely turn around and also stand up in the crate without hunching over. Do not compromise on your pooch's comfort, make sure he has enough room to stretch out.

Go the extra mile to cable-tie the crate's doors shut. Spring locks are hard to get open, but go the extra step to ensure no accidents happen.

Attach a latch water bottle with easy-to-use water dispenser inside of the crate. Do not place it on the outside as it could easily get knocked off as the baggage handlers transport your dog. Fill and freeze the water bottle the night before for dripless, refreshing hydration.

If your dog is hesitant to drink from the water bottle, then entice him by filling the bottle with lukewarm chicken broth. Water dispensers have a ball inside of the cap that rolls around when touched, releasing water. You might have to encourage your Brittany by rolling the ball around and releasing the irresistible scent of chicken broth. Reward him when he drinks from the bottle and slowly wean him off the chicken broth by replacing it with water.

Place visible identification and documentation on your dog's crate. Make sure the following information is attached to the crate: your full name, flight information, name of your pet, picture of your pet, your home and cell phone number, any medical considerations, dog temperament issues (if any), and veterinary information.

Make sure your dog has his collar on with his ID tag. Inside of the crate make sure your Brittany is comfortable with a soft blanket. Place some super-absorbent potty pads under the blanket just in case your dog has an accident or two.

UPON ARRIVAL

If your Brittany traveled in the cargo hold, pick up your checked luggage upon arrival and go straight to your airline's specified location for cargo. Airlines often state that dogs will be available thirty minutes after the flight's arrival. If your dog is not picked up within four hours of arrival, the airline will hand the dog over to a veterinarian or boarding facility at your expense.

Whether your Brittany flew in the cabin or the cargo hold, take him immediately for a walk, so he can stretch his legs and relieve himself in a designated relief area for pets either inside or outside the terminal. Even though the journey may seem complicated, you both will breathe a sigh of relief when you arrive at your final destination together.

Lodging Away from Home

Have dog, will travel. If your vacation or trip away from home is not complete without your Brittany by your side, you'll be happy to know there are many dog-friendly options to bring your pooch along.

HOTEL STAYS

Many hotel chains are not only dog-friendly nowadays but also give their canine guests the royal treatment. A recent survey by the American Hotel & Lodging Association discovered that almost 80 percent of luxury, mid-scale, and economy hotels in the United States now allow pets. Below are some tips to ensure your Brittany will be welcome at a hotel:

Talk directly with the hotel – Book directly with the hotel over the phone. This way, you will be able to ask any specific questions regarding the hotel's policies and fees for overnight pet guests. Ask the following questions:

- If there is a pet fee, is the fee per night or a flat rate for the entire stay?
- Does the hotel require a damage deposit?
- Is the entire hotel pet-friendly or only a designated floor? If the latter, ask whether the restaurants or lobby area are pet-friendly.
- Can you leave your dog in the hotel room alone or does he need to be supervised? If so, how long does the hotel's policy allow your dog to be left unattended?
- Does the hotel offer dog sitters or dog walkers? If so, what are the costs and availability for your stay?
- Are there any charges associated with damages from your pet?

The majority of hotels charge a nominal fee for dogs, $25 to $50 is a standard price per night. Many major hotel chains or boutique hotels offer discounts for pets during the off-season.

Take into consideration your Brittany's behavior – You will never really know how your Brittany will act when traveling until you try it, but taking into consideration his behavior at home will help you determine how he will act at a hotel. For example, if your pooch tends to bark at people walking past the window, then request a hotel room on a higher floor. Or if your Brittany gets nervous on elevator rides, request a room on the lower floor so you can just walk up the stairs.

If you have to leave your pup alone in the room, put the television on so he will not get nervous or excited by hearing people walking and talking in the hallways. If you are unsure how your pup will act, you can always plan a short-one night stay at a local pet-friendly hotel. Or if your Brittany loves the sound of his own voice, maybe consider staying at a pet-friendly rental property.

Have a backup plan if you cannot leave your dog alone – If the hotel policy is that you cannot leave your dog alone in the room, make sure you have a backup plan. Many hotels offer additional services, such as a dog sitter or a dog walker for hire. Another option is to take your Brittany to a day spa or groomer for the day.

If the hotel lets you leave your pooch alone in the hotel room, always give the front desk staff a heads up and leave them your cell phone number in case of any noise complaints or other issues. Also, do not forget to place a DO NOT DISTURB sign on the door, to prevent your pup from unexpectedly surprising the housekeeper.

Choose the right pet-friendly hotel – Just because a hotel lets your dog stay as a guest does not necessarily mean it is pet-friendly. Many boutique hotels provide amenities to cater to their four-pawed guests, such as a dog bed, a piddle pad, yummy treats, and food dishes at no extra charge. A few chain hotels even have a special dining menu for their canine guests, along with grooming and walking services for an additional fee.

Research pet-friendly restaurants and activities – If you cannot leave your pooch alone in the hotel room, you are going to want to find restaurants or activities that are pet-friendly. The majority of hotels will provide you with a list of nearby restaurants that allow pets. Often, if a hotel is pet-friendly, at least a part of the lobby or on-site restaurant will accommodate your pooch.

Look for fun activities to do with your Brittany that are dog-friendly, such as a walking tour of the city or spending the day exploring a dog beach or park. Many galleries, zoos, and wineries, are pet-friendly if your dog is leashed at all times and under your supervision.

TIPS FOR A QUIET HOTEL STAY

Trust me, you do not want to be that person whose dog barks inside of the hotel room. Nothing can be more embarrassing than being informed that your dog is disturbing the peace of other hotel guests. Plus, it can be an expensive inconvenience if the hotel requests you evacuate the property immediately.

If you must leave your furry friend alone in a hotel room, even if it is a short period of time, these steps will help you and your dog avoid any problems:

- Do not leave your Brittany alone until he has become acclimated to the new space. Take the time to establish in your dog's mind that this room is his "new home."

- Try doing a few practices by leaving the room for a few minutes then coming back inside. This will help your dog understand that if you leave, you will be returning promptly.

- Keep your time away as short as possible.

- If available, upgrade your room to a suite. By having two separate living spaces, you can place your dog's crate in the furthermost corner from the hallway. This will act as a buffer, giving your pooch some space from those strange noises outside of his door.

- Tired dogs make less ruckus. Be sure to take your Brittany for a long walk with plenty of opportunities to relieve himself outside.

- Pack something extra special to keep your dog distracted while you are out and about such as a toy stuffed with a delicious treat. If your pup's mouth is busy, he will be less likely to bark.

- Help your Brittany relax by playing classical music, and leave it playing when you go out to cover any hallway noises that may trigger barking.

STAYING WITH FRIENDS AND FAMILY

Today's society has become quite tolerant of dogs, but not everyone wants a dog at their next family gathering. No matter where you are planning on staying, your pup needs to learn to be a gracious house guest. The sooner you can start teaching your dog proper pet etiquette, the better.

Training is a critical aspect of whether your Brittany will make a gracious house guest. The better trained your pooch is, the more welcome both of you will be as guests. Ask yourself if your pooch has mastered the basic commands, such as: sit, stay, and come. It may seem like a long list, but they are key elements for your dog to be a charming guest.

You are taking your dog into someone else's house. Ask where your dog will be allowed to go and what areas are off-limits. Also, if your dog accidentally goes to the bathroom on their lawn, clean up after him promptly.

If things do not work out as planned, have a contingency plan, such as a pet-friendly hotel nearby or even a reputable boarding kennel. No matter how things go, send a thank-you card to express your gratitude and if necessary, to apologize.

No matter where you are planning on staying, these are some helpful suggestions on how to minimize friction:

Ask first – Never just show up to stay at someone's house with your dog in tow. Always ask permission to bring along your furry friend. Not everyone wants a dog as a house guest. Even dog lovers appreciate an advance warning, as it allows them to puppy-proof their home, such as putting away those collectible porcelain figurines on display.

The strain of an unwelcome dog can permanently damage relationships. So, even if your Brittany was welcome somewhere in the past, never assume he is welcome again – ask first!

Talk it over – Another factor to take into consideration is if the host or other house guests may be allergic to dogs, or maybe there are small children present who are uncomfortable around rambunctious pups, such as your Brittany. Take into consideration those who may be at high-risk of injury around a dog, such as your great aunt, who has already broken her hip twice.

Be considerate – If your Brittany is prone to bad behavior such as destructive chewing, nonstop barking, or house-soiling, it is unfair to expect your host to welcome your dog into their house.

CAMPING WITH YOUR BRITTANY

Camping with your Brittany will enhance the adventure of being outside in the great outdoors. Your Britt's joie de vie will remind you to drink in the moment. However, since camping is done on public land, there are a wide variety of rules and regulations that can vary depending on the destination.

The majority of developed campsites welcome dogs, allowing a specified number of pets per site. For instance, while your furry companion is not allowed on trails in Rocky Mountain National Park, the Acadia National Park offers hundreds of miles for dog-friendly trekking and camping. Be sure to do your research before you grab your sleeping bag and tent.

HELPFUL TIP
Hotel Help

Although more hotels are becoming dog friendly, many hotels still ban all dogs, while others have weight limits that could exclude your Brittany. Don't trust websites—you should always call hotels before you get there to find out if your Brittany will be welcomed.

Many states and counties throughout the United States provide an extensive list of dog-related information to help you pick an ideal camping destination for you and your Brittany. This is handy as some parks and campsites have definite rules for dogs year-round, while others have seasonal rules. For example, in the Sawtooth Wilderness near

173

Sun Valley, Idaho, dogs are required to be on a leash on trails from July 1 through Labor Day.

Rules for camping at regulated campsites or in the backcountry are quite similar. Here are some of the basics:

Co-sleeping – As there may be wildlife roaming near your campsite at night, the rules often will require your dog will need to sleep with you either inside of your car or inside of the tent. The last thing you want is your Brittany running into a skunk or a coyote. The best place for your pooch is right by your side at night. You can keep him safe and out of trouble and prevent barking.

Leave no-trace – Depending on the rules of the campsite you are staying at you may have to pick up your dog's waste and dispose of it later or bury it with dirt. Some parks require you to carry out your dog's waste to prevent the spread of noxious weeds, bacteria, and parasites.

Keep your pooch on a leash while at the camp – If you are staying at a public campsite, there are endless temptations for your pooch to explore, such as your neighbors' sizzling steaks or scurrying squirrels. Most campsites, whether regulated or in the backcountry, require all dogs be on a leash no longer than six feet long.

Constant supervision – Never assume you can leave your dog alone at the campsite while you run down to the marina to buy a bag of potato chips. Leaving your Brittany alone, whether tied up or kept inside of the car or tent, can be a disruptive disturbance to other campers. It can also put your furry companion in danger, as weather can change quickly, wildlife may wander into your campsite, or there could be other unforeseen circumstances.

Kenneling vs. Dog Sitters

You and your Brittany do everything together – from long walks in the woods to sitting in front of the fire on a cold winter day. You are two peas in a pod, which is why the very idea of leaving your tail-wagging best friend behind is so painful. Unfortunately, there will be occasions when you cannot take your Brittany with you, meaning you will have to choose between boarding your dog in a kennel or hiring a dog-sitter to watch over him while you are out of town.

Who will care for him? Will his caregiver give him plenty of cuddles and ear scratches? Is your dog better off at home with a professional dog siter, at a friend's house, or boarded at a local kennel? There is no ideal solution, but taking into consideration your Brittany's age, temperament, and needs will make the decision a little less worrisome.

Boarding Kennels

The best way to describe a boarding kennel is as a pet hotel for your Brittany.

Boarding kennels pride themselves in providing your dog with a safe environment. But just to be on the safe side, be sure to do your research beforehand to determine which kennel is right for your fur baby. Here are some things to consider:

How much space will your Brittany have?

Where will your dog stay? How big are the sleeping areas and the outside run? – Will he have enough space to stretch out, exercise, and play? Brittanys are high-energy dogs and do not do well locked in a small, enclosed space.

Will your Brittany have social time?

Some kennels have a common area for the dogs to exercise and socialize with other dogs for a specific time each day. It is important your Brittany gets at least three to four times of playtime a day; otherwise, he will feel cooped up. If your pooch is antisocial or aggressive, ask the kennel if they can provide a separate area for your dog to play.

How many caregivers will be around during the day and at night?

You are paying for the kennel to care for all of your dog's needs, so it is important your dog receives the proper amount of attention. Ask how many people work at the kennel throughout the day and how they interact with the dogs. Also, check into their experience and certification.

What are the fees, requirements, and inclusions?

Check out the kennel's fees and understand exactly what is included in the price per night. For example: Does the fee cover food and additional services, or do you have to provide the food and pay extra for grooming? Depending on the kennel's regulations, you might have to take your dog to a health screening to make sure he is up-to-date on his vaccinations before a kennel will accept him.

What is the kennel's reputation?

Look at the kennel website and, social media pages for customer reviews or testimonials. If you know any friends who have boarded their dogs at a certain kennel before, ask them for an honest opinion.

Your Brittany's stay at the boarding kennel includes grooming, attention, and daily exercise. Depending on the kennel you choose, they will offer a variety of packages and prices to cater to your pup's individual requirements. If you are considering this option, here are a few advantages and disadvantages:

ADVANTAGES TO BOARDING KENNELS

- Boarding kennels provide a secure environment with experienced, dog-loving employees who will constantly monitor your Brittany to prevent any incidents.

- Often a kennel will host other friendly canines, giving your Brittany plenty of fun opportunities to socialize with other dogs.

- Your pup will follow a strict schedule during his stay, which will reduce his stress levels. From your Brittany's first day there, he will be fed and exercised according to a schedule.

- Often there is a veterinarian on-site or on-call if there are any emergencies. This option is especially helpful if your Brittany has chronic health problems, as he will receive constant monitoring.

DISADVANTAGES TO BOARDING KENNELS

- With all the different dogs staying at the kennel, things can get quite chaotic and noisy at times, which can be stressful for sensitive dogs. If your Brittany tends to get nervous in a new environment or around other dogs, maybe boarding your dog might not be the best option.

- Although the kennel staff will do their best to keep everything in check, certain situations can get out of control. There is a small risk factor if your Brittany accidentally gets into a scuffle with another dog.

- Depending on the size of the boarding facility, staff could mix up food, toys, or blankets between different dogs. Often, this does not cause too many problems, except perhaps an upset tummy.

- Keep in mind, if you leave your Brittany at a boarding kennel, he will spend the majority of his time inside of his kennel.

All boarding kennels require that their doggy guests' vaccinations and immunizations be up-to-date. No matter the age of your dog, he is required to have received his rabies and Bordetella (kennel cough) vaccine at least seven days prior to your dog's planned arrival date.

Bordetella is an airborne upper respiratory infection. There are almost 60 different strains, and the current vaccine only protects against 14. There is no way to fully protect your Brittany from kennel cough as it is highly contagious. For this very reason, it is of utmost importance to search for a boarding kennel that prides itself on regularly sanitizing everything your pup might come into contact with, such as playground areas, daycare areas, toys, food and water dishes, etc.

Boarding kennels have the right to refuse the admittance to any dog if the pet owner lacks adequate proof of a dog's vaccinations or if the dog has serious health conditions or displays aggressive behavior.

Dog Sitters

A dog sitter is someone who cares for your dog in your home while you are temporarily absent. Typically, the dog sitter will stay in your house or drop by several times a day while you are away, allowing your Brittany to feel safe and secure in his own territory. Having a dog sitter stay overnight is the ideal solution if your pooch suffers from separation anxiety or if you prefer not to leave him alone at night.

ADVANTAGES TO A DOG SITTER

- While you are away, your Brittany is in the comfort of his own home. There is no need to worry about your pooch being exposed to a new environment, people, or other animals.
- The risk of accidents or injury is reduced because a single person is devoted to caring for your Brittany.
- Your dog sitter will carefully follow all of your care instructions for your dog and perhaps even water your plants if you ask them to. If you have a younger pup, you can teach the dog sitter how to work on your dog's obedience training and basic commands.
- A dog sitter will directly communicate with you if there are any problems, etc. The direct line of communication will give you peace of mind, so you can focus on your travels.

DISADVANTAGES TO A DOG SITTER

- A dog sitter needs to come into your house, and it is imperative you and your Brittany trust her or him. If your pooch is protective of his home or does not react well to new people, perhaps a dog sitter is not the best option.

- Having a dog sitter stay in your home requires extra preparation, such as readying the guest bedroom.

- During the holiday season, it can be almost impossible to find a reliable dog sitter. Be sure to book ahead of time.

- If you hired a dog sitter to drop by a few times a day, and there's bad weather, the person might not be able to get to your house regularly.

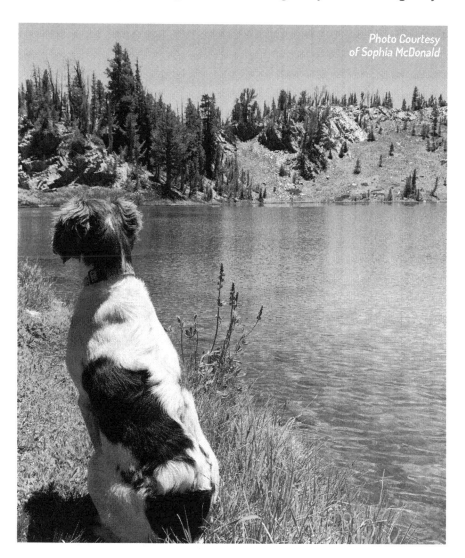

Photo Courtesy
of Sophia McDonald

Choosing the right sitter - Try to choose someone whose energy level and personality match that of your dog. For example, leaving your rambunctious puppy with an elderly relative is a recipe for disaster. Make sure you feel comfortable with the dog sitter and that he or she understands your Brittany's individual needs.

Finding a professional and responsible dog sitter should not be taken lightly; after all, the dog sitter will be responsible for your pup's welfare, and you are entrusting him or her with the keys to your house. Here are a few suggestions to help you find a reputable dog sitter for your dog:

- **Ask your veterinarian** – If your Brittany is elderly or has health issues, finding a dog sitter with a good recommendation from your vet will give you peace of mind, especially if there is a medical emergency.

- **Word of mouth** – Anyone can look good on paper, but a qualified, reputable dog sitter will come recommended by a close friend or a relative.

- **Ask for references** – Any reputable dog sitter will be able to provide you with a list of regular clients who would be more than willing to verify the person's professionalism.

- **Look for a certified dog sitter** – There are two nation wide agencies that train and certify dog sitters: Pet Sitters International (PSI) and the National Association of Professional Pet Sitters (NAPPS). Be sure to check out their webpages to locate a certified dog sitter in your locality, plus you can check out reviews from previous clients.

Location – Ideally, you want someone who can stay at your house to maintain your Brittany's regular routine and schedule. This involves keeping your dog on the same walking, feeding, and sleeping routine as when you are at home. If you must change your dog's routine, get him used to the changes a few weeks ahead of time to prevent separation anxiety or other issues.

If you plan on leaving your dog at a friend's house while you are away, you might want to get him familiar with the new location a few times before actually leaving your dog there for an extended stay.

Details – Just as parents leave a checklist for a babysitter, you can make a checklist for your dog sitter. Include important information such as the vet's phone number and address, any medications your dog needs to take while you are away, allergies, feeding schedule, the closest twenty-four-hour emergency veterinary clinic, and any behavioral problems.

Share with the dog sitter any house rules for your Brittany, such as whether he is allowed on the furniture and how often he gets a treat

– basically, any information you feel will keep your pup feeling happy, and secure while you are away.

Do not drag out goodbyes – Your Brittany is used to seeing you leave the house without him, so do not make a big production of your departure this time. If you do, you might make your pooch anxious. Be confident and casual when you say goodbye; both of you will be more relaxed.

Keep watch – If you are still uncomfortable about leaving your fur baby with a stranger, you could invest in a dog camera. Many smart dog cameras are designed to let you interact with your dog.

Relax – Now, take a deep breath and relax! You have taken all of the necessary steps to ensure that your Brittany has a pleasant experience while you are away, so enjoy your trip.

Carefully consider the advantages and disadvantages of each dog-care option. If you cannot decide which is the best choice for your canine friend, you can always try a short stay at a boarding kennel and another with a dog sitter before your actual planned trip to see how your dog reacts.

CHAPTER 10
Nutrition

A balanced and nutritious diet is essential to keep your Brittany healthy, but providing him with the right amount of nourishment can be tricky.

Obesity is one of the most common dog problems observed by veterinarians and often is due to an unbalanced diet of too many treats and not enough wholesome ingredients. In this chapter, you will learn everything you need to know about feeding your dog at every stage of his life.

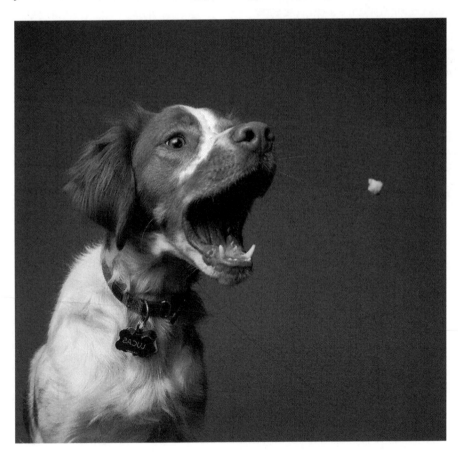

Importance of a Wholesome Diet

> *Your breeder has your pup on foods that work for them. I find my dogs do extremely well on the food we feed only to have an owner change the diet and have issues after that. So listen to your breeder, especially if they have been dealing with Brittanys for multiple decades.*
>
> **ARLETTE HENNESSEY**
> *K Nine Birddog Brittanys*

Every Brittany is different. Some Britts love to eat, while others are picky eaters or have a sensitive stomach, and there are also dogs with dietary sensitivities. Deciding on what to feed your dog is a very personal choice; however, his diet will have a direct impact on his health and happiness.

Just like humans, dogs require essential nutrients to develop properly and stay healthy. The wrong diet can lead to a life of health issues and obesity; on the other hand, the right diet can keep your dog slim, healthy, and in tip-top shape.

The old saying "you are what you eat" applies to your Brittany as much as yourself. Dog food made with high-quality ingredients equals a better quality of life, resulting in fewer infections, digestive issues, skin conditions, and so on. The impact of a wholesome diet does not end there as it can also directly impact your dog's personality and behavior.

Your dog's behavior is a direct result of activity in his central nervous center. If he is not receiving the necessary nutrients, he will be lethargic, moody, and inactive. Here are a few examples of how the food you give and the frequency by which you feed your Brittany will impact his mood and behavior.

Unbalanced diet – Many health and behavioral issues in dogs are caused by a poorly balanced diet. For example, a diet deficient in nutrients may cause your Brittany to suffer from frequent urinary tract infections that cause him to become irritable due to discomfort and pain. Make sure your Brittany only eats a well-balanced high-quality dog food to maintain good mental and physical health.

Inadequate food – If your Brittany is not consuming enough calories throughout the day, he will be hungry and may engage in disruptive behaviors such as scavenging through your neighbor's garbage or eating feces.

Dogs who are not receiving sufficient nutrients in their diet may develop a condition called pica, which causes them to eat non-food items such as soil and plants.

Pet food ingredients - The ingredients in your pup's pet food may also affect his behavior. For instance, research has found that senior dogs who receive a diet rich in antioxidants are able to learn complicated tasks faster than dogs who do not. Studies have shown that senior dogs who have always received a high-quality dog food suffer from fewer behavioral changes common to cognitive decline.

A well-balanced diet will promote stable blood sugar levels throughout the day, which will directly affect your Brittany's serotonin levels. Serotonin not only improves your dog's mood but also his concentration, behavior, and training response. Another advantage to a wholesome diet is your Britt's immune system will be in excellent condition.

Talk to your veterinarian before changing your Brittany's diet. Your vet will recommend a brand of food that is suitable for your dog's age, size, weight, medical history, and lifestyle. Nutrition has an extensive impact on your dog's overall health, so make sure you feed him a wholesome diet.

Here are some common health issues related to your Brittany's diet:

- **Heart disease** – Dogs often have issues with heart disease, especially if their diet is not well-balanced. Increased levels of sodium are one of the main factors of heart disease in dogs. Since high-quality commercial dog foods are low in sodium, the main source of sodium is probably coming from those table scraps you are slipping your dog under the table.

- **Diabetes** – Overweight dogs tend to develop diabetes as they age. There is no known cure for diabetes. A dog with diabetes will require daily insulin shots, a special diet, and extra medical attention. The best and only prevention is to keep your Brittany on a healthy diet and give him an active lifestyle. Avoid dog food that contains starchy fillers and sugar, which offer little to no nutritional value and will spike your dog's blood sugar level.

- **Obesity** – Obese dogs are prone to arthritis, diabetes, breathing issues, high-blood pressure, and cancer. Decreased life expectancy is linked to obesity in dogs. Your Brittany does not need excessive calories each day. Be sure to follow the instructions on the food bag for his weight, size, and age.

- **Pancreatitis** – Pancreatitis is caused by a diet high in fats. Consult with your vet to see if your dog's current dietary fat intake may be increasing his risk of pancreatitis.

FOOD ALLERGIES AND SENSITIVITIES

Food allergies and sensitivities are not the same thing. It is important to take into consideration how a particular food affects your Brittany. If your dog's energy level is normal for his age, if his coat and skin are healthy, if his stools are brown and well-formed, and if he appears to be healthy, then his food is doing its job.

However, if your Brittany has diarrhea, skin issues, or an extremely itchy coat, your dog may have a food sensitivity. In this case, discuss the issue with your veterinarian. He will be able to help you create a feeding plan that works best for your dog's health. Often, your veterinarian will place your dog on an elimination diet and slowly reintroduce foods to determine what foods are causing the allergic reaction.

A food allergy involves the immune system and is often caused by a protein molecule. Food allergies present an immediate immunological response, such as anaphylactic shock, which may mean your dog is having difficulty breathing. In this case, you should take your pooch to the nearest veterinarian clinic immediately. A less severe reaction may present with facial swelling, hives, or itchiness. If you suspect your Brittany has a food allergy, it is vital that you talk to your vet to identify the cause.

A food sensitivity is an abnormal response to a certain ingredient. Food sensitivities can easily be managed and often will disappear over time. If you suspect your dog has a food intolerance, talk to your vet; look for a hypoallergenic food that avoids common allergens such as beef or wheat, and choose a dog food with a single protein source.

Human Foods to Avoid

Slipping your Brittany, a morsel or two under the table may be tempting, but it can cause your dog some serious health issues or even be fatal. You might be surprised at some of the foods your furry friend needs to avoid at all costs!

Alcohol – Even the tiniest amount of any type of alcohol can be fatal for your Brittany. Alcohol causes dogs to have coordination problems, vomiting, diarrhea, breathing issues, and even death.

Avocado – All dogs are allergic to persin, which is found in high quantities in avocados. Persin is not only found in the flesh of the avocado but also in the leaves, peel, bark of the tree, seed, etc. If you have an avocado tree in your backyard, be sure to keep your dog away from it at all times.

Bones or fat trimmings – It might seem like second nature to give your pooch a bone to chew on, but dogs can easily choke on them, or the bone may splinter and become lodged in his throat or cut up his digestive system. Furthermore, pieces of grease or fat can cause your Brittany to develop pancreatitis.

Caffeine – All types of caffeine are fatal for your dog, including cocoa, energy drinks, Guarana, tea, caffeinated carbonated beverages, and soda.

Photo Courtesy of Lauren Marie

If your dog accidentally consumes a product with caffeine, go immediately to the nearest veterinarian office.

Chocolate – Dark, white, and milk chocolate are deadly for dogs. Even the smallest morsel can cause diarrhea, vomiting, cardiac failure, seizures, and even death.

Dairy products – Dairy products such as milk, whipped cream, and ice cream can cause your dog to experience digestive discomfort and diarrhea. Many dogs who are lactose intolerant have extremely itchy skin. That said, the majority of dogs can tolerate cheese and yogurt due to the natural digestive enzymes and probiotics.

Garlic and onions – Keep all types of garlic and onions far away from your pooch, including fresh, dry, powdered, dehydrated, or cooked. Even the smallest pinch can cause your Brittany's blood count to drop, causing him to become anemic.

Grapes or raisins – Grapes and raisins seem the perfect bite-sized treat for your dog, but a few can cause kidney failure. If your think your Brittany may have consumed some grapes or raisins, call your veterinarian if you notice any sluggish behavior or severe vomiting.

Macadamia nuts – Eating just three macadamia nuts can cause your Brittany to become seriously ill. Eating chocolate-covered macadamia nuts will intensify the symptoms, which will eventually lead to death. Macadamia nuts cause vomiting, muscle tremors, fever, and loss of muscle control.

Pitted fruits – Fruits such as peaches, persimmons, cherries, and plums have pits or seeds that can get lodged in your dog's intestines, causing a blockage. Some pits, such as from a plum or a peach, contain cyanide, which is fatal if consumed.

Raw eggs – Raw eggs are a source of bacteria, such as Salmonella or E. coli. Avoid feeding your Brittany raw or undercooked eggs or any type of raw animal products, such as fish, beef, pork, or chicken.

Raw yeast dough – Before baking, yeast dough needs to rise. If your Brittany eats some raw dough, it will continue to rise inside his stomach, stretching out your dog's abdomen, causing extreme pain. The yeast can also cause alcohol poisoning.

Salt – A word of caution: do not share your salted popcorn or pretzels with your furry friend.

Too much salt can cause sodium ion poisoning, vomiting, diarrhea, fever, or seizures, and may be fatal if left untreated.

Xylitol – Xylitol is a common sweetener used in baked goods, toothpaste, and diet products. It causes your dog's blood sugar levels to drop, which leads to liver failure.

If your Brittany got into the pantry and ate something he shouldn't have, call your local vet immediately or call the Animal Poison Control Center (ASPCA) at (888) 426-4435.

It is not advisable to make a practice out of giving your Brittany leftovers, bits of meat, or other scraps as he may begin to refuse to eat his normal food. Also, it can unbalance your dog's regular diet causing him to gain weight. Human foods can cause gas, which may not be a problem for your dog, but it could be for you!

Photo Courtesy of Tyler Toporowski

After all that talk about harmful human foods for your pooch, you are probably wondering: "Is all human food bad for my dog?" Although you may use great self-control to keep your Brittany on his canine diet, sometimes you may not be able to resist the urge to slip him a piece of cheese.

Before giving your dog any foods that are not on this list, do some research to make sure they are safe. If your pup experiences any sort of reaction or allergy, immediately consult a veterinarian. Here are some of the best human food choices for your four-pawed furry friend:

Peanut butter – Peanut butter is a favorite treat for Brittanys around the world. Also, it is an excellent source of protein, healthy fats, vitamin B, and niacin. Be sure to only use unsalted peanut butter. Make sure you are not using sugar-free or lite peanut butter, as it may contain artificial sweeteners such as xylitol.

Cooked chicken or turkey – Cooked chicken is a healthy source of protein and makes a great alternative to high-calorie treats used in obedience training. Plus, if you accidentally run out of dog food, it makes a healthy meal replacement.

Cheese – Cheese is an excellent snack for your pooch if he is not lactose intolerant. Choose low-fat varieties and do not overfeed, as most cheeses are high in fat and may cause constipation. Cottage cheese is typically a good option for Brittanys.

Carrots – Carrots are a yummy low-calorie snack for your dog and are great for your dog's teeth. They are also high in fiber, beta-carotene, and vitamins. You can feed your dog raw or cooked carrots; just be sure to cut them into small pieces to prevent him from accidentally choking on them.

Yogurt – Yogurt is high in calcium and protein. Also, its active probiotics can aid your dog's digestive system and improve his breath.

Salmon – Salmon is an excellent source of omega-3 fatty acids, which will help keep your Brittany's coat healthy and shiny and support his immune system. Try adding cooked salmon to your dog's kibble, or slip him some unwanted fish skins.

Pumpkin – Pumpkins are part of the squash family, all of which are excellent sources of fiber, beta carotene, and vitamin A. Plus, pumpkin can keep your dog's GI tract moving and aid with digestive issues.

Eggs – A scrambled egg will give your Brittany's diet a protein boost. Eggs are remarkably high in protein and a source of digestible riboflavin and selenium. Always thoroughly cook the eggs to avoid any risk of salmonella.

Green beans – Green beans are another healthy snack for your Brittany, as they are a source of protein, calcium, vitamin K, and iron. Raw and cooked green beans are filling and low in calories. Just remember to only serve them without salt or other seasonings.

Apple slices – Sliced apples are high in fiber and vitamins and are a healthy treat for your pooch. Additionally, apple slices are known for cleaning dogs' teeth and freshening their breath. Before giving your dog a few apple slices, make sure to remove the seeds and the core, as they can be a choking hazard.

Oatmeal – Cooked oatmeal is an excellent source of soluble fiber, which is especially beneficial to senior dogs with bowel irregularity issues. It is a fantastic grain option for dogs allergic to wheat. Always cook oatmeal before serving it to your pup, and only use oatmeal that has no added sugar or additives.

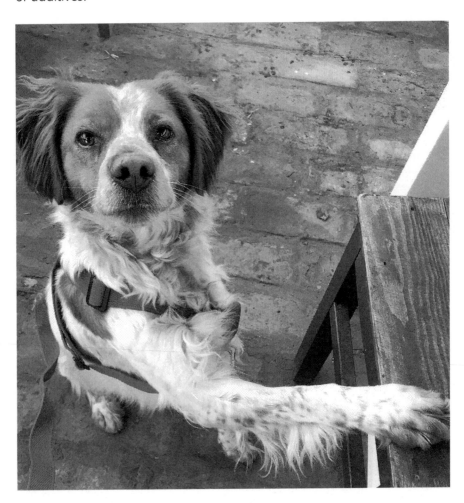

If you decide to give your pooch a treat or two from your table, make sure it is not seasoned, fatty, salty, or raw. Certain fruits, such as thin slices of apples, bananas, or watermelon, all make yummy treats for your Brittany. Be sure to remove any seeds, peels, or stems that could get stuck in your dog's digestive tract.

Cooked, plain white rice or noodles with a piece of boiled chicken might be the best solution if your pooch has an upset tummy.

Commercial Dog Food

> **"**
>
> *Being a sporting dog, a Brittany requires a different diet. Look for food that has 30% protein and 20% fat (we call this the '30/20 mix'). This will promote strength and protect against fatigue in your active Brittany.*
>
> STEVE ROGERS
> *Winding Branch Kennel*
> **"**

In the last few years, commercial dog food has improved enormously. A few decades ago, there were only a few generic brands of dog food on the shelves, whereas today, you can find countless brands, which cater to different breeds, ages, and dietary restrictions. However, with so many choices out there, it can be overwhelming narrowing down what type of dog food is best suited for your Brittany.

Learning about how commercial dog food is made will help you understand the nutritional value of the food you are feeding your Brittany. There are two main types of commercially prepared dog food: canned food and dry kibble. Commercially produced fresh dog food is a newcomer to the dog food aisle and is quickly gaining popularity but is not yet widely available.

WET DOG FOOD

Wet dog food may be sold in cans, boxes, or single-serving pouches, often consisting of 35 – 75 percent water, depending on the quality. Be sure to look for the moisture content on the label. Wet foods contain a variety of meats such as beef, chicken, lamb, salmon, or venison.

Once the can or package is opened, it must be refrigerated to maintain its freshness, and most dogs will not eat cold food. To solve this problem, you can warm up the meal portion before serving. Note that wet foods have the highest cost per serving, and cheaper brands of wet food are high in fillers, sugar, and fat.

Wet dog food is made using fresh and frozen meat. Many commercial brands use animal parts such as organs or fatty tissue. One of the advantages of these parts is they have a higher nutritional value than meats typically consumed by humans. The meat is then ground and mixed in large machines to ensure even distribution of the calories and nutrients.

The packaging method used for wet food uses a high heat sterilization method to kill off any bacteria, but an unwanted side effect is that it also destroys the nutrients and vitamins. The sterilization and vacuum-sealing process ensure a longer shelf life without the need to use harmful chemicals.

However, due to the processing method, wet foods are notorious for being void of nutrients. If you want your dog to get his daily nutritional requirements, you will need to give him a huge portion at each meal, which will eventually result in weight gain.

DRY FOOD

The vast majority of dogs throughout the United States are fed dry kibble.

Dry dog food contains similar ingredients as wet dog food, but instead of adding gravy and canning the product, the meat mixture is pulverized and mixed together to create a consistent mass of dough that can then be cooked. The dough can be manufactured by one of the following methods:

Baked – The dough is extruded through specially shaped holes and then baked at a low temperature. Once baked, the kibble is left out to dry and then sprayed with fats, oils, minerals, and vitamins – often baked kibble contains wheat gluten to aid in binding the ingredients together.

Cold-pressed – This is a newbie in the dog food aisle that is quickly gaining popularity with both pet owners and dogs alike. Cold-pressed dog food often prides itself on only using the freshest of ingredients. The manufacturer will grind the ingredients together, forming a thick, coarse paste, which is then left to dry before being pressed out to remove the excess moisture. It is then baked at a very low temperature to prevent any nutrient loss.

Extrusion – This method is similar to baking, except before extruding the dough through specially shaped holes, the mixture is first cooked in huge steam and pressure cookers to kill off any bacteria, etc. Then, when the mixture cools, it is pressed though an extruding machine, shaping the kibble. After this, the kibble is placed into a high-heat convection oven to remove any excess moisture.

It is worth mentioning that this type of kibble's double exposure to extreme heat removes the majority of the nutrients and vitamins.

Freeze dried – The fresh food is mixed together, then ground into a coarse paste, formed into small pieces of kibble, and placed inside a type of vacuum oven that removes all excess moisture. The process preserves the majority of the nutrients, making it one of the healthiest food choices for your Brittany.

Freeze-dried foods have a long shelf life without the need for harmful preservatives. Some freeze-dried foods may need to be re-hydrated with water before serving. This is one of the most expensive dry dog food options.

FRESH FOOD

Fresh dog food is quickly gaining popularity in the dog food aisle, as it is a convenient option to homemade dog food. Fresh dog food manufacturers pride themselves on using only fresh, organic ingredients and human-grade proteins. Many companies provide the option of using recyclable, reusable serving trays.

One of the main advantages of fresh dog food is the high nutritional value due to the low level of processing required. On the other hand, since it doesn't contain preservatives, fresh food has a maximum lifespan of seven to 14 days and will need to be stored in the refrigerator. It is not recommended to freeze fresh dog food, as many of the nutrients will be lost.

WET DOG FOOD VS. DRY DOG FOOD

As you can see above, both wet dog food and dry can be good choices, depending on the quality of ingredients and the process used to manufacture the dog food. However, they each offer different benefits and drawbacks depending on your Brittany's nutritional needs.

Benefits of wet dog food compared to dry dog food

- **Higher moisture content** – Your veterinarian may recommend a wet dog food diet if your dog frequently suffers from urinary tract infections or dislikes drinking water

- **Palatability** – Wet dog food is preferred by dogs who are finicky eaters. Also, wet dog food is ideal for concealing medications. It is ideal for elderly or sick dogs whose appetite has decreased.

- **Easier to chew** – Dogs who have dental issues or other oral abnormalities may find eating wet food easier than dry food.

- **Satiety** – Wet dog food tends to cause a longer-lasting feeling of being full. Increased satiety is especially useful in managing your dogs weight.

Benefits of dry dog food compared to wet dog food

- **Dental health** – One of the main advantages to dry food is it acts like a toothbrush, helping to remove and prevent the build-up of plaque and tartar on your dog's teeth.

- **Convenience and cost-effectiveness** – Kibble's popularity is due to the convenience for feeding and cost (as with most things, the larger the bag, the better the savings). In addition, it stays fresh longer than wet foods once the package has been opened.

- **Food enrichment** – Kibble is easy to use with food puzzles that help to keep your dog mentally stimulated and improve the quality of his life.

As you can see, there are quite a few factors to take into consideration when choosing the best dog food for your Brittany. Ultimately, choosing the right dog food is a very personal decision and depends on your budget and personal preferences. The right dog food for your Brittany will meet his nutritional requirements and keep him happy and healthy.

How to Read Dog Food Labels

The dog food nutrition label is similar to the nutrition facts on packaged food for humans. The label is designed to help you compare products and learn more about what you are considering purchasing and feeding your dog.

 Look past the attractive packaging and marketing; instead, learn to read the ingredients.

GENERAL RULE OF THUMB: *If humans are not allowed to eat it, then you should not feed it to your dog either.*

Just as with packaged food for humans, dog food must list the ingredients according to weight, starting with the heaviest. But a word of caution: if the first ingredient is a protein, keep in mind that proteins are typically about 75 percent water.

Dog food labels are required to contain:

- Product brand name

- Quantity displayed in terms of weight, liquid measure, or count, depending on the formulation of the dog food
- Ingredient listed in descending order by weight
- Feeding instructions for your dog's age, activity level, and weight
- Nutritional statement backed up by research and testing to prove the food provides the required daily nutritional requirements
- Manufacturer's name and address
- Calorie statement and the life stages the food is appropriate for

Continue reading to learn which ingredients to avoid and why they can harm your Brittany's health.

Artificial preservatives – Avoid dog foods that contain ethoxyquin, BHA, and BHT on the ingredient list. The National Institute of Health has deemed BHA and BHT to be carcinogenic and unfit for human consumption. Ethoxyquin is linked to cancer, chronic immune diseases, and kidney failure in both humans and animals.

Corn and rice fillers – Corn and rice fillers are commonly used for fattening up animals, and the last thing your Brittany needs is a carbohydrate-rich diet. A low-protein diet is one of the main causes of obesity in smaller breeds, such as your Brittany. A diet high in corn and rice can cause chronic digestive issues, such as bloating, gas, and diarrhea.

Food coloring – Many dog food manufacturers add food coloring to their kibble and/or treats to make them look more appealing and appetizing. But your Brittany is not concerned about the appearance or color of his food; he just cares whether it is tasty. Avoid dog foods that contain food dyes such as Blue 2, Red 40, or Yellow 5 because they are linked to allergies, hyperactivity, and cancer.

MSG – Monosodium glutamate (MSG) is a well-known flavor enhancer for Chinese food and dog food. MSG over-stimulates your dog's brain, causing him to produce a hormone called dopamine, making him become addicted to his food. Recent studies have shown when dogs regularly consume foods with MSG over time, they can develop brain damage, obesity, and behavioral issues.

Nondescriptive fats – Fat is essential for your Brittany's overall health. Many dog food manufacturers list generic animal fat as one of the ingredients, which often is fat derived from sick or rancid animals. Choose a dog food that specifies the type of fat used, such as salmon fat instead of fish fat or coconut oil instead of vegetable oil, etc.

Propylene glycol – Propylene glycol is a common ingredient for antifreeze and is extremely toxic for dogs. However, many dog food manufacturers add it to their product to reduce moisture from building up inside of the packaging, to prevent bacterial growth, and to lengthen the product's life span.

Rendered foods – Rendered meat is often listed on the ingredient list as animal by-product meal, which is a mix of animal parts such as blood, brains, spleens, entrails, and internal organs. More than often, it includes discarded animal parts that were considered to be unfit for human consumption. The nutritional value of rendered meat is extremely low and can be a source of salmonella and toxins.

Sugar – Many dog foods contain sugar to mask a bitter flavor and to improve texture. Once your Brittany is addicted to sugar, it is extremely difficult to switch him to a healthier, sugar-free alternative. Sugar additives to watch out for are cane sugar, beet pulp, corn syrup, sucrose, fructose-glucose, xylitol, molasses, and sorbitol.

Some dog owners shy away from buying food that contains synthetic preservatives such as BHA (butylated hydroxyanisole), BHT (butylated hydroxytoluene), or ethoxyquin. These synthetic preservatives prevent fat from turning rancid and can keep dry dog food fresh for at least a year. The FDA has approved these preservatives as safe for animals in small amounts.

Ethoxyquin came under scrutiny after a long list of complaints concerning some dogs who were given food with this preservative, such as skin allergies, reproductive problems, cancer, and organ failure. The FDA requested dog food manufacturers reduce the amount of ethoxyquin to half of the previously approved amount.

Some dog food manufacturers have opted to use natural preservatives such as vitamin E (mixed tocopherols), vitamin C (ascorbic acid), and plant extracts such as rosemary. These natural preservatives help to keep dry food fresh, but for a shortened lifespan. Be sure to check your dog food bag for the "best by" date on the label before buying or feeding it to your Brittany.

DECIPHERING TERMS

Recently there are so many new trends in the dog food market that it can be challenging to decipher the terms. Here are some terms that can be difficult to understand:

Organic – As of the moment this book went to print, the U.S. Department of Agriculture (USDA) was still developing official regulations regarding the labeling of organic foods for pets. In the meantime, dog foods that claim to be organic must meet the requirements established by the USDA's National Organic Program, which means organic dog food has to meet the same standards as organic human food.

HELPFUL TIP
Premium Nutrition

As active dogs, it's especially important to feed your Brittany a quality diet high in protein. Look for foods with whole meat as the first ingredient and avoid animal by-products and filler ingredients like corn, wheat, or soy.

Organic dog food must contain no artificial sweeteners, preservatives, flavorings, or food colorings. Plus, meat and meat by-products must be sourced from animals with no antibiotics or growth hormones. Generally speaking, dogs with sensitive tummies do better on an organic diet.

Note: "natural" dog food is not the same as "organic." The term "natural dog food," refers to the lack of artificial ingredients used in the product.

Grain-free – Recent studies by the FDA have discovered grain-free dog foods are linked to canine dilated cardiomyopathy (CDC), which causes the dog's heart to enlarge and prevents the blood from circulating freely throughout the body. The FDA recommends pet owners avoid feeding their dogs grain-free foods. Dogs need a diet based on high-quality proteins, natural fats, vegetables, and whole grains to meet their dietary needs.

New proteins – The term new proteins refer to new meats in the dog food market, such as bison, kangaroo, rabbit, lamb, and other exotic animals. At the moment, it is difficult to rate the benefits of this food due to a lack of research on the different nutrient profiles when compared with common proteins, such as beef, chicken, or fish.

Human-grade dog food – This is defined as legally edible and safe for human consumption. Human-grade dog food is tightly regulated by the FDA and the USDA. Also, the Association of American Feed Control Officials (AAFCO) requires that human-grade dog food be manufactured, packaged, and held in accordance with federal regulations for manufacturing, packaging, and holding human food.

Light, low-calorie, and low-fat – If labeled with one of these terms, dog food must have a significant reduction in fat or calories when compared to the brand's standard dog food. The AAFCO requires that any dog food label claiming to be light, low-calorie, or low-fat must show the reduction on the label and name the product in comparison.

Good foods to watch out for

Finding a wholesome, healthy, and delicious food for your Brittany may seem like a challenge, but it is not impossible. When choosing a dog food for your pooch, look for a variety of ingredients such as meat, veggies, grains, and fruits. Look for some of the following ingredients on the nutrition label:

Meat – Your Brittany is a high-energy dog, who needs plenty of healthy proteins to maintain his body, muscle, and immune system. Look for commercial dog foods made from human-grade proteins, such as beef, chicken, salmon, rabbit, etc.

Whole-meat meal – Often, meat meal is from by-products such as rendered meats, whereas whole-meat meal is a high source of protein and is simply a fancier way of saying ground beef. However, the ingredient list should specify the type of whole meat meal used, such as chicken, beef, etc. Meat meal contains more protein, as it is ground up, then dried to a 10 percent moisture level, making the protein level at least 65 percent and at least 12 percent fat.

Carbohydrates and grains – Whole grains are an exceptional source of energy for your Brittany, and they improve his digestion. Avoid dog foods made from corn, soy, or white rice; instead, look for higher quality ingredients, such as brown rice, whole oats, barley, and peas. Carbohydrates and grains should never be one of the first ingredients on the list.

Vegetables and fruits – Both provide essential nutrients, minerals, vitamins, fiber, and antioxidants. For example, sweet potatoes are an excellent source of potassium, vitamin B, and antioxidants. Unsweetened cranberries provide vitamin C, prevent urinary tract infections, and protect your pup's teeth from harmful bacteria.

Fats – Fats are necessary for your Brittany's overall health, proper cell function, and digestion. Fats help your Brittany to absorb minerals and vitamins and keep his coat and teeth in tip-top shape. Look for dog foods that contain wholesome fats like omega-3 and omega-6 fatty acids, canola oil, salmon fat, olive, and coconut oils.

WORD OF CAUTION

Pay attention to the product name, as it will give you a clue about the ingredients in the dog food you are considering. Most dog owners base their decision on a specific ingredient. Many brands will highlight that ingredient in the product's label.

Stay away from commercial dog foods that use the term "with," such as "with chicken'" or "with beef." Manufacturers are only required to use

3 percent of protein in the dog food. Avoid dog food whose labels include the wording "flavor," such as beef or chicken flavor, as this indicates it was made with an exceedingly small percentage of the actual product and mostly contains artificial flavoring.

Just because a dog food manufacturer claims to provide everything your Brittany needs for his optimum health, does not necessarily mean the food is really healthy. Take the time to carefully read the ingredient list and make a decision based on the ingredients, not based on the attractive packaging.

B.A.R.F. Diet

The B.A.R.F. diet stands for two common phrases: Biologically Appropriate Raw Food and Bones and Raw Food. B.A.R.F. was developed by nutritionist and veterinarian Dr. Ian Billinghurst, and the main principle behind the diet is feeding canines a diet similar to what they would eat in the wild. The raw diet is composed of proteins, vegetables, and fruits that are all uncooked.

The B.A.R.F. diet basically consists of a hearty portion of protein such as muscle meat, raw meaty bones, organ meat, and a moderate quantity of vegetables and fruits. Some pet owners also add supplements to their dog's diet, under the guidance of their veterinarian.

According to recent studies there are quite a few health benefits to feeding your Brittany a raw food diet:

- **Healthy weight** – Your Brittany will have a leaner, muscular build and will maintain a healthy weight.
- **Improved appearance** – Most pet owners who feed their dog a raw food diet noticed an overall improvement in the appearance of their skin and hair. Plus, their dogs have cleaner teeth and fresher breath.
- **Increased energy** – Many pet owners who feed a raw diet to their canines state their dogs have increased energy levels.
- **Improved bowel movements** – Dogs who suffer from diarrhea with a regular diet, often have firmer and smaller stools on a raw food diet.

However, there are many disadvantages to giving your Brittany a raw diet, such as:

- **An unbalanced diet** – An unbalanced diet can cause nutrient deficiencies and future health problems.
- **Bacteria and other pathogens** – Raw dog food, if not stored correctly or consumed immediately, becomes an ideal breeding ground for

potentially dangerous bacteria or pathogens that can make your dog very sick.

- **Cross-contamination** – The risk of contamination with raw meat can make humans extremely ill.

- **High cost and time investment** – Providing your dog with human-grade proteins each day can be very expensive, not to mention time-consuming to prepare.

If you decide to give your Brittany a raw food diet, be sure to consult with your vet beforehand to decide whether it is suitable for your dog's health and lifestyle. Your veterinarian will need to closely monitor your dog's overall health for the first few months to ensure he has no allergies or other health issues.

If you decide that a raw food diet is something you are interested in but do not feel comfortable in preparing your Britt's meals every day, ask your veterinarian to recommend a company that makes raw dog food in your locality.

Even though, what you decide to feed your dog is a very personal decision, you should be aware that a raw diet is not appropriate for every dog. For example, a raw food diet is not recommended for dogs with health issues such as kidney and liver failure. Dogs with cancer, on chemotherapy, or dogs with other immunosuppressive diseases also should not be on a raw diet. Due to the lack of calcium and the potential of harmful bacteria, raw food is not recommended for puppies.

Making Homemade Dog Food

Is homemade dog food healthier than commercial dog food? Many pet owners assume it must be better because eating a home-cooked meal is better than chowing down on fast food, but does this stand true for your Brittany?

Many dog food recipes fall short of the nutrients needed to keep your Brittany strong and healthy, such as iron, copper, calcium, and zinc. A recent study by the University of California, School of Veterinary Medicine tested more than 200 online recipes written by respected veterinarians. Unfortunately, the researchers discovered more than 90 percent of the recipes lacked essential nutrients for canine health.

One of the main advantages of preparing your own dog food is you know exactly what you are feeding your dog. Commercially made dog food is convenient and is a fantastic way to ensure your Brittany is receiving all of the necessary nutrients he needs. However, making your Brittany home-made meals involves more than just throwing a bunch of ingredients into the slow-cooker and hoping for the best. It involves careful planning to prepare a well-balanced and complete meal that meets all of your dog's nutritional needs.

If you decide to make your dog's meals yourself, be sure to consult with your vet before switching him over to the new diet. A homemade diet is not recommended for puppies or expecting mothers.

As I mentioned before, Brittanys are high-energy dogs and need a well-balanced diet to maintain lean muscle and support their immune sys-tem. Your dog's daily diet requires protein (animal meat, seafood, dairy, eggs, and so on), fat (from animal organs or oil), and carbohydrates (grains and vegetables). Your Brittany will also need calcium from dairy products or egg shells and essential fatty acids (oils, egg yolks, oatmeal, etc.).

The following guidelines will help you create your own balanced, home-made dog food recipe:

Meat products – Protein should make up 50 – 65 percent of your Brittany's diet. As it is the main component of your dog's meal, choose organic lean meats without skin and fat. Include in your dog's diet boneless chicken, beef, and fish. Make sure the meat is cut into small pieces as it will facilitate chewing and digestion. Adding up to 5 percent beef liver into your preparation is a nutritious and tasty addition.

Eggs – Eggs are an excellent source of protein; however, medium-sized dogs such as your Brittany should only eat one whole egg per day.

Dairy – The majority of dogs can tolerate plain yogurt, cottage cheese, and ricotta. If your pooch suffers from lactose intolerance, try substituting dairy products with goat milk. Avoid using other types of cheese as they tend to be high in cholesterol, fats, and calories.

Starchy vegetables – Beans, peas, potatoes, squash, and sweet potatoes are all great sources of fiber for your Brittany. If your pooch is overweight, you will need to reduce the percentage of starchy vegetables in his dog food. Cook all grains, beans, and starchy vegetables to make them easier to digest.

Other vegetables – Leafy veggies are high in fiber and low in calories, plus they are full of wholesome nutrients for your pooch. Avoid using raw, cruciferous vegetables, such as broccoli and cauliflower, as they can cause digestive issues for your dog. Chop and blend the vegetables together before adding them to the meat mixture when cooking.

Fruit – Fruit supports your Brittany's digestive health and provides a long list of vitamins, nutrients, and antioxidants. Apples, bananas, berries, and papaya are all excellent options. Avoid grapes and raisins as they cause kidney failure.

Grains – Whole grains such as quinoa, barley, brown rice, oatmeal, and pasta are all excellent sources of fiber. All grains need to be well-cooked so they can be properly digested by your Brittany. Note: white rice has low nutritional value and should only be used to settle an upset tummy.

Supplements – Even the best homemade dog food recipe, using the highest quality organic ingredients will still lack certain nutrients such as calcium. Another reason to add supplements to your dog's homemade food is if you are freezing the food into daily portions; many nutrients are lost when food is frozen then thawed. Closely follow the instructions on the supplement packaging for your dog's weight, size, and age. If you have doubts, talk to a pet nutritionist.

MAKE SURE THE HOMEMADE DIET IS WORKING

After your Brittany has been enjoying his homemade meals for one to two months, take him to the vet to make sure he is not gaining or losing too much weight. If your dog's weight has changed slightly, check it again in a few weeks. Your vet will regularly check your dog's coat, skin, teeth, and body condition for any issues that might be related to his homemade diet.

ARE MEATLESS DIETS SAFE FOR MY BRITTANY?

Due to climate change and ethical considerations, many people have decided to become vegetarians or vegans, and they often wonder if their dogs can be vegetarian or vegan too. Can dogs be healthy on a meatless diet?

Dogs are not considered to be obligate carnivores. Obligate carnivores, such as cats, have to eat animal proteins, as their body needs the amino acids found in animal proteins. This means, theoretically, dogs can eat a plant-based diet and get amino acids from plants or produce it themselves in their own liver. There have been a few pilot studies that have shown dogs, even sport dogs such as Brittanys, thrive on a meat-free diet.

One of the main side effects of meatless diets is they tend to make the dog's urine more alkaline, causing painful kidney and gallbladder stones that often need to be surgically removed. Veterinarians do not recommend feeding your dog a meatless homemade diet. Getting the right nutrients is difficult in a normal homemade dog food and almost impossible for a meatless diet.

The good news is there are quite a few meatless dog foods on the market and more are being launched all the time. There are some great meatless diets out there that are complete and balanced. If you do not want to purchase a meatless dog food, ask a veterinary nutritionist to help you plan a balanced recipe for your dog's lifestyle and age.

Remember, if your dog has any medical conditions or is prone to an upset stomach, it is best to discuss your options first with your veterinarian.

A Basic Recipe for Homemade Dog Food

The following recipe is a healthy alternative to canned dog food, as it is loaded with iron from fresh protein and veggies. It can be stored in the fridge for up to a week or be frozen and reheated later. The recipe below is a basic guideline, which you can adapt to your Brittany's personal preferences.

Dooggie Style Stew

Total: Makes four cups (32 fluid ounces)

- 1 pound chicken or beef, without fat, skin, or bones (cut into small pieces)
- 4 oz. of beef liver, chopped
- 1 medium, steamed sweet potato, chopped
- 1/2 cup steamed green beans, chopped
- 1 cup cooked quinoa or oatmeal
- 1 cup spinach, blended with a cup of water
- 1 tbsp. fish oil or coconut oil

DIRECTIONS

1. Sauté the meat and liver together with the oil in a large pot until thoroughly cooked.
2. Add the rest of the ingredients and leave to simmer on low heat for 10 to 15 minutes.
3. Let cool and serve.
4. Store the leftovers in the fridge for a maximum of five days.

As mentioned before, be sure to cook all animal products thoroughly to kill any harmful bacteria, and cook all grains, starchy vegetables, and beans to make them easier for your Brittany to digest. Before switching your dog to a homemade diet, be sure to discuss your dog's specific nutritional needs with your veterinarian. Remember that switching your dog's food to homemade from kibble is a slow process, so patience is essential.

Weight Monitoring

More than 60 percent of all dogs in the United States are considered to be overweight, and nearly all of their owners are in denial! Obesity is one of the greatest threats to your dog's long-term health.

Dogs, like people, have a harder time getting around if they are over-weight. Losing weight can be a challenge for dogs at any age, but even more so as they get older. Despite the challenges, weight loss for dogs of any age is worth the effort. Slender pups enjoy longer lives, show fewer visible signs of aging, and have less chances of developing canine arthritis.

Health problems that are more common in overweight dogs include pancreatitis, diabetes, heart disease, joint pain, ruptured ligaments, hip dysplasia, compromised immune system, and different types of cancer. If you cannot feel your Brittany's ribs and shoulder blades, if his waist is not discernible (a tuck behind his ribs), or if there is a roll of fat at the base of his tail, then it is time to face reality and put your pooch on a diet.

If in doubt, ask your vet for his professional opinion about your dog's weight.

Here are some weight loss tips for your Brittany:

Feed your dog more protein and fewer carbohydrates

When it comes to weight loss, the ratio of carbohydrates to fats and pro-teins matters more than calorie counting. Brittanys thrive on a high-protein diet, as it builds lean muscle and improves mood and mental agility. If your Brittany is overweight, look for a dog food that is high in protein, low in carbs, and moderate in healthy fats.

Avoid feeding your Brittany a high-fiber diet

Fiber will not satisfy your dog and can interfere with nutrient absorption. Instead, look for dog foods that contain whole grains such as quinoa, whole oats, and brown rice, as they are an excellent source of fiber and protein yet are low in carbohydrates.

Reduce your Brittany's portion size

Instead of making drastic changes, start slowly by cutting back your dog's meal portion size by 5 percent. Reduce this by 5 percent every three weeks until you are giving your pooch the amount of food specified for him on the dog food package. This strategy prevents your Brittany from los-ing weight too fast then gaining it back. Slow, steady weight loss means long-term success.

Measure everything your Brittany eats

One of the reasons your Brittany is overweight is probably because you have been eyeballing his dog food. The only way to accurately measure your dog's food is either by using measuring cups or even better, by using an electronic scale to weigh every meal. This takes a lot of discipline on your part, but you will be surprised to find that you were often feeding your dog twice as much as required. You can find a small scale at an office or kitchen supply store or online.

Make your dog's weight loss a family project

Feeding your furry friend a smaller portion will not help him lose weight if he is getting breakfast leftovers, an afternoon snack, and/or a treat or two throughout the day. Discuss your dog's diet plan with the entire family and be sure they cooperate. Allot each family member a certain number of training treats to give your Brittany each day, and encourage everyone to focus on calorie-free treats and rewards such as playing fetch, games, or praise.

Treats and rewards often have three to five calories and they can quickly add up in a training session. Instead of store-bought treats, try using pieces of cut-up skinless chicken breast. Most dogs are more concerned about the number of treats they are receiving and do not notice the size of the actual treat, so cut up chewy treats into smaller pieces. Use raw baby carrots, zucchini slices, or small slices of apple, banana, or melon for a healthier treat.

CHAPTER 11
Grooming Your Brittany

Good grooming helps your Brittany feel and look his best. Routine grooming sessions give you an opportunity to examine your pup's coat, eyes, teeth, ears, and nails for any health problems.

Brushing

> "
> The Brittany is a high shedding breed, and to manage this effectively, you must brush regularly. We recommend buying a good deshedding tool and brushing them out once or twice a week.
>
> **STEVE ROGERS**
> *Winding Branch Kennel*
> "

Adult Brittanys have beautiful, long feathered ears and silky hair under their chest, legs, and underbelly. This must be regularly brushed to keep it clean and free of knots. Regularly brushing your dog for a few minutes at a time can accomplish a lot in terms of keeping him clean, as it removes dirt, burrs, and grass.

Get your dog accustomed to being brushed while he is standing, as a groomer would, instead of lying down. If you have a hard time remembering to brush your Brittany daily, place his brushes in a place where you will see them, such as beside the television remote.

All dogs shed, and your Brittany is no exception. Excessive shedding can easily be prevented by providing your dog with a healthy diet, plenty of exercise, and fresh air. If you notice, while brushing your dog, that he is losing more hair than normal, the cause may be one of the following factors:

- Hot spots
- Sarcoptic mange
- Food-related allergies
- Parasites, such as fleas, lice, or mites
- An immune disorder, such as adrenal or thyroid diseases
- Cancer
- Anxiety or stress
- Pregnancy or lactation
- A bacterial or fungal infection, such as ringworm

Your Brittany will love running outdoors year-round, which means you will need to check him daily for ticks. In the following chapter, we will discuss how to remove a tick.

HELPFUL TIP
Low-maintenance Coat

The Brittany's medium-length coat doesn't shed or tangle much. Weekly brushing is enough to reduce shedding and prevent tangles from forming.

As you brush your pooch, look for sores, rashes, or signs of infection such as redness, swelling, skin inflammation, and tenderness. The same is true if you notice any patches of dry, brittle skin.

If you notice any foreign objects lodged in your dog's eyes, ears, skin, mouth, or paw pads, do not attempt to remove them yourself – always consult with your veterinarian beforehand.

If matted hair is an issue, leave your household scissors in the drawer where they belong. One wrong movement by a nervous pooch could result in injuring you or your dog. The best way to remove a knot or mat is by using your fingers, some pet-friendly conditioner, a comb, and a whole lot of patience.

Bathing

Your Brittany is an active dog and will need to be bathed at least every six weeks, sometimes more often. Regularly bathing your dog will help to keep his coat clean, short, and tangle-free.

Never spray your pooch with scents or perfumes. Dogs are very sensitive to fragrances, and most fragrances contain harmful ingredients that can make your dog very sick if he ingests them while cleaning himself. Fragrances can result in respiratory problems. The best way to keep your Brittany smelling his best is by regularly bathing him.

<u>How to give your Brittany a bath:</u>

(1) Before your Brittany's bath, take extra time to brush out any extra hair, debris, or heavy dirt. Place your pup in a large basin or tub filled with approximately four to six inches of lukewarm water.

(2) Thoroughly wet your dog down using a large pitcher or spray hose. If using a spray nozzle, make sure the water is neither too hot nor too cold.

(3) Avoid getting water or soap in your Brittany's eyes, nose, and ears. Use a damp washcloth to remove any dirt or debris around your pup's face.

④ Once your Brittany is completely wet, gently massage the pet-friend-ly shampoo into his coat. Start from the top of his head, working your way down to his tail. Pay close attention to under his legs, as Brittanys tend to sweat under these areas. Dilute the dog-formulated shampoo in water, so it is easier to rinse out.

⑤ Rinse and repeat if needed. Hold your dog still to prevent him from shaking the excess water out.

⑥ Take your Brittany out of the tub or basin and dry him off using a large, fluffy towel.

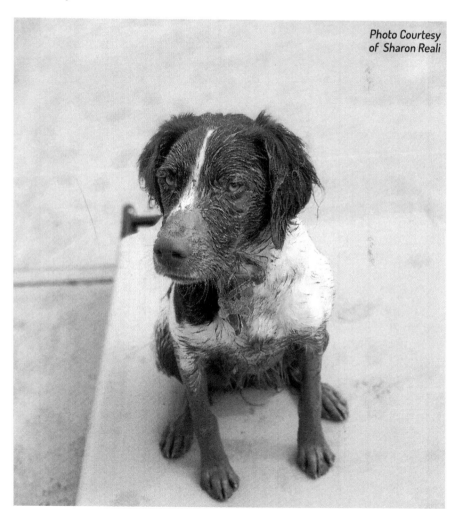

Photo Courtesy of Sharon Reali

Just a reminder – Never ever use human shampoo or conditioner to wash your Brittany, as it contains chemicals and fragrances that may irritate his skin. Instead, choose a high-quality shampoo specifically formulated for dogs. Avoid using inexpensive dog shampoos as they often are made with harsh ingredients.

Since your Brittany is a water dog, he can easily confuse bath time with playtime. If your dog has a hard time standing still, ask a family member to help you.

Nail Clipping

Most Brittanys are squeamish about having their nails trimmed, so do not expect it to be your favorite shared activity, no matter how many treats your pooch gets afterward.

Chances are your Brittany's nails will need to be trimmed every four to six weeks or so, unless he is running around on hard surfaces such as cement that keep his nails short. A general rule of thumb: if you can hear your pup's nails clicking against the floor or his nails get snagged on the carpet, then it is time for a trim.

If possible, get your Brittany used to having his nails clipped at a young age by rubbing your hands up and down his legs and gently pressing down between his toes each time. Never forget to give your pooch a yummy treat, followed by a big, boisterous "Good boy!" After about two weeks of massaging your Brittany's feet, you can attempt clipping his nails. This method works especially well if your older dog is ticklish or wary about having his feet touched.

If you are unsure about how to cut your Brittany's nails, ask your veterinarian or groomer; they will gladly give you a short demonstration on how to trim his nails to the right length.

There are two different types of nail clippers – scissor-type or guillotine. Both styles come highly recommended, so choose the style you feel the most comfortable with. Another option is a nail grinder, which sands the nails down; however, it makes a loud, grinding noise, and the vibration can frighten you and your dog.

Be sure to give your Brittany a vigorous workout to burn off excess energy before clipping his nails. If your dog is skittish, ask a family member to help you. There is no need to clip all of your dog's nails at once; you can clip one paw at a time, with breaks in between.

How to clip your Brittany's nails:

(1) Hold your Brittany's foot steadily but gently as you spread out each toe. Hold the nail clipper at a slight angle, snipping from the top to the bottom. Cut off the tip of the nail. Avoid giving the nail a blunt edge; instead, follow the natural curvature of the nail.

(2) Snip off the tip of the nail, avoiding the quick. The quick is the darker-colored circle inside of the nail, which is the blood vein. If you accidentally cut the quick, you will have one very unhappy dog.

(3) If you accidentally cut your Brittany's nail quick, use a nail cauterizer, such as cornstarch or styptic powder, which you can apply with a Q-Tip. Be sure to have a moist washcloth on hand to clean up the mess. Cutting your dog's nail quick hurts, and trust me – he will remember this unpleasant experience for a long time.

(4) Once you have finished clipping your Brittany's nails, do not forget to generously praise your Brittany with yummy treats and a healthy scratch behind his ears.

If you are using a nail grinder to trim your Brittany's nails, follow the method above; simply hold your pup's foot and grind a little off each nail. Do not forget to trim your Brittany's dewclaws. Since they do not touch the ground, they tend to grow longer and will eventually grow back into your dog's paw, which can be very painful and may cause health complications.

If your Brittany has darker nails, you will need to be extra careful because it is almost impossible to notice the nail quick. If you have a hard time keeping your hands steady or your pooch shows aggressive behavior while getting his nails clipped, feel free to ask the groomer to clip his nails for you.

Importance of Good Dental Care

You have probably heard the expression that a dog's mouth is cleaner than a human's mouth. The truth is a dog's mouth is no cleaner than a human's mouth; it just is home to an entirely different group of bacteria.

Your Brittany can develop dental issues such as tartar, plaque, and gingivitis. As if bad breath was not enough, these canine dental problems can lead to life-threatening infections, not to mention dental extractions, which can be very costly to treat. The only way to prevent this is by practicing good oral care.

Since your Brittany cannot brush his teeth on his own, you will need to brush his teeth regularly. Older dogs can learn to be comfortable with getting their teeth brushed, but you can make things easier for yourself by starting early with your dog when he is still a puppy.

Get your pooch used to having his teeth cleaned by gently massaging his gums for about 20 to 30 seconds daily for about two weeks. Once he is comfortable with you touching his gumline, do the same procedure daily but including his teeth for another two weeks.

How to brush your Brittany's teeth:

1. Place a pea-sized amount of canine toothpaste on the tip of your finger, then let your dog smell it and taste it.

2. Gently massage the toothpaste onto his gums. This will allow him to get used to the texture and the flavor.

③ Use a double-headed canine tooth brush held at a 45-degree angle to clean below the gumline.

④ Work on one spot at a time until your Brittany gets used to the feel of the toothbrush inside of his mouth.

Your pup may not be keen on getting his teeth brushed at first, but over time he will get used to it. Choose a time when he is more likely to sit still for the entire procedure, such as after a vigorous walk or a game of fetch outside.

Make sure you speak softly and soothingly throughout the entire process and do not forget to reward your dog with a yummy treat afterward. Be cautious not to overdo it the first few times or if your pooch becomes agitated. Take your time and increase the length of each session slowly.

If brushing your pup's teeth ends with tears, hurt feelings, or blood, there are still a few other choices you can make to improve his oral health. Dry kibble is better for your Brittany's teeth than soft or wet food, as soft food can become stuck between his teeth, causing tooth decay. There are also synthetic bones and chew toys that have been specifically designed to strengthen your dog's gums and teeth.

Never use human toothpaste or mouthwash for your Brittany, as it contains fluoride, which is toxic for dogs. Look for a specially formulated toothpaste at your local pet store; often, they come in a variety of flavors such as beef, chicken, or salmon. There is also dog mouthwash that is diluted in water to kill bacteria and prevent plaque buildup.

ROUTINE DENTAL CLEANINGS

No matter how disciplined you are about cleaning your Brittany's teeth, you will never really be able to give him a deep, thorough cleaning with just a toothbrush. Even if your dog has healthy teeth, it is wise to have your veterinarian give him an annual cleaning to remove any plaque and tartar buildup, clean the gum line, and polish his teeth.

Common Dental Issues in Brittanys

No matter how often you brush your Brittany's teeth, you should inspect the inside of his mouth at least once a week. If you notice any of the following signs, take your dog to the vet as soon as possible:

- Bad breath
- Constantly pawing at his face or mouth.

- A change of eating or chewing habits.
- Depression
- Excessive drooling
- Red, swollen, painful, or bleeding gums
- Bumps or growths inside of the gum line
- Yellowish tartar buildup along the gum line
- Discolored, missing, or misaligned teeth

Doggie dental care may be a hassle, but regular maintenance is a money saver in the long run and may even be a lifesaver. Letting your dog's teeth deteriorate leads to expensive and painful vet visits down the road. Many dogs will need to be given anesthesia to have their teeth and gums cleaned.

Gingivitis – Gingivitis is caused by an accumulation of plaque, bacteria, and tartar around the gum. Signs are swollen, bleeding gums, and extremely bad breath. Fortunately, it can easily be cleared up with regular brushing.

Mouth tumors – Mouth tumors look like small bumps or lumps on your dog's gums. They can be extremely painful and irritating for your dog while eating or drinking water. Mouth tumors will need to be surgically removed by a vet.

Periodontal disease – This gum infection results in tooth loss and a high risk of the infection spreading throughout the body, causing all sorts of maladies. Watch out for bad breath, nasal discharge, mouth pain, lack of appetite, and loose teeth.

Proliferating gum disease – This occurs when your dog's gum-line is over his teeth, causing a gum infection. It can easily be treated with antibiotics.

Salivary cysts – These are fluid-filled blisters located under your dog's tongue or along the corners of his mouth. They will need to be professionally drained and cauterized. Often the saliva gland will need to be surgically removed.

Moral of the story: Keep your Brittany's teeth sparkling white, and you will both be smiling.

Paws

Your Brittany's paws are made for stomping. Your pooch uses his paws for just about everything. You need to keep your dog's paws in tip-top shape by regularly checking them for pebbles, splinters, or any other type of debris that may get stuck in there. If you find a splinter, use a pair of tweezers to gently pull it out. Regularly trim the fur between your Brittany's toes as it could become matted, making it painful for your dog to walk.

Paw pads can crack and bleed if they get too dry. Never use lotions or moisturizers designed for humans on your Brittany, as they will soften the pads, leading to further injury. Instead, use a high-quality, dog-formulated paw moisturizer on his feet. Give your pooch a paw massage by rubbing the moisturizer between the pads on his feet.

Winter paws – Winter is not only harsh on you but also on your Brittany's paws. You need to worry about frostbite or hidden debris in the snow that could cut your dog's paws.

The salt used to melt the ice can burn your pup's paw pads, causing them to become chapped or cracked. Rock salt or other ice-melting chemicals are made from toxic chemicals that could be ingested by your pooch if he licks his paws. After coming in the house from a walk, wash your dog's paws in warm water to remove excess chemicals. Using doggy booties and limiting outdoor exposure are the best options.

Summer paws – Asphalt and pavement can get hot enough to scorch your pup's paw pads. Check the ground temperature with the palm of your hand; if you cannot rest it there comfortably for 30 seconds, then the ground is definitely too hot for your dog. Paw pads can easily become burned and blistered. If the ground is too hot, stick to grass or shady places when walking your pooch.

Ears

Your Brittany's long, drooping ears allow him to catch a scent while hunting. But those adorable floppy ears can also trap water and bacteria, leading to painful ear infections. Routine preventative care will reduce your pup's chances of infection and improve the overall health of his ears.

Plucking the ear hair is the best method as it removes both the strand and the root. However, since you have not removed the hair follicle, be aware that the hair strand will grow back. It is not recommended to trim the hair strands as the shortened hairs create a trap for bacteria, yeast, and debris.

Dog ear powder – This powder is designed for plucking hairs out of your pup's ears. The powder lets you grip the strands and makes for easier removal.

Hemostat – A hemostat is an essential tool designed to grip your Brittany's ear hairs; it is similar to a pair of tweezers but sturdier. It is not recommended to extract the hair strand using your fingers, as it will not extract the hair root, plus pulling the hair out with your fingers will be more painful for your dog.

How to pluck hairs from your Brittany's ears:

1. Choose a moment when both you and your Brittany are relaxed, such as when your dog has burned off some of his access energy with a vigorous walk or a game of fetch.

2. Position your dog so you have a clear view inside of his ear. Gently bend back the ear leather, sprinkle a light dusting of dog ear powder in the ear, and using a disinfected hemostat tool, grip a few hairs, lock, and quickly pull up.

3. Only pluck hairs you can see, as digging around in your dog's ear can cause more damage than good. Therefore, only pull out what you can easily see and grab.

4. Throughout the entire process, use a soft, calming voice, and be sure to reward your Brittany afterward with a nice, yummy treat.

Never insert a Q-Tip in your Brittany's ears, as it could easily slip deeper in the canal, causing injury. Another word of caution: do not clean your pup's ears too often as they could become irritated or infected.

How to clean your Brittany's ears:

1. If your Brittany's ears appear to be dirty or waxy, use a small piece of gauze or a cotton ball dampened in mineral oil or a liquid ear cleaner formulated for dogs.

2. Gently fold back your pup's ear and carefully wipe away any ear wax or debris you can see.

3. Instead of rubbing the ear to remove the debris or ear wax, gently wipe it away.

Most Brittanys need to have this type of ear cleaning every two to three weeks to keep bacteria and ear infections at bay.

Regularly check your Brittany's ears if you notice any of the following symptoms:

- Brownish or yellowish discharge
- Red and swollen inner ear canal
- Hearing loss
- Excessive shaking of the head or tilting to the side

- Scabby skin around the ear flap
- Strong odor emanating from the ear
- Loss of balance
- Ear scratching or wiping ears on the floor or rubbing ears against the furniture

If you notice a brownish or black build-up of earwax (that looks like coffee grounds) in your Brittany's ear, he could have microscopic ear mites. Be sure to make an appointment with your vet as soon as possible.

Eyes

Regularly check your Brittany's eyes. Have your dog sit in a well-lit part of the house, preferably with natural light. Your dog's eyes should appear bright and clear, and the area surrounding the pupil should be white and not yellow. There should be no crusty discharge at the corner of his eyes. Using your thumb, gently pull down the lower part of your dog's eyelid to observe the inner lining; it should be a pale pink color and not red or white.

On a daily basis, use a clean, damp cotton ball or dog-formulated eye-wipe to wipe any gunk away from your dog's eyes. Be careful not to touch your dog's eyeballs. If recommended by your vet, you can use canine eye drops to get rid of tear stains on your Brittany's face.

The following symptoms are clear indications your Brittany may have an eye infection:

- Crusty gunk and discharge around the corners of his eyes
- Cloudiness
- Swollen eyelid
- Unequal pupil size
- No desire to open his eyes
- Teary eyes and tear-stains

Keep the hair around your Brittany's eyes trimmed. Use a small pair of scissors, like cuticle scissors, to minimize the risk of injuring your dog. Long hair around the eyes can accidentally poke or scratch the pupils. Air conditioners will dry out your dog's eyes, causing irritation and possibly infection.

Anal Glands

Brittanys are prone to anal gland problems; unfortunately, this condition can cause painful sores around the anus. Both female and male Brittanys have a pair of anal glands found under the skin that surrounds your dog's anal muscles. Often, they are referred to as scent glands, odor glands, or stinky glands.

These glands hold an oily substance that is released in minute amounts when one dog meets another, which explains why dogs sniff each other's rear ends. The anal scent tells the other dog the unfamiliar dog's gender, health, and general mood. Also, the oily substance is released every time your dog has a bowel movement.

Often, when a dog is scooting his rear end on the ground after having a bowel movement, the anal sacs are engorged (swollen). Your Brittany will need your help to express his anal glands; otherwise, they could become infected or even break open, which will need to be treated by your veterinarian.

How to tell if your Brittany needs his anal glands expressed:

- Scooting his rear end on the ground
- Excessively licking or biting his butt
- Red, swollen skin around his anus
- Bleeding or discharge from around the anus

Most Brittany owners prefer to ask their groomer or vet to express their dog's anal glands. If your dog's anal glands have not been expressed in quite some time, and the oily substance has become solid (impacted), then your veterinarian will need to sedate your dog for the extraction as it is very painful.

Anal glands are expressed in a similar fashion as you would pop a pimple, but due to the location and the discomfort your dog is experiencing, it can be a challenge.

How to express your Brittany's anal glands at home:

To begin, you will need a pair of disposable latex gloves, Vaseline or a similar lubricant, paper towels, a warm, soapy washcloth, and someone to help you restrain your Brittany. The smell is not for the faint of heart.

① Place your dog on the table with his rear end facing you. Your dog should be standing on all fours. Have your helper gently restrain the dog by placing one arm underneath and around your dog's neck and the other arm hugging your dog's body.

(2) Put on your latex gloves and lubricate your index finger.

(3) Lift your Brittany's tail and insert your index finger about one inch into his rectum.

(4) Place your thumb on the outside of your dog's anus. Using your thumb and index finger, feel for a firm pea-sized object. The anal glands should be located at the four o'clock position and the other at the seven o'clock position.

(5) Once you have located the anal glands, using your other hand, place a paper towel in front of your dog's anus, as the glands tend to squirt outwards. Using light pressure, gently milk the anal glands. When you can barely feel the gland, it is completely expressed.

(6) Follow the same procedure with the other gland.

(7) Once you are finished draining both anal sacs, use the warm, soapy wash-cloth to clean the area.

(8) Reward your dog with some treats and lots of praise.

Professional Grooming

If you decide to take your dog to a groomer, be sure you research groomers that know how to trim a Brittany. I know it sounds crazy but not all of them know the proper way a Brittany should be trimmed. The internet is a great resource, especially the American Kennel Club website. You can always use photos as a visual guide. Remember a Brittany's grooming directly correlates to our breed's purpose and function.

JESSIE SCHULZ
Credit Brittanys

Grooming your Brittany may seem like an easy way to save money and bond with your pooch. But the grooming process is not for everyone, as it takes time, patience, and it is a whole lot trickier than it sounds. Thankfully, there is a stress-free option! Professional groomers have the skills and expertise to make sure your Brittany gets a trim and bath. After all, your furry friend deserves to be pampered.

There are pros and cons associated with taking your dog to a professional groomer. Here is the nitty-gritty:

ADVANTAGES

- Professional groomers have years of experience and can groom your dog in less time than you.
- Groomers use professional equipment and tools, ensuring a top-notch job.
- Groomers provide specialized treatments such as de-shedding and ringworm.
- They provide a quick medical exam, and upon request, they will pluck and clean your Brittany's ears and express his anal glands.
- Most groomers include nail trimming.

DISADVANTAGES

- The cost can add up, especially if your Brittany gets groomed every six to eight weeks.
- Some Brittanys suffer from anxiety and stress from being left alone at the groomers for two to three hours.
- Finding the perfect groomer for your Brittany takes time.
- Transporting your dog to and from the groomer may be troublesome if he does not enjoy long car rides.

In the end, the decision to use a professional groomer or not depends on your personal preference and situation. Ask yourself if you have the time and patience to groom your Brittany yourself or if you can financially afford to send him regularly to the groomer.

Many dog owners prefer combining both methods in order to save money, and in the meantime, they can gain experience grooming their dog themselves at home. For example, they may get their dog professionally groomed once every four to five months, and in between, they will do minor grooming touch-ups and baths.

Before you choose a groomer, take the time to research your options. Ask friends and colleagues for recommendations. Once you have narrowed down your options, be sure to ask the groomer the following questions to get a better picture of their operation. Feel free to ask any other questions that concern the well-being of your Brittany.

CAN I SEE YOUR FACILITY?

The grooming facility should be clean, well-ventilated, and modern. The wash-tubs and tables should be sturdy. Ask yourself as you observe the facility if you feel comfortable leaving your furry companion there. If the groomer is standoffish and refuses to let you into the facility, move on to the next option on your list.

DO THEY HAVE LIABILITY?

Any reputable groomer will have liability insurance, as they will be a registered business. Using a groomer with liability coverage will give you peace of mind if your Brittany has an unfortunate accident while in the groomer's care, as any medical expenses incurred will be covered.

WHAT IS THE TOTAL COST?

Never assume that one groomer will charge the same as another. Always ask what services are included in a basic grooming. Groomers often charge different fees depending on the dog's size, coat, and temperament. Often groomers offer discounts for regular dog clients.

WHAT TYPE OF TRAINING HAVE THEY RECEIVED?

Many groomers are self-trained. Be sure to look for a groomer who has been professionally trained through an apprenticeship, etc. Ask the groomer how long they have been professionally grooming dogs and if they have experience grooming Brittanys.

CHAPTER 12
Preventative Medical Care

By making your Brittany's health a priority, you will avoid a long list of medical issues and increase the overall well-being of your furry friend. Get the facts about preventative care, vaccines, parasites, and even alternative medical treatments to enhance your dog's quality of life.

Photo Courtesy of Bridgette Shaw

Choosing a Veterinarian

Choosing the right veterinarian for your Brittany is something you should carefully consider, as this person needs to keep your dog healthy and may even save his life. Both you and your pooch should agree about this person before making a commitment to work with him or her.

Before you start checking out different veterinary clinics in your region, make a list of your priorities for your Brittany. This will help you narrow down your options when choosing a vet and help you ask the right questions. Consider your dog's age, family history (if known), and any health concerns. For example, if your furry friend is getting older, look for a vet who specializes in geriatric dog care.

Here is a basic checklist of essential requirements for veterinarians (requirements may vary depending on your dog's needs):

- Proximity to your house – If there is an emergency, can you get to the veterinary clinic quickly?

- Pricing – Every veterinary clinic has different prices; make sure the clinic you choose fits your budget.

- Do the clinic's hours work with your work schedule, or will you need to take time off to take your Brittany there?

- Does the clinic have up-to-date facilities with cutting-edge medical technologies and care?

- Check for generous appointment times, as you do not want to feel rushed during the visit.

- A smaller practice means you most likely see the same vet every time you visit, plus your Brittany can develop a rapport with the medical staff.

- Does the staff have knowledge of alternative and holistic treatments?

- Is the staff involved in the local animal welfare community, such as pet rescue organizations?

Once you have narrowed down what you want from a veterinarian, it is time to start your search for potential candidates.

Ask for personal recommendations – The best place to start is by word of mouth. Ask fellow dog owners, whose pet-care philosophies are in line with your own, about their vets. Or ask a friend or family member for recommendations. Many veterinarian clinics offer a referral program, which may mean discounts for you and the friend who referred you.

Look for licensed personnel – Be sure to check out the American Animal Hospital Association (AAHA) website. There you will find an extensive list of accredited veterinarians in your region, as well as an evaluation of the facility, staff, patient care, and equipment. This is a great option if you have just moved to a new area and do not know who to ask.

Whether you get a referral from a friend or from an online search, you will want to make sure the veterinarian clinic is accredited with the AAHA. The AAHA regularly evaluates veterinary practices throughout the United States on their standards for patient care, pain management, facilities, surgery, medical records, cleanliness, anesthesiology, and more. While veterinary clinics are not required to be accredited by law, accreditation shows you a clinic is committed to maintaining only the highest standard of care or service.

Find a veterinary clinic that specializes in dogs – Not all veterinarians are created equal. Some veterinarians specialize in livestock, such as cows, goats, horses, etc. If you live in a rural area, be sure to verify that the veterinarian has expertise in treating dogs specifically; ask how much experience they have with canines before making an appointment.

Ask for a tour of the veterinary clinic – When you narrow the list down to one or two veterinary practices, ask to take a tour of the facility. Any reputable vet will be more than happy to show you around the clinic and make you feel comfortable. Notice whether the staff is caring, calm, and courteous. Another important aspect to observe is the cleanliness of the lobby, waiting rooms, and exam rooms.

In addition to getting a feel for the facility, ask plenty of questions. Vets appreciate when pet owners are interested in their pets' health and well-being.

Here are some questions you should ask when interviewing the vet:

- How are overnight patients monitored?
- Are all diagnostic tests like bloodwork, ultrasounds, X-rays, etc., done on-site or in another referred location?
- Are all of the veterinary technicians employed by the clinic licensed by the state to practice on animals?
- Does the facility refer patients to specialists if needed? (Their answer should be affirmative.)
- What types of payment plans does the practice accept? Are there special payment plans for major surgeries or treatments?

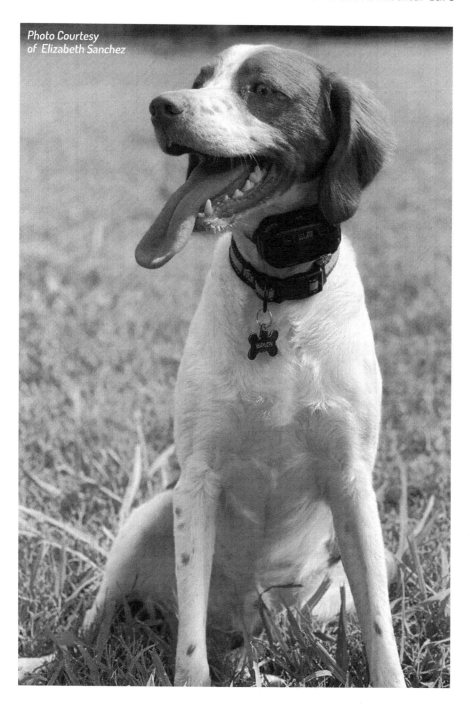

Photo Courtesy
of Elizabeth Sanchez

The questions above are simply guidelines. Feel free to ask any other questions that concern you and your Brittany.

Once you have decided on a vet, be a good client. Show up early for appointments to fill out any necessary paperwork. Be patient and understanding if you have to wait longer than expected. Your vet sometimes has to attend to emergencies, which take precedence over routine appointments. Be prepared to be your Brittany's advocate, but know when it is time to step back and let your vet take over.

If you or your dog do not feel comfortable with the vet, do not hesitate to switch facilities. Veterinary clinics expect clients to come and go. However, before your departure, be sure to request a complete copy of your Brittany's medical file. You can ask that your dog's health records be faxed or mailed to either you or the new clinic.

Microchipping

Each year, more than eight million pets end up in a shelter across the country, and fewer than 20 percent are reclaimed.

A microchip is about the size of a grain of rice. It is implanted in the loose skin between your Brittany's shoulder blades, and your dog will not even notice it is there. It is no more invasive than a vaccination. An average cost to get your dog microchipped costs around $30 to $50, depending on your vet.

The microchip itself does not have a battery; it is activated by a scanner that is passed over the location where the chip was implanted. The radio waves put out by the scanner activate the chip. The chip sends the scanner an identification number, which appears on the screen. The microchip is not a GPS device and cannot track your dog if he gets lost.

If your Brittany is found and taken to a veterinary clinic or shelter, one of the first things they will do is scan him for a microchip. Once they find the microchip registry information, they will quickly locate

HELPFUL TIP
Health Conditions

Like all dog breeds, the Brittany is more prone to certain health conditions than others. Some of these may affect a Brittany at any point in life, while other conditions are more prevalent in older Brittanys. Some health conditions Brittanys are prone to include:
- Hip dysplasia – a painful malformation of the hip joint
- Epilepsy – chronic seizures
- Hypothyroidism – not enough thyroid hormone for proper functioning

you to be reunited with your dog. Make sure to keep your dog's microchip data up-to-date with your personal information.

Another advantage to microchipping is if your dog is ever stolen, the thief will most likely remove your dog's collar and ID tags and toss them in the trash. Often, the thief will resell the dog to an unknown victim. With a microchip, you can prove the dog is yours.

Generally, the entire microchipping process takes only a few seconds, or about the time it takes to give your dog an injection. It will take more time for you to fill out all of the paperwork involved than it will to insert the microchip! Microchipping does not necessarily have to be completed by a vet, but it is highly recommended you use a vet's service.

If your dog is squeamish around injections and needles, you might want to consider getting him chipped at the same time he is being neutered. Most pet owners opt to have their pooches chipped when they are spayed or neutered for this very reason. The pain is similar to using a needle to draw blood; some dogs flinch, others do not.

Pet doors can be programmed to recognize your dog's microchip, letting him come into the house but keeping other animals outside.

Once your Brittany is microchipped, there are two things you need to do each year. First, ask your veterinarian to scan your pup's microchip at least once a year to make sure it is still working and can be detected. Secondly, keep your online registration information up-to-date. It only takes a few minutes to check the information, and you can rest easy that you have improved your chances of getting your Brittany back if the unexpected should happen.

Neutering and Spaying

There are numerous reasons to spay or neuter your Brittany. Neutering and spaying simplify pet ownership, as it prevents females from going into heat and according to some experts, improves dog behavior.

Many Brittany owners get their dogs spayed or neutered to comply with the breeder's contract. However, other dog owners opt to leave their dog's anatomy intact for personal reasons or because they plan on using their Brittany as a show dog. However, be aware that this presents occasional challenges. For example, your intact dog may be barred from some doggy day cares and boarding kennels.

Spaying and neutering have some direct health benefits for your Brittany. Testicular and ovarian cancers are nonexistent, and there is evidence that spaying reduces the risk of mammary cancer and uterine infections. Another benefit is fixed dogs live longer than intact dogs.

However, recent research shows that medium-to-larger sized dogs who were fixed before the age of six months have a much higher rate of orthopedic injuries and obesity. For this reason, many breeders request that you wait one year before getting your Brittany spayed or neutered.

Spaying is a simple surgical procedure performed by a qualified veterinarian. The procedure involves removing your female dog's ovaries and uterus. Here are a few reasons why you should consider spaying your Brittany:

- Spaying reduces the risk of urinary tract infections and breast cancer. It is highly recommended you spay your Brittany before her first heat to prevent health complications in the future.

- Spaying reduces unwanted pregnancies, which saves you from unplanned expenses.

- A spayed dog will not go into heat. A female dog in heat will urinate all over the house and yowl loudly while trying to attract a mate.

Neutering is a simple procedure performed by a qualified veterinarian which involves removing your male dog's testicles. Here are a few reasons why you should consider neutering your Brittany:

- Neutering prevents testicular cancer.

- Your Brittany will not roam about the neighborhood in search of a mate. An unneutered male dog will do everything in his power to find a mate, including digging a hole under the fence or running across a busy highway.

- A neutered dog will be less aggressive and better behaved than an unneutered dog. Also, he will not have the desire to mark his territory by spraying urine everywhere.

Many concerns you may have about getting your Brittany spayed or neutered are just misinformation. Consider the following:

Will your dog feel remorse or loss? No. Dogs do not suffer from emotional insecurities or experience societal pressures to have a family like humans do. They do not need to procreate to feel emotionally fulfilled.

Does spaying or neutering cause obesity? Contrary to popular belief, spaying and neutering will not make your Brittany fat. However, a lack of exercise and over-feeding will.

Are there negative side effects? As with all surgical procedures, there are certain risks, but these are minor and rare and often occur when the procedure is not performed by a reputable veterinarian.

Many states and counties have established low-cost programs for spaying or neutering, which makes these types of surgeries an affordable option for all pet owners. The webpage for the Humane Society will provide you with a list of local, affordable clinics and funding options to help you cover the cost of the procedure. If you are not planning on professionally breeding your Brittany, then you should definitely consider getting your Brittany neutered or spayed.

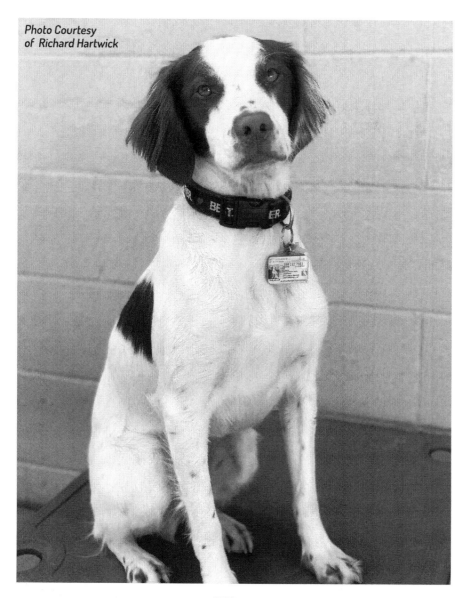

*Photo Courtesy
of Richard Hartwick*

Internal Parasites

Even though you may do everything possible to protect your pooch, he may be affected by parasites at some point in his life. These microscopic organisms carry disease and can cause serious health issues in your four-legged family member if not treated quickly. Some parasites can be passed to your dog from contaminated soil or other dogs' stool, and certain types of worms may even infect humans.

There are five main types of worms that commonly affect Brittanys: hookworms, whipworms, heartworms, roundworms and tapeworms. Most internal parasites in dogs are usually ingested and affect the dog's gastro-intestinal tract.

By familiarizing yourself with these common parasites, you will learn how to keep your dog safe. While each parasite affects dogs differently, there are some general warning signs that your Brittany may have parasites:

- Abdominal pain
- Vomiting
- Diarrhea that lasts longer than 24 hours
- Unexplained weight loss
- Pot-bellied appearance
- Extreme lethargy
- Dehydration
- Poor coat appearance, hair loss, or hot spots
- Coughing

Roundworms – Roundworms are one of the most common types of internal parasite in dogs, and can be transmitted to humans. Many puppies are born with roundworms as they are passed on from their mother. Roundworms can be diagnosed by your vet with a small fecal sample, and they are treated with deworming medications. If left untreated, roundworms can cause your puppy to become anemic, retard growth, and may be fatal in some cases.

Whipworms – Whipworms live in the large intestine and colon. Dogs can become infected by whipworms by consuming an infested substance, such as fecal matter, soil, food, water, or animal flesh. Eggs can survive in soil for up to five years, which is another reason to clean up after your pooch when he relieves himself. Severe cases of whipworms can cause weight loss, inflammation, diarrhea, and anemia. Often, three-monthly treatments will be required to eliminate whipworms.

Tapeworms – Tapeworms are intestinal parasites that can be transmitted through a flea bite or by consuming dead animals or fleas infested with tapeworms. When a dog consumes a flea infested with tapeworm eggs, the egg will attach itself to the dog's intestines and hatch. Infected dogs may scoot their rear end on the ground.

Often, it can be observed in an infected dog's stool, pieces of the tapeworm may break off and resemble small pieces of rice.

If you suspect your Brittany has tapeworms, take a stool sample to your vet for diagnosis. Treatment involves a combination of oral medicine, injections, and fumigating your houses for fleas.

Hookworms – Hookworms can be fatal in puppies if left untreated. There are several types of hookworms that attach themselves to the dog's intestinal wall to gorge themselves on blood, causing anemia. Your dog can get hookworms from ingesting contaminated fecal matter, or they can be passed on to puppies through their mother's milk. Humans can become infected with hookworms. Treatment involves a deworming medication, which will need to be administered twice.

Heartworms – Heartworms are transmitted through a mosquito bite but can be easily prevented by giving your dog regular heartworm medication. Heartworms grow and multiply at an extraordinary rate inside of your dog's heart, causing heart disease, heart failure, organ damage, and ultimately, a painful death. Mosquitoes carrying the heartworm parasite can be found in all 50 states.

The best approach to heartworms is prevention, as treating heartworms is extremely expensive and can have serious side effects. Also, treating heartworms requires keeping your dog confined without exercise for long periods of time in order to prevent heart damage. Even if your dog is regularly taking heartworm preventatives, he will need to be tested regularly for worms.

DIAGNOSING INTERNAL PARASITES AND WORMS

It is possible to observe some parasites, such as tapeworms, in your dog's fecal matter. However, the majority of internal parasites will need to be diagnosed by your veterinarian via a microscopic examination of your dog's stool. If you notice any of the symptoms mentioned above, your vet will ask you to bring in a small sample of your dog's stool. Even if your dog is not exhibiting any symptoms, it is highly recommended you take in a dog stool sample with you to your Brittany's annual check-up.

Your vet will set up a regular deworming schedule for your Brittany to treat different types of intestinal parasites, as well as prevent heartworms. The bottom line – prevention, flea control, and regular testing are the best actions to prevent consequences caused by internal parasites.

Fleas and Ticks

Your Brittany's soft, warm fur provides the ideal environment for fleas and ticks. These disgusting bugs feed on your dog's blood and may cause a long list of problems, such as allergic reactions and serious illnesses caused by a tick bite. Even though fleas and ticks are more prevalent during the warmer months, you will still need to ward them off during the colder months.

FLEAS

These pesky insects do not only set up home on your dog but will quickly invade your home. These blood-sucking insects have the ability to jump almost three feet and can survive in the harshest environments. An average life span for a flea can be 12 days to an entire year. During this time, a single flea can produce millions of baby fleas.

If not controlled, fleas can cause serious health complications for their host. For example, a flea consumes approximately 15 times its body weight in blood each day, causing your Brittany to become anemic. Some dogs have an allergic reaction to flea bites, which is called allergic dermatitis.

Flea warning signs:

- Hair loss
- Allergic dermatitis
- Flea eggs look like white grains of sand
- Flea droppings look like tiny dirt particles
- Excessive biting, licking, or scratching
- Hot spots or scabs

Flea droppings can be found throughout your Brittany's coat. Use a fine-toothed comb to detect them, especially around your dog's abdomen, ears, mouth, and tail.

Fleas are expert stowaways. They quickly attach themselves to animals while outside or can jump from one dog to another. If not controlled, fleas can invade your house within a day or two.

If your Brittany has fleas, all of your resident pets will need to be treated. In some extreme cases, the inside of your house will need to be fumigated. Your veterinarian will confirm your suspicions and most likely will suggest one or two of the following treatments:

- Oral or topical treatment or dog-formulated shampoo for your Brittany

- Thoroughly cleaning your house, including bedding, rugs, and upholstery. A severe infestation will require professional help, which means you and all your pets will have to temporarily evacuate your home.
- If your Brittany gets reinfested every time he goes into the backyard, you may need to fumigate your lawn.

How to prevent fleas:

- Wash your Brittany's bedding at least once a week in hot, soapy water and brush him using a flea brush.
- Rake up any grass clippings or leaves in your backyard, as fleas tend to conceal themselves in dark, moist areas.
- There are preventive flea-control measures available either by prescription or over-the-counter. Be aware some flea collars can be carcinogenic for animals and humans. Always consult with your vet beforehand.

TICKS

Ticks are considered to be parasites as they feed on the host's blood. Ticks are experts at concealing themselves by burrowing into their hosts then gorging on their blood. Ticks can transmit serious diseases to both animals and humans. Transmission varies by certain areas and climates. Ask your vet what types of ticks are in your locality.

Your Brittany loves running through the grass, which makes him an easy target for ticks. You will need to be alert year-round, but be extra vigilant during late spring and early summer.

How to check your Brittany for ticks:

Ticks are very small, making them very easy to miss until they bite your dog and begin to swell up with all the blood they have sucked. Carefully run your fingers through your Brittany's coat, paying extra attention to warm spots such as inside of his ears and around his feet and face. Be sure to repeat this every time your pooch comes inside from playing.

Health complications caused by tick bites:

- Blood loss and anemia
- Tick paralysis
- Allergic dermatitis

If you find a tick attached to your Brittany, it is essential you carefully remove it, as the tick's blood may infect you or your dog. Humans may contract Lyme Disease from deer ticks; these ticks are the primary carrier of Lyme Disease. The illness causes depression, fever, loss of appetite, painful joints, and kidney failure. Lyme disease needs to be caught in time to be successfully treated with antibiotics.

Follow these instructions to safely remove a tick:

(1) Prepare a glass jar with rubbing alcohol inside. This allows you to take a tick in for testing at your veterinary clinic. Put on latex gloves and ask a family member to distract your Brittany while you extract the tick.

(2) Using a pair of disinfected tweezers, gently grasp the tick as close as you can to the dog's skin. Pull straight upward, using even pressure, then place the tick into the jar with rubbing alcohol. Do not twist the tick out, as this could leave the head attached inside the dog or cause the tick to regurgitate infected fluids.

(3) Disinfect the bitten area and the tweezers; wash your hands with warm, soapy water afterward. Monitor the area for the next few weeks for any signs of an infection. If there is a sign of infection, take your Brittany and the tick to the veterinarian for a check-up.

Many products used to treat or to prevent fleas are also useful in killing ticks. Keep your yard tick-free by keeping the grass cut and by removing any large weeds that could be hiding places for ticks.

Holistic Alternatives to Conventional Veterinary Medicine

Holistic veterinary care is often combined with conventional medicine to aid a dog's healing process. For example, if your Brittany has a hip or knee replacement, he will need to take medications such as antibiotics to prevent infection. But some veterinarians recommend combining the treatment with holistic care such as acupuncture or massages to naturally ease the pain and hasten the healing process.

Below are some of the most popular holistic treatments recommended by veterinarians and used by concerned pet parents. Be aware that few of these treatments have been scientifically proven in treating canines. Before starting any type of holistic treatment, be sure to talk over the risks and details with your veterinarian.

CANINE ACUPUNCTURE

Acupuncture uses needles to stimulate pressure points to release the buildup of certain chemicals in the muscles, spinal cord, and brain, thus promoting better health. There is plenty of anecdotal proof that acupuncture can relieve dogs of joint and muscle pain, encourage healing post-surgery, and even treat cancer or other types of traumas.

HYDROTHERAPY

Hydrotherapy means physical therapy in water. This type of therapy is highly recommended for dogs in need of low-impact exercise due to joint pain from arthritis or recovery from an injury or surgery. Hydrotherapy is proven to build muscle, improve mobility, decrease stress, and increase circulation.

CHINESE HERBAL MEDICINE

Chinese herbal medicine combines certain herbs to relieve pain, improve and restore organ function, and strengthen the immune system. Many pet owners rave about Chinese herbal medicine's effect on their pets. As with all herbs, make sure they are safe to use alongside your dog's conventional medications, such as blood thinners or diuretics.

MAGNETIC FIELD THERAPY

According to the Veterinary Clinics of America, magnet therapy is gaining popularity in the United States to treat illness and injury; however, there is not much evidence that the application of magnets can heal your Brittany. Magnet field therapy is affordable, non-invasive, and has virtually no side effects.

CANINE MASSAGE

Canine massage encourages healing, improves circulation, stimulates nerves, relieves stress and relaxes your dog's muscles. One of the biggest advantages of a doggy massage is that it makes your pooch feel good and strengthens the bond between a person and the dog. Massage will not cure your Brittany's cancer or injury; it will, however, make him feel relaxed and loved.

NUTRITIONAL SUPPLEMENTS

Nutritional supplements are required if you are feeding your dog a homemade or raw diet to make up for any nutritional deficiencies. Look for nutritional supplements that include calcium, omega fatty acids, vitamins, and amino acids.

When choosing a holistic treatment or supplement for your dog, be sure to use good judgment and always consult with your veterinarian to see if the treatment will help your dog. Note: just because an herbal substance claims it is healthy and beneficial does not mean that it is harmless. Always thoroughly research a product before giving it to your dog.

Vaccinations

Vaccines are a primary prevention against infections and diseases. Your vet will establish a vaccination regime for your Brittany by taking into account his age, health, lifestyle, and where you live.

Vaccinations are designed to help your dog fight off organisms that cause diseases. Vaccines are made up of antigens, which the immune system identifies as the same disease-ridden organism, but without actually causing your dog to become sick. When the vaccine is introduced into the body, it is instructing the immune system how to fight off the real virus in its entirety, hence building antibodies.

The American Animal Hospital Association (AAHA) recommends all dogs receive core vaccines throughout their lives. Your veterinarian may recommend other noncore vaccines depending on geography, lifestyle, and the current prevalence of the disease. For example, a noncore vaccine for kennel cough is required for dogs who frequent doggie daycare, kennels, grooming facilities, and so on.

PUPPIES

When puppies are about six to eight weeks of age, they will receive a series of three core vaccinations administered by a veterinarian at three-to-four-week intervals. The final dose should be administered when your Brittany is 16 weeks of age.

ADULT DOGS

Your Brittany will require annual vaccines or booster shots every two to three years.

RABIES

In the United States, it is mandatory for all dogs to be vaccinated against rabies. However, each state and county have different laws regarding how often your dog will need to be vaccinated. For example, some states require an annual vaccine while others stipulate doses are required once every three years.

The majority of dogs experience no side effects from being vaccinated. However, there are exceedingly rare cases of severe side effects. Reactions are often short-lived and rarely require veterinary care. Here is a list of common reactions:

- Lack of appetite

- Sluggishness
- Vomiting
- Swelling, pain, redness, or hair loss around the injection site
- Fever
- Diarrhea

Schedule your Brittany's vaccinations when you will be around to monitor him for a few days. If your dog experiences any severe symptoms, like seizures, difficulty breathing, or lameness call your vet as soon as possible.

Pet Insurance

No matter how careful you are with your Brittany, unexpected accidents do happen, and often they are not cheap.

Veterinary costs are higher than ever. According to the American Pet Product Association, an average dog owner spends almost $250 for annual check-ups. What happens when the unexpected occurs? Costs can quickly

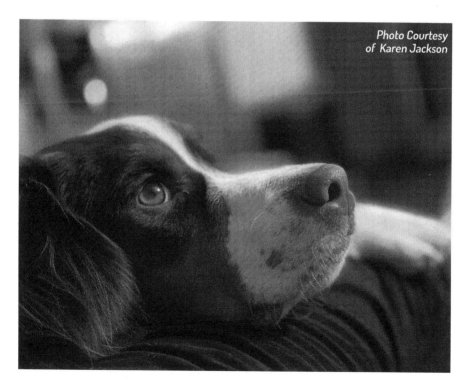

Photo Courtesy of Karen Jackson

add up! For example, for an active dog such as a Brittany, the cost to repair a cruciate ligament tear in the knee (which often happens when the dog comes to a sudden stop while playing fetch) was about $1,200 five years ago. Today, it can cost a whopping $5,000 each knee.

Pet insurance can help defray these costs. Pet insurance was once a specialty niche, but in the last few years, it has gone mainstream. Currently, there are more than 15 different insurance companies in the United States that offer pet insurance, but less than 1 percent of dog owners purchase this type of insurance.

Just as you can pick a health plan that matches you and your family's needs, you can also choose an insurance plan that is the best fit for your Brittany. Most insurance companies offer three types of coverage: accident and illness, accident only, and a wellness plan. Wellness plans often cover preventative care such as annual check-ups and routine vaccinations. You can purchase one type of plan or add on an accident or illness policy.

The final price of pet insurance depends on your Brittany's age and the type of coverage you choose. You can expect to pay a monthly premium of about $20 to $50 a month. The deductible depends on the type of policy you choose.

Here are a few benefits and drawbacks of pet insurance:

PROS

- It gives you peace of mind knowing you have the resources for any unforeseen medical costs if your Brittany becomes injured or ill.

- Pet insurance gives vets the opportunity to give your pooch top-notch care without having to worry about incurring too many medical costs for you.

- Pet insurance helps your dog live a longer and healthier life, as you will not hesitate to take your dog in for medical treatment before his condition worsens.

CONS

- Some insurance companies look at factors such as the dog's age, whether he is a purebred or a designer breed dog, and the dog's living environment. Depending on these factors, the monthly insurance premium could increase.

- Many insurance companies have a 48-hour waiting period before approving accident insurance and a 14-day waiting period before approval for illness insurance.

- Depending on the fine print of the insurance plan, it may exclude pre-existing illnesses, pregnancy and/or birth, routine vaccines, and dental maintenance.

- The majority of pet insurance plans require that you pay for the entire veterinary cost up-front and, afterward, submit a claim for reimbursement.

Note: Your pet insurance will be void if your Brittany is not up-to-date on his vaccinations and deworming. Also, if your dog gets sick from something that is preventable by being vaccinated, most insurance companies will not cover the expenses.

CONSIDER SELF-INSURING

If you decide that pet insurance is too expensive for your monthly budget, then another practical option is to set up a personal savings account for your Brittany. You can always deposit a certain amount of money in the account each month and only withdraw from it for your dog's medical care. This is an excellent option if you are disciplined with money.

The bottom line – veterinary care is not cheap and it can quickly add up, especially if your Brittany needs expensive diagnostics, care, and treatment. If you do decide to purchase pet insurance, take your time and read the fine print very carefully to make sure you completely understand what you are getting yourself into.

CHAPTER 13
Breed-Specific Diseases

All dogs, purebred and mixed breeds, are prone to diseases and abnormalities, which may be genetic. Your purebred Britany is no exception.

Many of these health issues can be unapparent to the average person for years and can only be detected by a medical screening performed by a veterinarian.

Understanding some of the predisposed health problems that may affect your Brittany, can help you take precautions to avoid future troubles. For example, if a certain dog breed has an inherent risk for intervertebral disc problems, then precautions can be made to avoid having him running up and down the stairs or jumping off the furniture.

Photo Courtesy of Christie Limbeck-Dishaw

Common Hereditary Diseases and Illnesses for Brittanys

By purchasing your Brittany from a reputable breeder, you will be able to verify the health of at least up to three generations of your puppy's family health. However, if your pooch was adopted from a shelter, he most likely will not come with a pedigree ensuring a clean health background, so it will be even more useful to be aware of which breed-related health problems to watch out for.

Acral Mutilation Syndrome

Acral mutilation syndrome (AMS) is a serious but very rare hereditary disease. AMS causes progressive degeneration of the sensory neurons of the dog's spinal cord, resulting in a loss of pain sensation of the outer extremities such as the hind legs. Dogs with AMS will often chew, bite, and self-mutilate their outer extremities, resulting in bacterial infections and ulcers.

Puppies with AMS are often much smaller in size when compared to their littermates. Often by the age of three months, the puppy will begin excessively licking, biting, and chewing on his hind feet. The puppy will have no pain or temperature sensation in his feet.

Unfortunately, there is no known treatment for AMS, but there are ways to prevent the dog from mutilating himself, such as Elizabethan collars or cones, bandages, doggie booties, and muzzles. Topical application of specially formulated ointments that taste bad may deter the dog from licking a certain area. Talk to your vet for additional alternatives. If all attempts to prevent the canine from self-mutilating are unsuccessful, then your vet may suggest euthanasia.

AMS is an autosomal-recessive condition, which means the affected dogs must inherit two copies of an abnormal gene (one from each of the parents). If a dog inherits only one abnormal gene from one of his parents, he will have no symptoms of the disease, but the dog will be a carrier and will pass the abnormal gene off to any future offspring. Reputable breeders will test both parents prior to breeding for AMS. The Kennel Club Breed Register also has a record of DNA results tests carried by different breeders.

Even though this condition is extremely rare, make sure the breeder tests the parent dogs prior to breeding for AMS. Also, in the breeder's contract make sure there is a clause that you will be refunded your money if the dog has a genetic disease such as AMS.

Progressive Retinal Atrophy

Progressive retinal atrophy can refer to a group of different degenerative diseases that affect a dog's vision. This disease causes the light-sensitive layers of cells inside of the eye, the retina, to slowly deteriorate over time, eventually leading to blindness. Retinal dysplasia is diagnosed in puppies around two to three months of age, and a later onset form is diagnosed in dogs between the ages of four to nine years.

Progressive retinal atrophy is an inherited disease that occurs in a long list of breeds and mixed dogs. Affected dogs should not be used in breeding. If a dog develops progressive retinal atrophy, its parents and all of its siblings from previous litters should be prevented from breeding. Unfortunately, there is no known cure for progressive retinal atrophy.

Cone Degeneration (Day Blindness)

Cone degeneration is often referred to as day blindness, as affected dogs experience temporary blindness when exposed to daylight. Cone cells are responsible for helping a dog see in high light, and rod photoreceptors are responsible for helping canines see in low light. Affected dogs have normal vision in low light, and light sensitivity begins eight to twelve weeks after birth. By the time an affected dog is an adult, it will have completely lost all cone cells; however, it will be able to see normally in a low-light situation.

As this is a genetic condition, and some dogs may be carriers without showing symptoms, many reputable breeders will test the parent dogs for this mutation. Dogs with this genetic defect are recommended to be eliminated from breeding lines. There is no known cure.

Joint Dysplasia

Joint dysplasia is a deformity of the joint that occurs during growth. Joint dysplasia often occurs in the hip joint. During growth, the thigh bone and socket for the pelvis need to grow at the same speed. However, in joint dysplasia, this growth does not occur, resulting in a loose joint, which is followed by osteoarthritis or degenerative joint disease as the body tries to stabilize the loose joint.

Joint dysplasia is a genetic disease, but the extent of damage can be affected by diet, environment, exercise, growth rate, and hormones. Medium-sized and larger dogs are most prone to joint dysplasia. Care should be taken to keep your dog at a healthy weight, especially during his growth cycle by feeding him a healthy, balanced diet.

Other Common Diseases or Health Conditions

Not all diseases and health conditions are hereditary. Diet, lifestyle, and just plain bad luck are all factors that can affect your dog's long term health.

Aortic Stenosis

Aortic stenosis is a hereditary cardiovascular condition. Affected dogs are born with a narrow aorta, which prevents newly oxygenated blood from being pumped out of the heart into the body. Consequently, the narrowed aorta causes the entire heart to work twice as hard to provide the body with oxygen-rich blood needed to perform bodily functions.

Symptoms of aortic stenosis often are identified early, including fainting, poor growth, sluggishness, and exercise intolerance. Since the dog's heart is constantly over-working, it grows bigger and bigger overtime. Affected dogs tend to develop a constant cough as the heart takes up more space and pushes against the lungs, causing breathing difficulties and heart rhythm abnormalities. Sadly, sudden death is a likely outcome for affected dogs with aortic stenosis.

Vets often identify this condition within the first year of a dog's life via a simple medical exam. The vet will hear a characteristic murmur known to be caused by aortic stenosis. If your Brittany has aortic stenosis, your vet will recommend reducing the impact of the heart's work by reducing exercise to a bare minimum, along with beta-blockers to reduce a dog's blood pressure.

Discoid Lupus Erythematosus

Discoid lupus erythematosus is an autoimmune disease that causes the immune system to attack its own skin, causing painful inflammation and tissue damage. Discoid lupus erythematosus is the most common type of lupus in dogs but is still extremely rare. Dogs with this autoimmune disorder develop a crusty scab around the nose, as well as skin pigmentation loss.

The underlying cause of discoid lupus erythematosus is unknown. Veterinarians have observed that prolonged exposure to ultraviolet light appear to worsen the condition. Affected dogs respond well to a topical steroid medication or ointment. Apply the cream when your dog is distracted, such as during meal-time, to prevent him from licking it off.

242

Von Willebrand's Disease

This is one of the most common hereditary canine disorders, as it has been reported in more than 50 different dog breeds, including the Brittany. This disease is a blood disorder, which prevents the canine's blood from clotting properly. Most dogs with Von Willebrand's disease show no signs or symptoms and may go years before the condition is discovered when a dog has surgery or gets injured.

In very rare and severe cases, symptoms may begin to occur in dogs younger than 12 months of age. Some common symptoms may be spontaneous nosebleeds or bleeding from the gums, excessive bleeding from the vagina during the heat cycle, bloody stools, or visible blood in the urine.

If your veterinarian diagnoses your Brittany with von Willebrand's disease, he will know to use medications while operating on your dog to

Photo Courtesy of Paul and Heidi Heide

stabilize bleeding and promote blood clotting. Your vet most likely will tell you to avoid giving your dog certain medications that have anti-platelet or anticoagulant properties, such as aspirin, NSAIDs, ibuprofen, and more.

Yeast Dermatitis

Yeast dermatitis is a common cause of skin disease in dogs and is caused by a fungus called Malassezia pachydermatous. This fungus is normally found on a dog's skin, but an overgrowth can cause dermatitis or skin inflammation. Common clinical signs of this condition may be itchy, crusty, and flaky skin. Left untreated, it can cause thickened skin resembling elephant skin, hyperpigmentation, and chronic ear infections.

Yeast dermatitis is not contagious. There are different treatments for yeast dermatitis depending on the severity of the dog's condition. Your veterinarian may recommend a medicated anti-fungal shampoo. You will need to bathe your dog using this shampoo for a period of two to twelve weeks every three days. For more severe conditions, your veterinarian will recommend an oral treatment for a period of six months.

Gastric Dilation Volvulus

Gastric dilation volvulus is a life-threatening condition in dogs, as it causes the dog's stomach to expand to the point that neither food nor gas can be expelled. This condition is believed to be caused when a dog eats a large meal; however, the actual cause is not completely understood. An expanded stomach can rotate inside of the abdomen, which is called volvulus. When a rotation occurs, it can lead to a blockage in the blood supply to the dog's spleen and stomach.

When this condition occurs, your vet will need to quickly stabilize your dog by decompressing the stomach, followed by surgery to return the stomach to its original place. During the surgery, the vet will evaluate any damage to the surrounding organs. If this painful condition is left untreated, it can result in a ruptured stomach wall, put excess pressure on the lungs, causing decreased breathing, and finally, it can be fatal.

Hepatitis

There are two types of hepatitis in dogs: infectious canine hepatitis and canine chronic hepatitis. Infectious canine hepatitis is a contagious disease

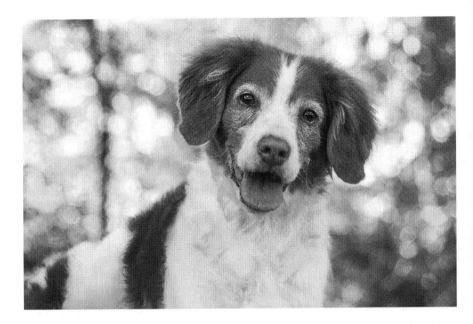

caused by a canine adenovirus, and symptoms can vary from fever to lethargy, thirst, or death. If infectious hepatitis is left untreated, it causes chronic hepatitis, affecting the liver to the point of causing inflammation and cell death (necrosis).

If your dog has a fever for more than one day, take him to see the vet immediately. The sooner your dog starts treatment, the better the outcome. This condition can be prevented by routine vaccinations. However, dog owners must stay vigilant and keep their dogs' vaccines up to date, as the disease can develop quickly.

Myasthenia Gravis

Myasthenia gravis is a condition that causes a miscommunication between the nerve and muscle signals. Affected dogs will exhibit extreme lethargy and muscle weakness. Dogs with congenital myasthenia gravis are usually diagnosed between six to eight weeks of age. Acquired myasthenia gravis is more like an autoimmune disease and is not hereditary. It tends to be diagnosed in dogs between two to four years of age.

Most affected dogs can be treated with medication they will need to take for the rest of their lives. If left untreated, the affected dog will eventually have difficulty swallowing food, and it may accidentally inhale food, liquid, or vomit, which will result in aspiration pneumonia. Aspiration pneumonia is extremely serious and requires costly veterinarian care until the dog's condition can be stabilized.

Cruciate Ligament Disease

Cranial cruciate ligament disease occurs when the tough fibrous tissue attached to the hip and knee bone prevents the knee from moving forward, and at the same time, it does not prevent the knee joint from over-extending or rotating. The precise cause of this condition is unknown, as the ligament degenerates slowly over time, similar to a fraying rope. Factors such as obesity, hormonal imbalance, and inflammatory conditions of the joint may play a role in this condition.

One of the most common signs of cruciate ligament disease is a dog limping after exercise or standing up after sitting for a long period of time. In severe cases, affected dogs cannot stand up and may be erroneously suspected of having a neurological issue. Your vet will most likely recommend noninvasive treatment measures such as anti-inflammatory painkillers, physiotherapy, weight management, and exercise modification. If the condition worsens, your vet may recommend surgery.

Pan-osteitis

Pan-osteitis is a painful condition that causes inflammation of the outer surface of one or all of the leg shafts. Often called growing pains, it can move around from one bone at a time, causing temporary lameness in the impacted leg. This condition affects puppies, who are growing quickly and can have recurrent episodes until they are two years of age.

Your vet will most likely recommend analgesics and/ or anti-inflammatory drugs. Lameness will not be permanent and generally will last a few hours to a day or two. The condition will resolve itself when the dog's bone density normalizes.

HELPFUL TIP
Pet Insurance

As such active dogs, Brittanys may be more prone to injuries than couch potato pups. You may want to consider buying pet insurance to cover accidents or illnesses. Pet insurance always has a waiting period before coverage starts, and it doesn't cover preexisting conditions, so you should sign up as soon as you bring your Brittany home.

CHAPTER 14
Caring for a Senior Brittany

"

Brittanys typically do not slow down until after 10 years of age, unless they are sick. Continue to keep them active if they are happy doing so, and monitor their weight. They are happiest being with you and going for their walks.

DARLENE VANHOEVE
Shamrock Brittanys

"

According to the American Society for the Prevention of Cruelty to Animals (ASPCA), of the 79 million dogs owned in the United States, more than one-third of these furry companions are senior dogs. Aging varies from dog to dog. Some dogs stay physically and mentally active as they age, while others become lethargic and senile. This is just the natural process of growing older.

Physical and Mental Signs of Aging

Unfortunately, dogs age faster than their pet owners. Generally, a medium-sized dog like your Brittany will enter into his senior years at around eight or nine of our years. The more aware you are of typical signs of aging, the sooner you can make your dog's golden years more comfortable.

Senior Brittanys experience physical and mental signs of aging such as bathroom issues, hearing loss, poor mobility due to aches and pains, and so on. Some of these changes may affect your dog's behavior. For example, your mellow companion might suddenly turn into an old grouch. He may be in pain from arthritis. Or maybe your hyperactive Brittany suddenly wants to sleep all day long. Senior dogs need more rest, so – let him sleep.

Your senior Brittany may also begin to display symptoms of cognitive decline, such as forgetting where his water dish is or simply barking at nothing. Your dog may seem to be going senile, which is entirely possible as dogs can develop cognitive problems just like humans. Many behavioral changes are caused by canine cognitive dysfunction syndrome (CCDS). CCDS is similar to Alzheimer's disease and affects around half of all dogs over 11 years of age.

At around 14 years of age, almost 70% of all dogs begin to experience symptoms associated with CCDS. Some behavioral changes your Brittany might display are:

- House soiling
- Increased anxiety
- Fear of familiar people and objects
- Compulsive behaviors

- Excessive barking and vocalization
- Change in activity level
- Insomnia, sleep walking, or restlessness

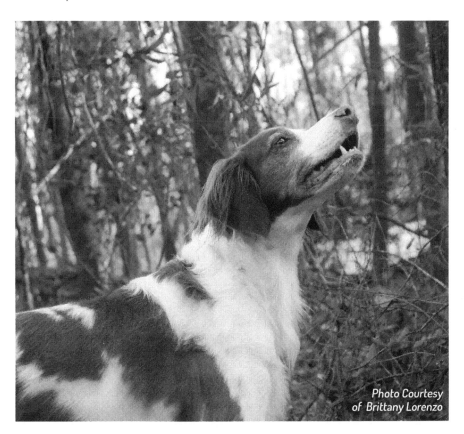

Photo Courtesy of Brittany Lorenzo

If you observe your Brittany displaying any of these symptoms, consult with your vet. Your vet will make a diagnosis by asking you a few questions during the visit. There is no cure for CCDS; however, there are medications and therapeutic options such as dietary therapy, nutritional supplements, and maintaining a healthy and stimulating environment.

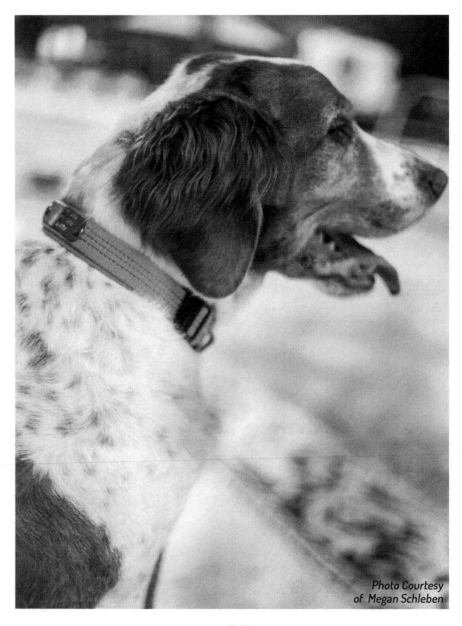

Photo Courtesy of Megan Schleben

Illness and Injury Prevention

> *The average Brittany lives to 14 years and they are generally a very healthy breed. Make sure that they get the best nutrition and continue exercising their bodies and minds for as long as possible. Make sure they see a vet regularly to keep on top of any health problems you might not have noticed. Give them all the hugs and love you can and treasure the memories!*
>
> DIANA L KUBITZ
> *Renegade Brittanys*

Strained muscles, sprains, and pulled ligaments are all common senior canine injuries. As your Brittany ages, he will become more susceptible to injury due to brittle bones and arthritis. Research shows dogs experience a similar pain threshold as that of humans. You can easily reduce injuries by incorporating the following strategies into your dog's daily life:

Avoid extreme temperatures – Elderly Brittanys are more sensitive to extreme temperature changes. They can suffer more easily from heatstroke, frostbite, and hypothermia than younger dogs. If the weather outside is too hot or too cold, keep your pooch inside.

Daily exercise schedule – Even though your senior Brittany has gotten slower in the last few years, that does not mean he does not need regular exercise. Switch up your dog's exercise routine by taking him for shorter walks. Instead of walking on cement, take your canine for a walk on a dirt or grass path, as it will be softer on his sore joints.

Ramp up – Climbing stairs, jumping up on the couch, or getting into the car may become a challenge for your senior dog. At your local pet supply store, you can find a variety of ramps to help your pooch.

Slip proof your home – Your Brittany may lack the agility he once had during his younger years. Your hardwood or tile floors may cause him to slip, causing injury. Place rugs in the areas your dog spends the majority of his time to help him feel more secure and sure-footed.

Soft, fluffy bed – Your Brittany will thank you for a soft, fluffy bed that supports his old bones and joints. Invest in a doggy bed with soft sides, so your senior pooch can rest his head on a soft surface while he observes his surroundings.

Take it slow – Your elderly Brittany will need extra time for eating, walking, going to the bathroom, etc. Be patient with him and give him the time he needs. Your furry friend also will appreciate any extra attention, love, and affection from you, like cuddling on the couch.

Weight control – Since your senior Brittany is less active, he is burning fewer calories, meaning unwanted weight gain. Extra weight puts pressure on your old dog's bones, joints, and heart, which can cause additional health problems. Consult with your vet for recommendations to improve your dog's diet.

SIGNS OF ILLNESS OR PAIN

Each dog will display pain and suffering differently. Any change in your Brittany's behavior may be an early indication that he is ill or in pain.

When your dog is in pain or is ill, his eating or drinking habits will often change. He might lose interest in food or drink excessive amounts of water. He may become withdrawn, be aggressive when petted, or seem unwilling to go for a walk. Your dog may display one or more of these signs of ill health:

- Runny nose, crusty eyes, or discharge coming from the ears
- Excessive drooling
- Vomiting
- Diarrhea
- Constipation
- Difficultly urinating
- Coughing
- Hot spots, excessive scratching, or skin sores under his coat
- Limping, swelling, and lack of mobility

If you notice that your Brittany is displaying any of these symptoms for more than forty-eight hours, consult with your veterinarian about any health issues.

Age-related Diseases and Conditions in Brittanys

During your dog's golden years, he may begin to experience age-associated illnesses and diseases. Many of these conditions can be treated if identified early, so be sure to consult with your vet immediately. The following health issues are commonly associated with geriatric Brittanys.

Arthritis – Just like people, dogs develop arthritis as they age. The most common type of arthritis in aging Brittanys is osteoarthritis, also called degenerative joint disease. This condition affects the hips, knees, shoulders, and elbows. The changes in joints result in pain, stiffness, and lack of mobility. Osteoarthritis is progressive, meaning there is no cure, but there are many treatments, such as chiropractic, hydrotherapy, and acupuncture, which are known to slow the disease progression and ease joint pain.

Cancer – Unfortunately, cancer is common in older dogs. Different types of cancer can cause a variety of symptoms. Often, symptoms may be dismissed as signs of aging, such as lethargy or a lack of appetite. As your Brittany ages, it is vital that he receives routine wellness screenings. Lab work, additional diagnostic imaging, and exams can pick up on anything that is unseen to the naked eye. The sooner the cancer is caught, the better the chances of your dog's survival.

Cataracts – Cataracts cause your Brittany's eye to lose transparency, causing them to appear cloudy. The cataract prevents light from passing through your dog's lens, blocking his vision. Most elderly dogs who develop cataracts will not completely go blind, and they can adjust to their loss of vision. Your vet will need to diagnose the cause of the cataract before coming up with a treatment plan.

Glaucoma –Your dog's eye is made up of a jelly-like substance called aqueous humor. This liquid is constantly being produced by the eye. Normally, the eye drains itself of the old fluid, but if this does not occur, then glaucoma happens. Glaucoma in dogs can have one of many causes, so be sure to consult with your vet to find the correct treatment for your dog.

Watch out for the following symptoms of glaucoma in your Brittany:

● A cloudy cornea

● Continual blinking or squinting of the eye

● Pupil does not respond to light

● Pupils are a different size in each eye

● Increased sleeping

Diabetes – Brittanys are prone to developing canine diabetes. Diabetes occurs when the pancreas stops producing normal amounts of insulin and may be caused by heredity, diet, obesity, and certain medications, such as steroids used for treating allergies. Diabetes can easily be regulated with insulin shots and a change in diet.

Incontinence – Age takes a toll on your dog's organs, muscles, and nerves, making it more challenging to hold his bladder and bowles the way he used to. Incontinence may be an indication of other health complications, so you will need your vet to rule out some issues first. If the vet does not find any health problems, you may need to let your Brittany out more often for potty breaks or have him wear a doggy diaper.

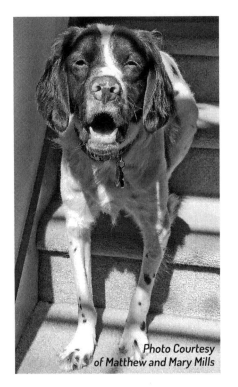

Photo Courtesy
of Matthew and Mary Mills

Kidney Disease – Kidney disease often develops slowly, starting off as renal insufficiency and progressing to full renal failure. Once this disease starts to progress, there is no cure, but if caught in time, it can be successfully treated to slow the progression. Signs of kidney disease include increased thirst, frequent urination, lack of appetite, vomiting, and lethargy.

Lenticular Sclerosis – This condition is often confused with cataracts as it also causes the dog's eyes to form a white, cloudy reflection. Lenticular sclerosis, however, does not affect your Brittany's vision. But to be on the safe side, get your dog's eyes checked out by your vet.

Muscle Atrophy – Muscle atrophy is common in older Brittanys as they become less active with age. This condition causes rear leg weakness, limping, ataxia, paw dragging, flabby muscles, and weight loss. Muscle atrophy can be caused by a number of conditions such as arthritis, injury, and sore muscles from lack of exercise. Your vet will need to give your dog a checkup to diagnose the cause of your Brittany's muscle atrophy before treating him.

Lifestyle Modifications

> *Brittanys age extremely well. They are known to maintain their activity level much longer than other breeds. As your dog ages don't restrict their activities based only on how old they are, you don't want to take away what they love to do most. Always remember to enjoy every moment, those memories will last a lifetime.*
>
> **JESSIE SCHULZ**
> *Credit Brittanys*

As your Brittany ages, his mobility is going to decline. However, this does not mean he should not be getting any exercise. Actually, by helping your senior dog maintain an active lifestyle, you are decreasing his risks of geriatric ailments such as arthritis and muscle loss. Although your old pup may not chase the ball as fast as he used to, there are still plenty of safe physical activities for him to engage in.

Here are a few suggestions to keep your senior Brittany active:

DO

- Establish a regular exercise regime. The more active your Brittany is, the more agile he will feel, even if it is several short walks a day instead of one or two long walks.

- Consider the climate before going for a trot around the block. Elderly dogs are more sensitive to extreme weather conditions. During the warmer months, take your Brittany for a walk in the cooler times of the day. During the colder winter months, buy your dog a doggy jacket.

- As your Brittany ages, he may lose his hearing and eyesight, so stick with familiar walking routes. New surroundings may cause your furry friend to become anxious and confused.

- Be sure to consult with your vet about whether your Brittany is receiving enough exercise, especially if he has a medical condition.

DON'T

- Never stop taking your Brittany for daily walks! Maybe your pooch will not be able to endure longer strolls, but he will still be grateful to go for shorter walks. Walking gives your dog the opportunity to stretch his legs, sniff out his surroundings, and enjoy the fresh air.

- Do not set the pace; instead, let your Brittany set the pace. If your dog needs to sit or lie down for a minute or two, then let him rest.

- Do not forget that indoor playtime is exercise. If the weather outside is too extreme, then keep your Brittany active by playing hide-and-seek inside.

- Do not assume your dog can keep up with you or go long distances. Just because you don't feel like you are getting a work out does not mean it is not difficult for your dog.

Regular exercise helps to keep your Brittany's mind stimulated, helps him maintain a healthy weight, and keeps his body agile. Regardless of your furry friend's physical limitations, there are plenty of appropriate exercises for your senior dog.

Walking – Your Brittany will love going for a walk, despite his age or health limitations. Walking is a low-impact exercise if you take into consideration the footing, so grass and dirt are preferable surfaces. Avoid asphalt or rough surfaces that may damage your dog's paws.

Swimming – Swimming is the lowest impact exercise for your elderly Brittany, as it puts zero pressure on his joints while providing him with a total body workout. An added bonus is your Brittany adores water and will be the world's happiest dog while he paddles around in a dog-friendly pool or lake. Swimming is often used as a form of physical therapy for dogs who have undergone major surgery for injuries.

There are plenty of other ideas to keep your senior dog active, such as playing fetch in the backyard or sniffing games that lead him to a treat. Give your Brittany time to follow his surroundings by sniffing out every shred of grass. However, whatever type of physical activity you choose for your dog – do not overdo it!

How much exercise is too much?

Each dog's physical tolerance levels vary depending on weight, lifestyle, exercise history, and overall health. Your Brittany may be pushing himself past his comfort zone just to please you. Here are a few tell-tale signs your dog has pushed himself past his physical limitations:

Excessive drooling or panting – It is perfectly normal for your Brittany to pant a little after playing a game of fetch; however, excessive panting and drooling are a clear indication that he is dehydrated or overheated.

Reluctant to play – If your Brittany stops playing and wants to sit down, then he is telling you he is tired and needs to rest.

Limping or muscle atrophy – If your Brittany starts to favor his hind legs by limping while exercising, stop immediately! Observe your dog for the next twenty-four hours, and if the limp does not go away, take him to see your vet as soon as possible.

Coughing or hacking – If your Brittany begins to cough or hack while exercising, it may be a sign of his trachea collapsing or other health conditions. Repeated hacking can sound like your dog is honking. If your dog begins to make coughing or hacking sounds while exercising, stop immediately! If you notice the coughing noise returns every time that your dog exerts himself, consult with your vet.

It helps to keep an exercise journal of your Brittany's daily exercise regime and adjust his routine as needed. Whenever you notice your dog is experiencing pain or discomfort, slow down his workout. Do not hesitate to check in with your vet if you have any questions or concerns.

OLD DOG, NEW TRICKS

You have most likely heard the saying, "If you don't use it, you lose it!" Elderly people play sudoku, do crosswords, or complete brain teasers to keep their minds sharp and alert. Your faithful old companion needs to keep learning new activities to keep his mind stimulated. When your dog is asked to focus on something, it tends to slow down cognitive degeneration.

Here are some ideas to keep your canine's mind sharp:

- Explore new places, such as parks, beaches, or a ferry boat ride.
- Teach your Brittany new tricks or reinforce old ones.
- Reactivate old instincts with a game of tug-of-war.
- Take your old companion swimming or, even better, to a local natural hot spring.
- Play a short game of fetch or hide-and-seek.
- Introduce new toys or games that involve sniffing out a yummy treat.

Grooming

Should your senior Brittany still get groomed? The answer is unabashedly "yes!"

Grooming is essential throughout your Brittany's life but even more so as he gets older. Grooming sessions are an excellent opportunity to observe any changes in your dog's overall health, as many underlying health issues are revealed through the health of his skin and coat. Fur can begin to thin, and skin irritation, new growths, or lumps may start to appear.

One of the best gifts you can give your aging Brittany is grooming him daily, as it keeps him looking and feeling his best. Plus, your pooch will drink up the extra attention from you. Your dog is never too old to be pampered!

Elderly dogs who loved getting groomed in their younger years may suddenly start to resist the process due to joint pain. Senior dogs may squirm and bark to vocalize their objections to being groomed. However, at the end of the grooming session, your Brittany will be prancing around like he was still a puppy!

Your older Brittany will thank you for his grooming session. A warm bath will relieve those itchy sections your dog is no longer able to reach. Plus, your Brittany will drink up the extra attention and the treats during the grooming and afterward. Nothing is more satisfying than to see your freshly groomed old companion swagger away, feeling completely renewed and refreshed.

If you prefer to take your Brittany to a professional groomer, avoid using a discount service that may neglect your dog. Not every groomer has the ability or the patience to deal with your faithful old companion's aches and pains, so choose carefully. Look for a groomer who has experience with grooming geriatric dogs.

If you decide to groom your Brittany at home, carefully review the detailed information found in chapter 11 of this book and take into consideration the following tips to adapt the process to your old friend. These tips can go a long way in ensuring your elderly dog will receive the level of care and respect he deserves.

Keep sessions short – Lengthy grooming sessions can cause unnecessary discomfort, pain, and stress for your older dog. Many reputable groomers with experience grooming geriatric dogs will schedule multiple grooming sessions instead of one. For example, the first session may include a bath, and the following week a haircut and brushing.

Watch for signs of discomfort – Your older dog will communicate his discomfort through body language or by vocalizing. If you notice your Brittany whimpering, squirming, shivering, or even growling, then you need to stop the grooming session. Let your dog take a short rest or find a more comfortable position. If your Brittany becomes agitated or stressed, then discontinue the session and continue another day.

Understand your dog's limitations – It is more than likely your senior Brittany may not be able to handle the same grooming regimen as when he was younger. Pressure sores and benign fatty tumors mean your dog's coat cannot be trimmed as short as usual. Or if your Brittany has poor eyesight, clipping too close to his face may cause him anxiety.

Bathing – If you decide to bathe your elderly Brittany at home, there are a few precautions you can take to ensure his well-being and comfort. When bathing your dog, place a non-skid mat in the bottom of the basin or tub to secure his footing. Make sure the water is warm enough that your Brittany is not shivering during the bath. Often, geriatric dogs need a special shampoo to treat dry skin or other conditions.

After thoroughly rinsing out the shampoo, dry your dog with warm, fluffy towels. Before using the blow dryer, let your Brittany shake himself off. Never use the blow dryer on the hottest setting. Instead, use the cool setting. Be sure to get your old dog as dry as possible, as water trapped close to the skin may cause hot spots.

Brushing – Before you start brushing your Brittany, inspect the brush to make sure it's in good condition. If the brush's teeth are bent or broken, it is best to discard it and get a new one, as the teeth can scratch an older dog's thin, vulnerable skin or damage his coat.

Arthritis and joint pain may make it difficult for your dog to stand in the same position for long periods of time. Place a blanket on the floor and have your Brittany lie on his side while being brushed. Matted, tangled hair does not provide your dog with extra insulation as much as clean, tangle-free hair will.

While brushing your Brittany, be on the lookout for bare patches and brittle hair. This may be an indication of underlying health conditions. Also use your fingers to feel for any new lumps, warts, or sores on your dog's skin. If you notice anything suspicious, consult with your vet.

Nail trimming – Your elderly Brittany will need his nails trimmed more frequently than when he was younger. If your old dog suffers from arthritis or joint problems, it is even more reason to keep his nails trimmed, as the nail length affects your dog's posture and can force him to torque his spine, causing additional discomfort. In the past, his long walks on the sidewalk naturally kept his nails trimmed, but nowadays, because of his shorter strolls, he needs some extra help.

Sanitary areas – The glands and groin area are normally cleaned by your dog daily, but with old age, he may need some help. Regular trimming of the groin area will prevent any fecal matter or urine from getting trapped. Typically, all dogs express their anal glands when they defecate. But smaller breeds such as the Brittany may need help to express their anal glands as they age.

Nutrition Needs

Your Brittany's nutritional needs will vary throughout his lifetime, and once he reaches his golden years, it can become a challenge to understand his new dietary needs. However, switching your dog's regular brand of dog food for a senior one may not be enough.

Watch those calories. As your dog ages, he begins to slow down which means he burns off fewer calories and those unneeded calories are stored as fat. Research shows senior dogs require 20 percent fewer calories than an adult dog in order to maintain a healthy weight. However, if your Brittany starts losing too much weight, you may need to give him extra calories to help him stay healthy.

Protein is vital for your Brittany's overall health. As your dog ages, he begins to lose muscle mass, even if he is still leading an active lifestyle. As his muscle mass is depleted, so are his protein reserves, causing his immune system to weaken. As your dog's immune system weakens, so does his ability to fight off infections and illnesses. Your senior Brittany's diet should be made up of 40% protein. Avoid dog foods that contain fillers. Instead, opt for foods rich in lean red meats, fish, chicken, and dairy products.

Your senior Brittany will need a low-sodium diet if he has hypertension, cardiac, or kidney problems. Most commercial dog food is extremely high in sodium, so look for brands that are low in sodium or make your own homemade dog food. For more information on how to make your own dog food, see Chapter 10 of this book.

IF YOUR SENIOR BRITTANY WILL NOT EAT

It is common for senior dogs to lose interest in food. Try adding one to two tablespoons of bone broth or a small amount of canned food to entice your dog. If your elderly pooch refuses to eat for more than forty-eight hours, consult with your vet to rule out any underlying health problems.

Bone broth is a delicious, nutrient-dense superfood that will improve your Brittany's health and is guaranteed to get him to gobble up his dinner. Bone broth is a stock made from simmering raw bones for several hours, either in your slow-cooker or on low heat on your stove. Bone broth is jam-packed with nutrients that will improve your dog's overall health, plus he will devour his food.

How to make bone broth for your Brittany:

INGREDIENTS

- 4 pounds of raw bones with marrow (you can use chicken, turkey, rabbit, beef, or oxtail bones)
- 1/3 cup fresh parsley, chopped
- 3 stalks of celery, chopped
- 1/4 cup organic apple cider vinegar (helps to pull the marrow and minerals out of the bones)
- 6 to 7 quarts of water

(1) Place all of the ingredients in a large pot or the slow cooker.

(2) Cook on low heat for 8 to 12 hours on a low simmer or for 24 hours in the slow cooker on the lowest setting. Stir occasionally and add extra water if necessary.

(3) Allow to cool. Remove the bones, celery, parsley, and discard. Note that you should never feed cooked bones to your Brittany.

(4) Once the broth is completely cool, place in the refrigerator overnight. It will form a layer of fat on top which can easily be skimmed off and discarded.

(5) Freeze in small portions in zip-lock baggies, then thaw before serving your Brittany. Give him one to two tablespoons with each meal.

Choosing a Premium Senior Dog Food

The FDA has not established any official regulations for senior dog foods, which is why you need to educate yourself on how to find a premium-quality dog food for your Brittany.

Beyond the caloric intake and protein content, there are several ingredients that can benefit your Brittany's overall health. Here are a few key ingredients to look for when choosing a premium dog food.

- **Glucosamine and Chondroitin** – These supplements help your senior dog's cartilage and joints so he can move around with less pain.

- **Antioxidants** – Antioxidants provide much-needed support for your elderly pup's immune system, helping him to fight off diseases and illnesses.

- **Decreased levels of sodium and phosphorus** – Lower phosphorus helps to maintain healthy kidney function, and lower sodium levels keep your Brittany's blood pressure normal.

- **L-carnitine** – Recent studies have discovered that foods rich in L-carnitine help elderly dogs to burn off stored fat for energy. L-carnitine is found in lean red meats, chicken, fish, healthy fats, and dairy products.

- **Omega-3 fatty acids** – Healthy fats found in fish, nut, and plant oils help to decrease inflammation caused by arthritis and improve kidney and liver health.

- **Extra fiber** – Many senior Brittanys suffer from constipation, so extra fiber may help. However, too much fiber can cause other problems, so the best way to control constipation is to make sure your dog gets enough exercise. Some beneficial soluble fibers for your dog are sweet potatoes, carrots, brown rice, milled flaxseed, wheatgerm, kale, and kelp.

When choosing a senior dog food, it is important to consider your Brittany's individual needs and recognize that these needs can change over time. So, just because one type of senior dog food is suitable for your dog

Photo Courtesy
Patricia Branson

now does not mean it will always be. The right dog food will have a direct impact on your dog's health, so take your time to do your research and talk to your vet to find the best diet for your faithful companion.

Look for a senior dog food made from premium quality ingredients, such as human-grade organic lean red meats, free of artificial preservatives. No matter how healthy your Brittany is, there is no need to put a strain on his immune system by feeding him poor-quality, generic dog food with little to no nutritional value.

Transition your pooch slowly to a new senior dog food. It is best to start gradually by adding a small amount of the new food to his current food. Each day you can add a little more of the new food. Ideally, it should take seven to ten days to completely switch your dog to the new food.

Listen to your vet's recommendations, especially if your dog has been diagnosed with a condition such as diabetes, kidney, liver or heart disease, arthritis, etc. Your vet will most likely recommend a prescription diet. While these diets often do not include the word "senior" in the title, they are formulated to manage disease conditions commonly seen in elderly dogs.

Saying Goodbye

"Dog's lives are too short. Their only fault, really." – Agnes Sligh Turnbull

For every person who loves and shares their life with a Brittany, the dreaded and inevitable day will arrive when you have to ask yourself whether or not to intervene in how and when your best friend's life must come to an end. The very thought of having to say goodbye to your four-pawed companion for the last time is beyond heart-wrenching.

Often, when we begin to observe signs that our dog is suffering and dying, we start to second guess ourselves or even go into denial. This often causes our beloved dogs to suffer far longer than they should have. The question is, how do you know? When is the right time to put your best friend into a forever sleep?

TELL-TALE SIGNS YOUR BRITTANY IS DYING

Prolonged lethargy or disinterest – One of the most common signs of the dying process is finding your dog lying in the same spot (often not where he would normally rest), barely acknowledging you or other family members. Dogs may become lethargic due to other health conditions, but if the veterinarian has ruled this out and the lethargy lasts for more than a few days, then maybe it is time to consider saying goodbye.

Stops eating or drinking – Another classic sign something is wrong with your Brittany is when you offer him the tastiest treat imaginable, and he refuses to even sniff it. Often at this point, the dog will stop drinking water, as his organs are starting to shut down. Try keeping your dog hydrated by giving him water using a dropper or turkey baster, but if he still refuses to swallow, there is not much you can do at this point. Be sure to rule out other health conditions with your vet.

Lack of coordination – The next sign is when your dog begins to lose balance and motor control. When your elderly Brittany tries to stand up, he may be very wobbly or disoriented. Or he could shake or convulse while lying down. In this case, make your dog as comfortable as possible and remove any objects he could knock over if he tries to stand up. Note: Saying goodbye to your dog means protecting him, creating a safe area for him, and providing whatever help he needs.

Incontinence – When a dog is dying, often, he will not even move from the spot to relieve himself even if he has diarrhea. This is an indication that your dog's organs are starting to shut down. During this stage, make sure you keep him and his bed clean and dry.

Labored breathing – As heartbreaking as it sounds, toward the end, many dogs display labored breathing. Your dog's breathing may become difficult, with lengthy gasps between each breath. This is an extremely hard moment; as you know, at this point your dog is suffering.

Seeking comfort – This is one of the hardest moments, as despite your dog's quickly deteriorating health, he will look for comfort from his people – from you. During these final hours, be with your dog, reassuring him of your love and affection.

MAKING THE DECISION

The signs above are not always consistent and will vary, as some dogs suddenly pass away in their sleep without any indications of ill health. Part of preparing to say farewell to your Brittany is realizing you may have to make the difficult decision for your dog by intervening. Before making a decision, talk over all of your options with your family and come to a mutual agreement.

Once you have come to the decision to intervene to end your dog's suffering, discuss the options with your vet.

Veterinarians are required to follow a set of guidelines called the "Humane Euthanasia Protocol," whether the euthanasia is performed inside of the clinic or in the tranquility of your own house. The entire process is painless and stress-free for your Brittany. The Humane Euthanasia Protocol is considered the kindest way to put your dog to sleep.

The Humane Euthanasia Protocol:

1. The veterinarian will inject your Brittany with a pain tranquilizer.
2. Once your dog is relaxed and sedated, then your vet will insert an IV to administer the euthanasia solution.
3. The vet will leave you alone with your dog for a few minutes for any final goodbyes, then return to administer the final drug to stop your Brittany's heart.

In certain parts of the United States veterinarians are not required by law to adhere to the Humane Euthanasia Protocol. Instead, they practice a quicker and more affordable method to stop the animal's heart with a single injection of barbiturates. Barbiturates cause the animal's central nervous system to slow down, causing a painful death. This type of euthanasia is not humane, as it is not pain-free, causing the animal short-term distress and anxiety.

Ensure your veterinarian agrees to apply the Humane Euthanasia Protocol to your dog. If not, look for another veterinarian who will.

Most dogs are euthanized inside of the veterinary clinic, but many vets will make house calls. If your vet is unable to make house calls, you can find an extensive list of reputable veterinarians throughout the United States and Canada online at the In-Home Pet Euthanasia Directory. (www.inhomepeteuthanasia.com)

Here is a quick overview of the pros and cons of getting your Brittany euthanized at home versus at the clinic.

At-home euthanasia may be the right choice for you if:

- Your Brittany is too sick to be transported comfortably to the veterinary clinic.
- You personally feel more comfortable with grieving at home.
- Car trips or visits to the veterinary clinic cause your dog anxiety and stress.
- Money is not an issue, as at-home procedures cost more.

Vet clinic euthanasia may be the right choice for you if:

- You want your usual vet to perform the procedure, but they are unable to perform house calls.
- You prefer a more neutral environment for the procedure.
- You dog is still mobile enough to be comfortably transported in your car.
- Cost is a concern.

Whether you decide on euthanasia at-home or at the veterinary clinic is a very personal decision. There is no right or wrong answer.

The cost of clinical euthanasia can be between $80 to $350 depending on where you live. The cost of at-home euthanasia can cost between $300 to $800. The higher cost may include add-ons, such as cremations, funeral services, or getting the vet to take an impression of your dog's paw to cast into a memento.

It is highly recommended you pay for the euthanasia before the procedure as emotions can be running high when the procedure is final, and the last thing you need is to relive the heartbreak by receiving the bill later. When it is all over, you can request the veterinary clinic to dispose of your dog for an extra cost. Some clinics offer cremation or a professional burial service at a nearby pet cemetery.

Take your time grieving your Brittany and coming to terms with your loss. Everybody does it in their own way. Saying goodbye to your Brittany does not mean forgetting about him. With time, you may start thinking about opening up your heart to another dog.

> **"**
>
> *How lucky am I to have something that makes saying goodbye so hard.*
>
> WINNIE THE POOH
>
> **"**

Made in the USA
Coppell, TX
22 February 2022